金融稳定
监测与管理
——来自FSAP的经验
和改进FSAP的建议

主 编 ◎ 刘士余

Monitoring and Managing
Financial Stability
Lessons from and for the FSAP

中国金融出版社

责任编辑：戴　硕　李　融
责任校对：潘　洁
责任印制：程　颖

图书在版编目（CIP）数据

金融稳定监测与管理：来自 FSAP 的经验和改进 FSAP 的建议（Jinrong
Wending Jiance yu Guanli：Laizi FSAP de Jingyan he Gaijin FSAP de Jianyi）／刘
士余主编 . —北京：中国金融出版社，2012.7
　ISBN 978 - 7 - 5049 - 6491 - 5

　Ⅰ.①金… 　Ⅱ.①刘… 　Ⅲ.①金融管理—研究—中国 　Ⅳ.①F832.1

　中国版本图书馆 CIP 数据核字（2012）第 153972 号

出版
发行　**中国金融出版社**

社址　北京市丰台区益泽路 2 号
市场开发部　（010）63266347，63805472，63439533（传真）
网 上 书 店　http：//www. chinafph. com
　　　　　　（010）63286832，63365686（传真）
读者服务部　（010）66070833，62568380
邮编　100071
经销　新华书店
印刷　北京松源印刷有限公司
尺寸　185 毫米×260 毫米
印张　16.75
字数　264 千
版次　2012 年 7 月第 1 版
印次　2012 年 7 月第 1 次印刷
定价　38.00 元
ISBN 978 - 7 - 5049 - 6491 - 5/F. 6051
如出现印装错误本社负责调换　联系电话（010）63263947

前　　言

金融部门评估规划（Financial Sector Assessment Program，FSAP）由国际货币基金组织和世界银行于 1999 年 5 月联合推出，旨在加强对国际货币基金组织成员经济体金融脆弱性的评估与监测，减少金融危机发生的可能性，同时推动金融改革和发展。经过逐步发展和完善，目前 FSAP 已成为国际广泛接受的金融稳定评估框架。

为落实我国在二十国集团（G20）峰会上的承诺，从国际视角审视我国金融体系稳健性，2009 年 8 月，我国正式接受国际货币基金组织和世界银行进行中国首次 FSAP 评估。鉴于首次评估，为加强协调、提高效率，中国人民银行牵头会同 11 个部门成立了 FSAP 部际领导小组和部际工作小组，建立了相应的工作机制和工作原则，全力做好各项评估工作。2010 年以来，国际货币基金组织和世界银行的中国 FSAP 评估团，两次集体来华开展现场评估，评估团部分成员多次来华进行专项评估和后续磋商，先后与国务院相关部门、部分地方政府、部分金融机构、中介机构等举行 400 余场会谈，就中国宏观经济、金融风险和金融体系脆弱性、金融法律与规则、金融监管环境、金融体系流动性和金融稳定、金融市场基础设施建设、金融发展和金融服务可获得性、应急预案和危机管理安排等诸多方面内容展开深入交流。

经过两年多的努力，中国首次 FSAP 评估于 2011 年 11 月圆满完成。为交流和借鉴中国的经验，推动其他发展中国家开展相应的金融稳定评估，国际货币基金组织多次致函中国人民银行，希望与中国人民银行共同举办研讨会。2011 年 12 月 9～10 日，国际货币基金组织和中国人民银行在上海联合举办了"金融稳定监测与管理：来自 FSAP 的经验和改进 FSAP 的建议"高层研讨会。出席会议的有来自韩国、日本、印度、印度尼西亚、澳大利亚等 17 个亚太国家（地区）中央银行、金融监管部门的高级官员，金融稳定理事会、巴塞尔银行监管委员会、国际证监会组织和国际保险监督官协会等国际组织的代表，以及美国、英国、日本、北欧等八个选区驻国际货币基金组织执行董事。中国人民银行和财政部、银监会、证监会、保监会、外汇管理局以及部分金融机构有关负责同志出席了研讨会。

研讨会上，来自各国（地区）、国际组织的代表，从不同角度对 FSAP 评估的经验、教训进行了热烈讨论和交流，对加强系统性风险监测取得的进展，以及在确立宏观审慎制度框架方面的经验进行了总结。研讨会的召开增进了参会各国（地区）和国际组织对中国金融业改革、发展和金融稳定工作的了解，对促进亚太地区加强金融稳定监测和管理的协调合作起到了积极作用。

鉴于此次研讨会的重要性，经商各位发言人，我们将其发言内容进行了整理并翻译出版，以飨读者。

编者
二○一二年七月十日

目　　录

Session Ⅰ The Financial Sector Assessment Program – The Role of an Independent Review

Keynote Address

Session Ⅱ New International Regulatory and Supervisory Standards—Their Role in Addressing Systemic Risks

Session Ⅲ Prevention and Response – How Prepared Are We for the Next Crisis?

Keynote Address

Special address

Session Ⅳ Macroprudential Policy—What Are the Implementation Issues?

Session Ⅴ Connecting the Dots and Key Takeaways

欢迎词

周小川
中国人民银行行长

女士们、先生们：

早上好！非常高兴与新老朋友相聚在上海，分享和交流我们开展金融部门评估规划（FSAP）的经验与收获，探讨如何维护金融稳定。应国际货币基金组织和中国人民银行的邀请，这次研讨会汇聚了来自国际金融组织、亚太地区多个国家中央银行、财政部、金融监管部门的代表以及市场参与者。我们还特别邀请了美国加州大学伯克利分校的 Barry Eichengreen 教授。

此次国际金融危机的爆发凸显了对金融稳定进行监测和评估的重要性。危机发生以来，各国政策制定者都把维护金融体系稳定、促进经济恢复增长作为经济工作的重中之重。由此，国际货币基金组织和世界银行联合推出的金融部门评估规划，成为国际社会广泛接受的金融稳定评估框架。在华盛顿召开的第一次二十国集团（G20）峰会上，G20 领导人一致承诺对本国开展 FSAP 评估。

中国于 2009 年 8 月启动 FSAP 评估。为做好这项工作，中国人民银行会同 11 个部门建立了相应的工作机制和工作原则。两年来，由国际货币基金组织和世界银行组织的中国 FSAP 评估团，对中国金融体系和制度框架进行了全面评估，提出了很多有益的建议。评估专家在评估期间表现出的专业水准和敬业精神给中方留下了深刻的印象。在此，请允许我向他们表示衷心的感谢！

中国政府高度重视 FSAP 评估。对评估团的评估结论以及提示的风险因素和政策建议，温家宝总理、王岐山副总理十分重视并做出重要批示，要求有关部门以此次评估为契机，充分重视国际金融机构提出的需进一步改进的意见和建议，结合中国金融体系发展、改革和风险防范工作实际，巩固成绩，查找不足，提出整改措施。

总体来看，中国 FSAP 评估进展顺利，取得了丰富的成果。中国 FSAP 成果报告——《中国金融体系稳定评估报告》（FSSA）和《中国金融部门评估报告》（FSA）已于 2011 年 11 月 15 日分别由国际货币基金组织和世界银行公布。总体来看，评估报告对中国金融体系的评价是客观、积极、正面的，对中国金融体系未来改革建议是富有建设性的。我相信，这次 FSAP 评估，对于中国继续推进金融改革和维护金融稳定必将起到积极的推动作用。

此次国际金融危机使国际社会深刻认识到，只强调关注单个金融机构稳健运营的监管安排，未能捕获金融市场的发展趋势和关联风险。为弥补这一缺陷，加强宏观审慎管理成为危机后国际组织和各国金融监管改革的共同政策主张。国际金融危机以来，一些国际金融组织，如金融稳定理事会（FSB）、国际货币基金组织（IMF）以及巴塞尔银行监管委员会（BCBS）等，积极推动金融监管理念重塑和监管体系重构，支持加强宏观审慎管理，促进各国加强监管合作，推动金融领域国际标准与准则的修订和切实执行，在推动全球金融体系和金融监管改革、强化金融稳定制度框架等方面发挥了十分重要的作用。

当前，国际金融危机深层次影响仍未消散，包括强化监管在内的各种纠正市场的行动都应充分考虑经济金融形势的脆弱性和复杂性，这就需要各国加强深层次的协调与合作。今天，在国际货币基金组织的倡议下，我们齐聚一堂，希望在进一步总结和交流 FSAP 评估经验的基础上，共同深入探讨金融稳定监测与管理，认真分析最新国际监管标准以及最近一轮国际金融监管改革的影响，反思如何更好地加强金融稳定框架、识别和监测系统性风险，交流在建立宏观审慎制度框架方面的经验。这些议题都颇具挑战性，是很有时效性的题目，值得深入讨论。

预祝会议圆满成功！

谢谢大家！

开幕词

朱 民

国际货币基金组织副总裁

各位尊敬的来宾，早上好！欢迎参加我们这个关于金融部门评估规划（FSAP）的座谈会。我非常高兴大家可以来上海出席我们的会议。亚太地区的高级决策者们能够齐聚一堂，就应对本次全球危机的努力和国际货币基金组织在促进金融稳定方面的作用彼此交换意见，这本就是一个十分难得的机会。这次研讨会的举办还离不开中国人民银行的鼎力合作。我衷心感谢周小川行长和央行工作人员的辛勤工作和热情招待。

就在我们共坐一堂之时，全球各地的决策者正又一次地进入应急状态。当初的金融部门危机转变为了一场主权债务危机，现在又演化为全面的信心危机。市场对主权风险与金融部门疲弱之间持续存在的恶性反馈循环尤其不安。为了降低主权风险，各方需要作出重大、果断的政治决策。但是，我们也需要付出更大努力来加固先进经济体和新兴经济体的金融系统。我们相信，经过改进的 FSAP 可以在这个进程中发挥必不可少的作用。你们的意见和建议将有助于我们进一步改善 FSAP，使其成为一个切实有效的监督和危机预防工具。

在详细讨论 FSAP 之前，我想先谈一下当前国际金融危机对先进经济体和新兴经济体的影响。主要先进经济体看来已进入了经济活动疲弱、金融困顿、公共债务和赤字居高不下的恶性循环。相形之下，新兴市场经济体显示了较好的基本面，这些要素迄今为止支撑了全球经济增长。但是，这些经济体并非完全不受影响。事实上，它们的脆弱性正在增加，其经济前景正由于来自先进经济体的潜在溢出效应而被削弱。也正因为如此，很多亚洲决策者公开警告说，经济下行风险正在增加，并且他们也已经开始调整政策态势。

由于世界各大中央银行上周采取了协调行动，为全球金融体系注入美元流动性，投资者的担心有所缓和，尽管如此，各主要先进经济体的疲弱和新兴经济体的周期性经济降温加在一起，已给金融市场带来压力。Euro Stoxx 50 指数自 2011 年初以来下降了 15% 以上，即使是那些通过"购买世界各地股票"来分散风险的投资者，其股票价值用 MSCI 世界股票指数衡量，也在 2011 年下降了接近 7%。市场波动性已经增加，一个体现就是，被称为"恐惧指数"的 VIX 指数自 6 月以来急剧上升[①]。有些人甚至开始疑问，全球经济是否即将进入比 2008—2009 年期间更为严重的衰退。

问题的核心是欧元区危机。核心的欧洲国家现正受到压力。外国投资者正在逃离欧洲主权债务市场，西班牙和意大利债务的长期收益率因此升到 6%，已接近通常认为可持续的边界水平。德国的债券资产掉期利差最近达到了自雷曼兄弟公司倒闭以来的最高水平。

随着主权债务市场条件恶化，欧洲各银行在批发市场筹借资金越来越困难，成本越来越高。与此同时，这些银行还面临着大量即将到期的债务，一些分析人员估计，明年到期的债务将超过 6000 亿欧元[②]。这意味着，欧洲的银行正越来越依赖欧洲中央银行提供的短期流动性；最近的估计数据显示，欧洲中央银行提供的资金自 2011 年 6 月以来增加了大约 1250 亿欧元，自 9 月以来增加了大约 500 亿欧元。

在这些情况下，欧洲银行将难以达到欧洲银行监管局新规定的 9% 的核心一级资本目标。由于欧洲的金融股票价格自 2011 年初以来下降了几乎五分之一，利用股票市场融资的空间非常有限[③]。风险在于，银行将更有可能削减放贷或出

---

① VIX 指数：危机前，2008 年 7 月 1 日：23.65；危机顶峰，2008 年 11 月 20 日：80.86；目前，2011 年 12 月 8 日：30.6。

② 市场估计数据显示，在这即将到期的 6000 亿欧元中，德国占 1570 亿欧元；意大利占 2060 亿欧元；法国占 990 亿欧元；西班牙占 500 亿欧元。荷兰、比利时、奥地利、芬兰、葡萄牙和爱尔兰占其余部分。

③ 金融部门股票价格年初至今（12 月 1 日）的下降幅度：全世界（−21%）；欧洲（−19%）；美国（−28%）；日本（−21%）；中国香港（−25%）；韩国（−22%）。

售资产。由于存在着这种去杠杆化趋势，金融部门、实体经济和欧元区内外财政状况之间的恶性反馈循环进一步加剧的风险很大。

实体经济也已很明显地受到了压力。欧洲的广泛的经济信心指数在最近几个月恶化，商业景气指数也是如此，而产能利用率预计将在第四季度下降。欧洲各国政府和经合组织都已大幅度下调增长预测，调整后的预测接近衰退水平。

欧元区的危机有可能通过金融和贸易联系对世界其他地区产生溢出影响。在美国，经过修正的第三季度 GDP 增长率为 2%，低于预期。即使是这个水平，也难以在第四季度保持，原因是：收入增长无力，失业率高居不下，住房价格不断下降，且消费的增加主要是通过减少储蓄实现的。关于财政政策的政治分歧久而不决，正在抑制美国市场的信心。美国的超级委员会最近未能就减少财政赤字达成协议，可能意味着将要总共削减 12000 亿美元的支出，而如此大规模的财政调整将冲击经济增长。这使得信用评级机构再次发出下调评级的警告。

其他的主要发达经济体，尤其是日本和英国，面临着同样困难的情况。日本的工业生产于 2011 年 9 月急剧下降，而 10 月的采购经理指数显示，第四季度的经济扩张温和，增长前景不强。在英国，2012 年的经济增长率预测已经向下修正至不到 1%，如果欧元区经济收缩，英国可能难以避免衰退。

我想强调的一点是，虽然亚洲迄今为止在这场危机中相对安定，但仍不能掉以轻心。我们并不认为新兴亚洲已经"脱钩"。实际上，更加疲弱的全球需求和更加困难的国际金融状况可能会暴露出亚洲的基本脆弱性——驱动这些脆弱性的往往是迅速的信贷增长。已有迹象显示，新兴亚洲的增长速度正在放慢。来自中国和印度的制造业采购经理指数报告显示，经济活动与 2011 年早些时候相比已有所放缓。另一些规模较小的经济体的贸易数字下滑则说明了：不断转弱的外部前景可能会压抑本地区原本很强劲的经济增长。

国际货币基金组织最近的溢出效应报告显示，亚洲在来自贸易渠道的冲击面前仍然非常脆弱。欧洲是包括中国、印度和菲律宾在内的一些亚洲国家的最大出口市场之一。虽然地区内贸易正变得日益重要，但这种地区内贸易中的一部分和亚欧贸易同属一个供应链。2008 年危机的经验显示，与欧洲和美国的贸易如果受到破坏，也会殃及地区内贸易。

此外，亚洲也通过金融渠道受到影响。一直以来，外国投资者在亚洲的股票和债券市场发挥着重要作用，该区域很多国家通过贸易信贷额度、银团贷款和其他批发融资，对欧洲银行有很大的风险敞口①。越来越多的证据显示，在新兴市场活动的一些主要欧洲银行正在撤离，这会给通过这些渠道的信贷供应产生重大影响。与此同时，为寻求建立流动性缓冲，新兴亚洲的银行正继续进行着近年开始的去杠杆化过程。

正如大家所知，基金组织大量参与了当前危机的管理。这属于我们的应急工作。与此同时，我们正在加紧努力，通过改进 FSAP 之类的监督工具来预防未来的金融危机。

让我现在详细阐述一下 FSAP 的作用②，我们认为，它将成为全球金融稳定的一个必不可少的支柱。FSAP 于 1999 年针对亚洲金融危机创立，目标是帮助各国政府查明金融部门的脆弱性并制定较长期的政策和改革措施。对于先进经济体，FSAP 提供了一个独特的机会，以根据当前危机的教训加强和改革金融部门。在新兴经济体，FSAP 可有助于各国政府预防今后的危机。

FSAP 通常侧重于以下三个核心领域：

1. 首先，是根据公认的国际标准评估金融监督工作的效力。本次国际金融危机突出表明，需要改进标准和准则，以防范系统性风险。这些监管方面的改革给各国政府和基金组织带来了重任。问题在于：“我们是否做好了准备，以实行包括巴塞尔Ⅲ在内的更严格的新准则？”

2. 其次，FSAP 将评估宏观金融稳定所面临的主要风险的来源、发生概率和潜在影响。FSAP 将全面观察金融体系及其与实体经济之间的各种联系。这包括对银行乃至整个金融体系进行量化的压力测试。FSAP 除了提供定量的分析结果

---

① 欧元区银行对以下三个国家的债权超过或略低于它们的 GDP 的 10%：澳大利亚、新西兰和越南。对于新兴工业化经济体、东盟成员国、日本和印度，这个比率接近 5%。欧元区银行对中国的债权较小。欧元区银行还提供亚洲贸易信贷的约 50%。

② 新兴市场和发展中经济体的 FSAP 是与世界银行联合举办的，具有两个构成部分：国际货币基金组织负责金融稳定评估，世界银行负责金融发展情况评估。对于先进经济体，评估由国际货币基金组织负责，侧重于金融稳定。

之外，还对政府监测和查明系统性风险的能力进行定性评估。在这方面，FSAP可用于制定和完善宏观审慎政策，以限制金融失衡的加剧和预防系统性风险。

3. 第三，FSAP 将评估政府管理和解决金融危机的能力。它提供了一个框架，用以评估应急预案和金融安全网的充分程度（包括跨境问题），以及用于制订行动计划，来处理那些失去偿付能力的金融机构。

直到 2010 年，参加 FSAP 仍是自愿的，此后二十国集团领导人决定，对于那些其金融部门被视为"具有系统重要性"的经济体，将强制进行 FSAP。通过每五年进行一次的强制性 FSAP，国际货币基金组织将能够更为密切地监测那些一旦发生危机，很可能对系统稳定性产生最严重影响的成员。

本次国际金融危机之后，就国际货币基金组织监督任务的现代化问题进行了长达一年的辩论，而决定为具有系统重要性的经济体强制进行 FSAP 是这场辩论的主要成果之一。这是一个具有里程碑意义的决定，它把金融部门问题正式纳入了基金组织的双边监督工作的核心，并弥补了基金组织的两个主要监督工具，即第四条磋商和 FSAP 之间的缺口。

自从创立 FSAP 以来，已有 138 个国家（地区）自愿参加这个规划［很多国家（地区）不止一次参加］，当前正在进行或正在筹划的 FSAP 共有 35 项。2007—2008 年金融危机开始以来，对 FSAP 的需求急剧增加。最近的一次调查显示，四分之三的答复者表示，对 FSAP 的总体功用感到满意或非常满意。

我们最近的内部分析显示，FSAP 作为一个独立检查工具发挥了很好的作用。在最近的国际金融危机开始之前，FSAP 的评估能够确定出主要的风险来源。随着危机的展开，FSAP 小组还迅速调整了评估范围，以侧重于诸如危机管理、流动性支持安排和跨境传播这样的关键问题。FSAP 提出的建议为部分地缓和危机影响提供了帮助。

当然，仍有一些教训有待吸取。过去五年的经历显示，需要在评估中更多地注意流动性风险以及跨境和跨市场联系。我们最近的检查得出结论认为，FSAP虽然准确地查明了风险，但其发出的警告的有力度和清晰度还有待提高。我高兴地说，我们正在参考这些经验教训调整 FSAP，并在以下几个方面加强其有效性：

- 首先，FSAP 已变得更加灵活，能考虑到各国的具体情况。

- 其次，FSAP 的分析工具箱已经过改进，能涵盖种类更多的风险、宏观—金融反馈和跨境溢出效应。

- 第三，正在加强"非现场"工作，以提高评估的延续性和"现场"检查的有效性。

我们认为，经过改进的 FSAP 可以在亚太地区发挥特别重要的作用。尽管 FSAP 是在亚洲金融危机之后创立的，但亚洲对它的支持似乎不如其他地区那样热烈。只有一半的亚洲基金组织成员完成了一次 FSAP，与此相比，所有欧洲成员、68% 的西半球国家，81% 的中东和中亚国家以及 59% 的撒哈拉以南非洲国家完成了该规划。

但是，这一情况正在转变。国际金融危机开始以来，大多数具有庞大金融部门的亚洲成员已完成了 FSAP 或即将进行该规划。这也符合这样的现实，即亚洲正在诸如基金组织和二十国集团这样的多边机构中发挥着更大的领导作用。基金组织为能够加深与我们的亚洲成员的合作而感到高兴和自豪。

一个很好的例子是，我们在过去两年中首次为中国和印度尼西亚进行了 FSAP。FSAP 赞扬了这两个国家过去十年里在金融体系改革方面取得的显著进展。这些改革有助于它们承受住 2008 年国际金融危机的最严重影响。但是，问题仍然存在。中国应该改善其金融市场和金融服务的广度和深度，以形成一个更为多样化和更为创新的、基于商业化原则的金融部门；在印度尼西亚，当务之急是推进法治并消除透明度和治理方面的弱点。

最后，我确信，经过改进的 FSAP 将带来双赢局面，它不仅将大大提高基金组织监督职能的能力和有效性，而且还将大大加强各国政府监测和管理金融稳定的能力。

我们相信，FSAP 将继续演进，特别是，它将根据亚太地区当局的需要而调整。本地区今后的某些 FSAP 很可能成为其他国家借鉴的榜样。我们仍有很多问题需要处理。例如：

- 基金组织是否应该鼓励其成员进行更多的 FSAP 和 FSAP 更新？

- 如何应对基金组织和各政府面临的资源限制？

- 改进 FSAP 的最好办法是什么（自下而上还是自上而下）？

- 我们可以通过何种方式来照顾迅速增长的新兴经济体的需要？

- 我们是否做好了准备，来推行重大的监管改革，包括巴塞尔Ⅲ？

在接下来的会议上，大家将有机会讨论这些问题和许多其他问题。我坚信，座谈会结束时，我们作为个人和团体都能获得宝贵的经验见识。我希望大家的讨论富有成果，引人入胜。谢谢！

第一部分

金融部门评估规划
——独立评估的作用

- 如何进一步提升FSAP在以下方面的作用：(1)识别系统性风险和提升系统性监督能力；(2)识别微观审慎监管存在的缺陷；(3)评估危机管理框架中的优缺点？

- 在基金组织给出评估结果以及与受评国持续开展后续对话时，如何提升FSAP政策建议的影响力？

- FSAP应加强哪些方面工作，以提升其地区针对性？

□ 何塞·比亚斯（José Viñals）
国际货币基金组织金融顾问和货币与资本市场部主任

金融部门评估规划的现在与未来角色

金融部门评估规划（FSAP）开始于 1999 年亚洲金融危机后，作为工具帮助当局解决以下 3 方面问题：（1）在广泛接受的标准下，评估金融监管的有效性；（2）识别宏观金融稳定主要风险的来源、可能性和影响；（3）协助各国当局管理和化解金融危机。其基本思路是与各国金融监管当局开展非常坦诚的对话，目的是不仅要发现金融脆弱性，还要提出一系列建议，有助于当局在短期和中期内解决脆弱性问题，提高金融体系的稳定性。

为了考察 FSAP 对成员国的实际效果，我们最近进行了一个内部的 FSAP 成效检验，检验的结果是既有好消息也有坏消息。好消息是，我们发现在此次国际金融危机中，FSAP 能够在许多情况下揭示风险的主要来源，且一般情况下 FSAP 的建议有助于避免危机恶化产生最为严重的后果。但我们也发现，危机前 FSAP 存在一些缺陷，距离一个完美的工具还相差甚远。其主要缺点是低估流动性风险和系统性流动性风险，FSAP 可能未将某些重要问题考虑在内，例如跨境和跨市场的联系，产品、市场和金融机构之间的相互影响。因此，在许多情况下我们未对系统性风险进行评估。这就是为什么我们最近进行了一些改进，以确保目前的 FSAP 保持过去的优势，克服其以往的缺陷。

FSAP 现在已经更加注重地考虑各国的具体情况，成为一个更灵活的工具。这也得益于改进后的分析工具箱，其中涵盖了各类风险、跨境溢出效应、金融部门与其他经济主体之间的相互作用。类似系统性风险、宏观审慎政策框架、主权风险和金融体系之间的联系或资本流动突然停止引发的系统性影响等要素，都在如今的 FSAP 中得到体现。我们力求使危机管理更加公正和透明。如果让我总结新 FSAP 的关键要素，那就是：FSAP 是严格而公平的，它将以一种非常明确的方式提供给各国当局。也许最近 FSAP 最重要的变化是遵循着由二十国集团领导人去年做出的决定，其金融市场被金融稳定理事会（FSB）认定为具有系统重要性的国家将强制接受 FSAP 评估。这 25 个被认定为具有系统重要性的国家的金融体系将每 5 年接受一次 FSAP 和更新 FSAP 的审查。基金组织需要通过其监督机制监测这些国家的系统稳定性，以便更好地理解造成全球金融不稳定的风险组成和来源，并提出相应政策建议以更好地维护全球稳定。因此，这是基金组织监督全球金融部门的真正核心。

改进后的 FSAP 在亚太地区特别有用，自此次国际金融危机以来该地区对 FSAP 的需求显著增加。基金组织已对中国和印度尼西亚开展首次 FSAP，与相关国家的合作非常成功。

不断发展的 FSAP 和国际金融体系的不断变化意味着，我们有很多东西需要学习。这是一个"干中学"的过程，我们有很多要学习，以确保 FSAP 总是比学习曲线领先一步，而不是落后于曲线。这就是为什么我们很欣赏大家坦诚建议的原因。

□ 刘士余

中国人民银行副行长

加强协调合作　继续拓展 FSAP 作用

尊敬的朱民副总裁，来自各国央行和监管当局的各位同事，女士们、先生们：

大家上午好！

刚才周小川行长在欢迎词中已经介绍了中国"金融部门评估规划"（FSAP）的一些经验和做法。我作为中国 FSAP 工作的参与者在此也谈一些体会，与各国朋友分享。

FSAP 自 1999 年推出以来，逐步成为一项卓有成效的国际评估项目，已被国际社会广泛认可，并在监测、管理全球金融风险，推动有关国家（地区）金融改革和发展等方面作出了积极贡献。中国从 2003 年开始按照 FSAP 的框架和相关国际准则进行了自评估。自评估结论表明，中国注重深化金融改革、发展金融市场、加强金融监管，并取得了良好进展。在 2008 年 11 月的二十国集团华盛顿峰会上，胡锦涛主席正式承诺中国将接受国际货币基金组织和世界银行对中国进行 FSAP 评估。这项工作于 2009 年 8 月正式开始，到 2011 年 11 月顺利完成。在此我特别感谢来自国际货币基金组织和世界银行的评估团，他们以杰出的专业水准、敬业精神和团队精神与中国同事密切合作，顺利完成了评估工作，给中国的同事留下了深刻印象。

这次评估有助于世界加深对中国金融体系的认识和了解，也有利于中国金融部门对自身面临的挑战做出清醒的认识。在此，我愿与各位分享中国通过推进改革、加强监管和鼓励创新，促进金融业持续健康稳定发展的一些实践和经验，具体有以下三个方面：

一是按照市场化方向，不断深化金融改革。

努力保持金融机构微观财务健康，是中国的重要经验。特别是亚洲金融危机后，中国深深感到深化金融改革的紧迫性和重要性。在改革过程中，我们非常重视金融机构微观财务健康。在中央政府的统一领导下，2003 年以来，我们已经基本完成了各类主要大型金融机构的财务重组工作，将其由国有独资机构改造成股份公司，并且上市。在股份制改造过程中，政府向四家大型国有银行注资共 800 亿美元。从近几年情况来看，大型银行的公司治理不断规范，风险控制机制不断提升，财务指标持续改善，从而使中国金融体系的整体稳健性发生了质的变化，这也是中国金融体系在此次国际金融危机中保持稳定的重要基础。

国际货币基金组织副总裁朱民先生在中国银行工作期间，主要负责中国银行的股份制改造，相信他能深深地体会到在金融机构内部进行微观财务重组的难度，当然他到中国人民银行担任副行长之后也更能体会到从宏观层面推动金融机构进行财务重组的难度。

二是不断加强宏观审慎管理。

无论是亚洲金融危机，还是尚未结束的本轮国际金融危机，其重要启示就是单个金融机构的微观财务健康十分重要，但是宏观的系统重要性金融机构或者说易于引发系统性风险的机构的风险防范则更为重要。中国《国民经济和社会发展第十二个五年规划纲要》已明确提出要构建逆周期的宏观审慎制度管理框架，建立健全系统性风险预警、评估体系和处置机制。众所周知，今年以来中国金融宏观调控的任务非常重，一方面我们要继续深化改革，保持金融稳定，同时我们要把治理通货膨胀作为宏观调控的首要任务。在本轮治理通胀、促进金融发展的过程中，中国宏观管理部门、中央银行和金融监管当局已经尝试运用一些宏观审慎管理的工具和手段，并且取得了较好的效果。比如，我们对资本消耗过快、贷款增长过快的金融机构实行差别存款准备金率，在贷款拨备方面也提出了相应的要求，这将有利于此类机构在微观层面的审慎管理，从而为国家整个经济系统的审慎管理作出贡献。此外，中国支持巴塞尔Ⅲ的严格执行，进一步提高会计标准和信息披露要求，并将加快建立存款保险制度，完善系统性风险处置机制和方法。

这也是 FSAP 评估团对中国提出的非常重要的一条建议。

三是鼓励金融创新，提高金融市场在资源配置中的效率。

中国正处于工业化、市场化的过程中，国际化、信息化、城镇化迅速推进，全社会对金融产品和金融服务的需求日益多元化。近年来，我们在充分借鉴国际金融市场发展经验的同时，努力通过制度创新和产品创新来促进整个金融市场的发展，特别是债券市场快速发展，很快地改变了中国债券市场在中国资本市场发展中的落后程度，以及整个中国债券市场与其他国家债券市场相比较的落后状况。按照国际清算银行（BIS）的统计，中国债券的存量和每年新增发行量在全球基本处于前五位，这是近年来我们在制度创新和产品创新方面推动金融市场发展的重要成果。

同时，评估团也指出了目前中国金融体系的一个问题，就是服务小微企业、服务农业、农村和农民的金融体系处于发展当中，尚未形成富有竞争性的市场。这一评估结论是符合中国现状的，我们要予以高度重视。实际上自 2001 年，特别是 2003 年以来，中国人民银行和金融监管部门就非常重视这一问题，努力构建富有竞争性的、面向小微企业和农业、农村、农民的金融服务体系，但效果还不是太理想，我们仍在努力。因此我们鼓励各类资本，包括国际资本、民间资本和大型企业资本进入中国中小金融机构，以利于这类金融机构数量的增加，并提高服务的广泛性。

另一方面，在此我也非常想向来自亚太国家的各位同仁介绍我们在 FSAP 操作层面的几条具体经验：

第一，评估双方应注重沟通和交流。这项工作好比一个人去医院接受体检，受评国必须和评估团坦诚相见，客观、历史地介绍本国经济、金融的发展过程、历史以及文化。

第二，要做好这项工作，必须加强协调和组织领导。中国在承诺接受国际货币基金组织和世界银行的评估之后，成立了跨部委的领导小组，由周小川行长担任组长，主要任务是加强协调。这种协调分为三个层面，分别是正部长级、副部长级以及司局级的协调。中国金融体系有很多技术概念和操作与其他市场经济国家不完全一致，在接受评估的过程中，我们要对一些原有数据按照新口径做出修改，这些事情很繁杂，离开细致的协调是不可能完成的。此外，中国银监会、证监会和保监会在评估时也都成立了相应的工作小组。

第三，要有专门的工作层面的机构。中国在人民银行金融稳定局设立了FSAP办公室，该办公室不仅在评估期间配合国际货币基金组织和世界银行的工作，在评估结束后仍将保留，以利于深入研究国际货币基金组织和世界银行的评估结论，学习和借鉴其他国家和地区的经验，进一步促进深化改革，接受国际货币基金组织和世界银行的下一次评估。

第四，做好这项工作还需要预算上的支持和安排。中国政府非常重视FSAP评估工作，财政部专门做出相应的预算安排。

希望上述微观操作层面上的四条经验能为在座尚未接受评估的国家做好FSAP工作提供一定借鉴。我相信国际货币基金组织和世界银行能够继续拓展和改进FSAP，使其具有更加广泛的影响力，成为国际金融体系中的权威评估机制。在此，我提出三点建议，供各位参考：

第一，立足实际，尊重各国国情。希望FSAP立足受评国的经济发展阶段和特点，充分理解一国金融体系和市场格局的历史、文化和现状，尽量避免用传统的模式来评价一国/地区金融市场发展和管理的现状，这也有利于吸引更多的国家和地区主动接受FSAP评估、更好地运用评估结论。

第二，突出重点，加强对主要经济体系统性风险的监测和管理。国际金融危机以及欧洲主权债务危机还在影响着全球经济复苏，也对包括中国在内的新兴市场国家的经济平稳增长产生持续影响。这表明，一些系统重要性经济体的风险具有巨大的溢出效应。吸取危机教训，FSAP应强化对系统重要性经济体风险的监测和管理，对其提出更高的标准和要求。

第三，与时俱进，增强合作。评估团和受评国之间的合作至关重要。在评估过程中，受评国应当向评估团全面客观地介绍本国的金融情况，同时评估团也应当倾听受评国的意见，以此加深双方理解。

女士们、先生们，各位同事，在这次研讨会上，我相信来自各个国家（地区）中央银行和金融监管当局的同事，以及来自国际货币基金组织、金融稳定理事会等国际组织的朋友将会介绍各自的经验和真知灼见，我和来自人民银行以及中国其他部门的同事会认真学习和借鉴大家的经验，也愿意和各位代表一道共同努力，把 FSAP 评估工作向更加深入的方向推进，不断促进全球各地区金融业发展，为承担维护金融稳定的使命作出应有的贡献。

谢谢大家！

□ 梅格·伦萨格（Meg Lundsager）

美国驻国际货币基金组织执行董事

引言

很高兴在此发表演讲！我想从 2010 年美国 FSAP 评估经验以及我作为国际货币基金组织执行董事的经历出发，与大家分享我对 FSAP 附加价值的看法，FSAP 在哪些方面做得不错，在哪些方面还需进一步改进。

过去几年的经历让我们对宏观金融联系有了深刻的认识。IMF 应当利用其掌握的各国经验，让成员国认识到改革的重要性。我们积累了相当多的负面经验，尤其是最近这几年，一些国家未能采取有效行动应对金融脆弱性。IMF 关注实体经济与金融部门之间的联系，这对改善未来经济增长和创造就业是非常重要的。

对 FSAP 价值的思考

FSAP 全面把握金融体系及其运行环境，重点关注系统性风险，这是其独特之处。FSAP 试图指出一国金融系统脆弱性大致状况，而这些脆弱性可能来自国内，也可能来自国外。这些脆弱性往往被忽视了，金融危机让我们意识到解决这些脆弱性的重要性。

IMF 在对美国经济和金融体系的监督中引入了一些新工具，评估国内脆弱性可能对其他国家产生的溢出效应。IMF 应当将这种做法向其他国家推广，这当中不仅包括大国，还包括小国，因为小国也会通过金融部门间的联系影响邻国。

FSAP 的另一大优点是关注监管漏洞。IMF 认识到，监管漏洞可能存在于法律层面，也可能存在于执行层面，即监管机构具备法律赋予的相应权力，但却未能有效执行该权力。

另外，FSAP 还评估一国对国际金融监管标准和准则的实施情况。这项评估对国内监管机构具有重要意义，监管机构能够得到有关全球最优做法的最新信

19

息，并获得客观公正的外部评估促进其改进监管。

美国 FSAP 评估的意义

2010 年美国 FSAP 评估对美国进行了一次系统和独立的评估，以找出造成这次国际金融危机的根本原因。这对美国当局来说是非常有意义的，因为处在危机当中的美国当局很难站到局外对美国进行全面分析，而 FSAP 评估团却能够这样做。FSAP 指出了美国金融体系存在的主要问题以及可能的解决方案。尽管评估中的很多发现与美国内部评估结论一致，FSAP 仍有助于我们理清思路。

FSAP 评估团对美国的银行进行了压力测试。而在此之前，美国监管机构于 2009 年推出监管资本评估项目（SCAP），也对美国的银行进行了压力测试，被市场认为是高度成功和可信的。作为独立、可信的评估团队，FSAP 评估团的压力测试为 SCAP 结果提供了进一步支持，增强了对美国金融机构的信心。

另外，FSAP 评估有助于增强美国监管机构间的协调与沟通。美国当局成立了 FSAP 协调委员会，是美国新成立的宏观审慎政策协调机构金融稳定监督委员会（FSOC）的前身。

通过共同参与 FSAP 评估，美国监管机构将它们看做是一个系统，而不是互不相干的部分。这在尊重不同监管机构职责及独立性的基础上有力地促进了机构间合作，并让监管机构树立起维护金融稳定的集体责任感。现在，共同维护金融稳定是 FSOC 的核心，监管机构可利用同行压力敦促彼此采取必要行动解决潜在的脆弱性问题。

另外，美国 FSAP 评估提高了对标准和准则执行情况的评估标准。我们希望，将来的评估也将继续采取严格的标准。

如何进一步改善 FSAP

我想，今天我们将讨论包括 FSAP 在内的 IMF 监督的影响力。一般来说，IMF 建议很难切合一国的实际情况。在一国当局来看，FSAP 评估是发现了一些基本问题并提供了多项可能的解决方案，但通常情况下，这些建议并没有清楚地表明该国当局应如何将这些建议转变为适合该国国情的具体政策方案。

我想就如何增强 FSAP 的影响力提几点建议。

第一，FSAP 评估团要认识到，无论是何种监管结构，都没有有效监管重要。例如，美国保险行业监管结构繁杂，有很多州层面的监管机构，但实际上，美国保险监管系统运转良好，美国保险监督官协会（NAIC）有效地促进了国家层面的对话。

第二，IMF 应确保在进行评估前，FSAP 评估团和评估人员清楚地了解一国制度结构和执行机制。这将增强 FSAP 评估的影响力，使受评国当局相信 FSAP 针对该国具体国情提出的政策建议将发挥有效作用。

第三，FSAP 评估团在建议受评国进行改革时，应提供可信的逻辑，说明为什么这些改革是必要的。仅仅以"其他国家如此"为由是不够的。为什么某项政策行动在另一个国家有用或者没有用？评估团需对此作出解释。为此，评估团需了解现有结构的历史和政治背景。

第四，IMF 可充分利用其积累的经验，提供令人信服的解决方案。IMF 员工对各国政治经济有着深入的了解。一项政策方案可能听起来不错，但很难具体应用到某个国家。应充分利用 IMF 员工已有经验帮助各国了解如何才能开展必要的改革。具体而言，在一些国家，改革带来的利益曾使既得利益集团对解决金融部门监管缺陷持支持态度，FSAP 评估团应充分利用其在这方面的知识。

除增强评估影响力外，IMF 应多利用其他国家的例子帮助一国当局认识到其面临的问题。例如，IMF 员工可能会联想到另一个国家也面临类似问题，从而可建议一国当局与这个国家共同探讨政策应对，有关政策是如何发挥作用的或为何未能发挥作用。

另外，FSAP 评估者的工作还需进一步改善。IMF 依靠外部评估者完成《关于标准和准则遵守情况的报告》（ROSCs）。这具有重要意义，但 IMF 需要对各国 ROSCs 的一致性和质量做好监督。IMF 应确保对 RSOCs 的主导权，RSOCs 应当是 IMF 的评估，而不仅仅是评估者的评估。

最后，FSAP 还需改进其后续工作。目前，我们在这方面已取得了一些进展，但我们仍认为 IMF 员工可通过第四条款磋商等机制深入了解 FSAP 建议是否已被采纳。另外，IMF 还应在考察已进行的改革是否如计划中有效的基础上制定未来的政策建议。判断一项监管结构是否有效不应局限于形式，IMF 要认识到，不同形式的监管结构可能同样有效。

□ 迪帕克·莫汉提（Deepak Mohanty）
印度储备银行执行董事

大家上午好！

首先，我想感谢此次研讨会的举办方——中国人民银行和国际货币基金组织（IMF）邀请我参加这次重要会议。由 IMF 和世界银行联合进行的 FSAP 越来越重要，尤其是在当前欧元区金融问题有逐步蔓延迹象之际。FSAP 是在亚洲金融危机后于 1999 年启动的，并在最近这次金融危机后于 2009 年 9 月进行了一次改进。改进后，25 个拥有系统重要性金融部门的国家每五年进行一次 FSAP，该项评估成为在第四条款双边监督下的一项强制性内容。作为 G20 成员国和拥有系统重要性金融部门的国家之一，印度正积极参与这个项目。

主持人先生，在讨论 IMF—世界银行 FSAP 评估前，我想先介绍下印度在维护金融稳定方面的经验。印度是 2001 年参与 FSAP 项目试点的为数不多的国家之一。过去十年，印度进行了多次比较全面的、前瞻性的自评估。这种自评估基于三大互相促进的支柱：金融稳定和压力测试，法律制度和市场发展，国际金融标准和准则的实施。自评估是一个不断学习的过程，需要相关部门密切配合。

除进行自评估外，印度还成立了一批高级别委员会和小组，考察金融部门问题，妥善实施有关政策建议。印度并没有因国际金融危机而放弃引入公司债信用违约掉期。印度同时还致力于解决与微观金融机构运行有关的监管问题。可以说，印度金融部门改革是个循序渐进的过程。当然，也有人批评印度金融改革过于缓慢。

现在全球都在讨论是否应将金融稳定确立为央行的目标之一。而印度早在国际金融危机前就已将维护金融稳定确立为央行的货币政策目标。自 2000 年初印度将维护金融稳定确立为央行目标以来，印度一直在积极运用货币政策和监管政策实现这一目标。作为金融系统监管机构，印度储备银行能够有效协调宏观审慎监管与微观审慎监管。早在发达国家爆发金融危机前，印度储备银行就曾采取多项审慎措施，降低银行体系在敏感行业的风险敞口，调整对不同资产的风险权重。为央行设定多重目标可能会带来一定利益冲突，但会产生更大的协同效应和利益融合，这些效应远超过利益冲突。

现在，印度又在进行 FSAP 评估。在这个背景下，我想强调几个问题。

第一，印度一直在根据自评估弥补监管漏洞。我们在一些领域取得了积极进展，但在其他一些领域要做的工作还很多。尽管我们在监管方面取得积极进展，但破产程序执行、债权人权利执行和破产体系应用的推进工作进展缓慢，因为这不仅涉及法律层面还涉及政治层面。

第二，印度在积极参与由 IMF、巴塞尔银行监管委员会（BCBS）、金融稳定理事会（FSB）和二十国集团（G20）领导的国际金融监管改革。我们为实现改革目标采取了几项改革措施，如积极实施巴塞尔协议Ⅲ，加强对金融集团（即印度的系统重要性金融机构）的有效监管，发布稳健薪酬政策指引，健全反洗钱措施等，我们对我们在 G20 监管改革框架下取得的进展感到满意。

对目前印度正在进行的 FSAP 评估，我们已经提交了我们对 FSAP 评估报告、技术文本以及备忘录的意见。

我们非常期待将 FSAP 的重要建议付诸实施。为进一步改进 FSAP、提高 FSAP 评估的有效性，我想提几点建议。换而言之，应在哪些方面进一步开展工作？

第一，不应因过度强调以风险为基础的评估方法而将监督资源集中在系统重要性金融部门，从而使针对所有国家的标准评估受到影响。近期欧洲边缘国家的情况表明小型、不具系统重要性国家的主权债务问题可能产生较大的溢出效应、破坏金融稳定。有鉴于此，为维护全球和区域金融稳定，应当重视对所有国家的标准评估。

第二，有必要梳理后危机时期建立的几个评估机制。比如，目前 G20 主导的全球监管改革非常注重同行评估，改革事项包括薪酬改革、影子银行体系等一系列问题；FSB 分别就每个具体问题对全球执行国际标准的进度进行了评估。这就容易导致评估泛滥。事实上，FSAP 可与 FSB 就评估事项进行交流，避免重复评估。

第三，FSAP 应成为一个双向学习的过程。我们希望 FSAP 向我们介绍压力测试等技术手段，这会帮助我们建立并完善我们自己的分析框架。同时，我们也希望 FSAP 评估团能从印度金融系统中获得一些有用的经验，比如，现在全球许多国家开始将宏观审慎监管作为逆周期政策工具，而印度在这方面取得了很大成功。再比如，为监测传染风险，印度引入了可有效分析关联性和系统性风险的网络模型，IMF 可参考印度这方面的经验，并与其他国家分享。

第四，立足于不同国家的具体情况提出政策建议有助于提升 FSAP 建议的认可度。FSAP 应考虑不同国家的需要运用更为灵活的评估模型，而不是用最优做法套用所有国家，这将使 FSAP 更易于被受评国接受。在定义最优做法时，我们应拓宽视野，世界各国的做法都有可能成为最优做法。如果 FSAP 能解决各国特别关注的问题，FSAP 建议将更容易被各国所接受。

第五，我要特别提一下金融部门在推动一国发展方面所能发挥的作用。除了评估金融部门的稳定状况，改进后的 FSAP 评估还有一项重要目标是评估金融部门对一国增长和发展的潜在贡献。在印度，我们通过推动金融包容性增长实现发展目标，即金融中介和正规渠道的渗透性需满足印度这个人口特点的大陆经济的需要。这种发展战略强调填补物质和社会基础设施缺口。所有这些要求 IMF 和世界银行在评估新兴市场国家时采取更加灵活的方法、开展更多的工作。

在总结前，我想强调除采取措施加强审慎法规制定、改善客户服务、强化监管外，我们还发起一些政策讨论，探讨新银行许可证的发放、外资银行在印度的发展路线、大型金融企业的控股结构以及监管过程审核。我们还对金融监管结构进行了大刀阔斧的改革，成立了金融稳定和发展理事会（FSDC）。为进行立法改革，我们还成立了金融部门立法改革委员会（FSLRC）。而危机后，为完善监管结构，我们采取了一系列行动。我们希望 FSAP 能根据不断达成的国际共识，在认真审视其与印度国情的关联性的基础上，在构筑后危机时期行动计划的过程中发挥重要作用，强化法规和监管制度。

谢谢大家！

□ 宣昌能
中国人民银行金融稳定局局长

感谢主持人给我这次机会做一个非常简短的发言。首先，我想向国际货币基金组织、世界银行和中国 FSAP 评估团，尤其向今天在座的各位表示感谢。Jonathan Fiechter、Udaibir Das、Keith Hall 等为中国 FSAP 的圆满完成作出了重要的贡献。

刚才刘士余副行长简短介绍了中国 FSAP 评估的经验。正如他所提到的，我们和其他部门，尤其是三个监管委员会，通力协作，确保评估工作有效开展。

刚才 Meg 谈到如何提升 FSAP 评估结论和建议切合一国实际的程度，我想就此谈一谈我的看法。刘士余副行长在介绍中国 FSAP 评估经验时也提到同样的感受，尤其是对于一些重要的教训。对于一国应该做什么、采取什么措施的争议较少，难以达成一致的问题在于行动的时机和先后顺序。在这方面，我认为中国 FSAP 评估团做得非常好，特别是考虑到了中国的具体情况，就像在美国 FSAP 评估中的做法一样。

例如，我们与中国 FSAP 评估团谈论过 FSAP 的影响力、美国 FSAP 评估对《多德—弗兰克法案》的影响。他们表示，虽然美国 FSAP 评估对这一法案的立法进程有一定的影响，但评估团刻意很巧妙地规避了对具体问题加以指点，比如，是否应该建立统一的银行业监管机构，是否应该向保险业发放联邦许可证。这样做很明智，因为如果建议过细，考虑到复杂的立法程序，执行起来也许会很困难。再比如，对于期货业的监管，如果提出要将美国商品期货交易委员会和证券交易委员会合并，那将涉及复杂棘手的问题，关系到参议院的金融委员会以及众议院相关委员会的管理权限问题。

在中国的 FSAP 评估中，我们和评估团就改革的时机和先后顺序进行了多轮讨论。他们在报告中提出的建议都和中国"十二五"规划的相关表述有高度的相关性，可以说"十二五"规划已包括了所有重要的要素，准确把握了未来中国金融体系发展中需要做哪些工作。我们和评估团的不同观点主要在于什么时候行动和如何行动，当然，我们之间对于监管框架也还有些不太大的分歧。但从总体看，中国 FSAP 评估团的工作非常出色，在需要进行什么改革、如何实施、实施的时机和先后顺序等几个问题间达成了平衡。Meg 就美国 FSAP 经验发表的观点，我深有同感。这些观点是非常重要的。今后，关键问题是提升 FSAP 评估的有效性，使 FSAP 评估被更广泛地接受。FSAP 评估所使用的方法可能需要进一步考虑如何使评估更切合实际。我对刚才其他几个国家代表的发言深表赞同，我认为这些观点都非常重要。谢谢！

□ 赤松典孝（Noritaka Akamatsu）

亚洲开发银行地区经济一体化部门副主任

FSAP 最初关注的重点是金融机构的微观审慎监管，但是现在看来，已经加强了对金融稳定的宏观审慎评估，这一点值得肯定。但是，很有必要持续跟进以帮助各国实施 FSAP 建议。鉴于 FSAP 评估间隔时间较长而且给受评国带来沉重负担，应建立单独的机制确保其持续发挥作用。虽然已经有了支持能力建设的金融部门改革和强化倡议（FIRST），但仍需与各国建立持续的政策对话以促进 FSAP 建议的实施。

亚行在其发展中成员国开展金融部门规划活动，可以此为平台为持续政策对话和能力建设提供支持。因此，亚行相信自身能有所贡献。但是，要发挥这样的作用，亚行须参与到 FSAP 评估中，原因有二：一是亚行目前无法看到 FSAP 的大部分评估结果，只能看到金融体系稳定评估报告（FSSA）和其他零星报告，这导致亚行所支持的改革有可能与 FSAP 建议相悖；再者，如果亚行也开展与 FSAP 类似的评估，一方面将加重受评国的负担，另一方面，由此造成的人力、物力重复投入既没有必要亚行也承受不起。因此，这一做法不可行。

亚行成员国进行 FSAP 评估时，有时会邀请或建议亚行参与。亚行认为，将这种参与制度化有助于提升 FSAP 的有效性。亚行认为不必也不可能成为这一全球规划中 IMF 和世界银行的正式合作伙伴，而是希望，只要在任一亚行成员国进行 FSAP 评估，亚行可以制度性地派专家参与 IMF/世界银行评估团。由于对 FSAP 评估团成员的保密要求，这样的安排并不能完全解决亚行接触不到 FSAP 评估结果的问题，但亚行认为这样做对于改善亚行相关规划与 FSAP 间的协调大有裨益，亚行成员国也将从中受益。因此，亚行建议 IMF 和世界银行考虑将此项安排付诸实施，同时希望 IMF 和世界银行以及亚行成员国在建立妥善保密安排的基础上向亚行开放全部 FSAP 评估结果。

主旨发言

FSAP与金融稳定——中国的实践与经验

周小川　中国人民银行

□ 周小川
中国人民银行行长

FSAP 与金融稳定——中国的实践与经验

女士们、先生们，中午好！

2008 年以来，金融稳定已成为国际金融组织和各国金融管理部门最优先考虑的议题之一，尤其是 2010 年爆发的欧洲主权债务危机更凸显了这一议题的重要性。实际上早在亚洲金融危机爆发后，中国金融界和政府部门都已认识到，深化改革和加强监管是防范和管理金融风险、维护金融稳定的重要基础。当然，此次国际金融危机的爆发进一步加深了这种认识。

今天的研讨会提供了一个很好的机会，来自亚太及其他地区的代表，济济一堂，共同分享在 FSAP 评估和促进金融稳定等方面的经验，并探讨如何在以往实践的基础上进一步完善相关的工作。我想借此机会，向大家介绍一下中国在 FSAP 评估、金融改革和金融稳定等方面的观点及做法。

一、国际金融危机凸显了宏观经济稳定与金融风险评估的重要性

此次危机暴露出主要经济体在系统性风险监测与评估、政治行动意愿和危机管理框架等方面还存在薄弱环节。为此，加强金融稳定评估和早期预警体系建设已成为国际社会的共识。

FSAP 是由国际货币基金组织和世界银行于亚洲金融危机之后建立的，用于全面评估成员经济体金融稳定。一直以来，FSAP 提供独立的评估结论，逐渐成为广泛接受的评估机制，也是受评经济体官方自评估的重要补充。此次金融危机以来，二十国集团（G20）峰会和金融稳定理事会（FSB）及时有效地进一步提升了 FSAP 的合法性，并强化了对基金组织开展 FSAP 的授权。相关国家的领导

人先后在 G20 华盛顿和伦敦峰会上两次承诺将对本国进行 FSAP 评估，FSB 成员经济体也一致承诺将以身作则，每 5 年进行一次 FSAP 评估。

这次国际金融危机同时让大家认识到，FSAP 自身也需要不断完善。在这方面，基金组织做出了不少努力，不断完善 FSAP 监督框架，FSAP 评估范围和评估重点也与时俱进，特别是在危机管理、防范跨境风险传染等方面，更加适应当前的需要。比如，FSAP 所关注的评估对象已由危机前的新兴市场国家转向了系统重要性经济体和金融中心；参加 FSAP 评估现在已成为 25 个具有全球系统重要性金融部门的经济体应尽的义务。

总体看，亚洲国家和地区对 FSAP 的参与程度相对较低一些，但主要的经济体，包括中国、印度、印度尼西亚、日本、韩国和中国香港等，都已开展了 FSAP 评估，其中日本和印度正在进行更新评估。我相信，随着亚洲的广泛参与，FSAP 在加强风险监测、维护亚洲乃至全球金融稳定方面将发挥日益重要的作用。

二、提升并落实有关金融体系健康性的国际标准

此次危机的一个重要启示是，要不断提高并完善国际标准。实行新的国际标准意味着所有成员经济体都要进一步深化改革，并加强国际合作。

（一）FSAP 有助于推动国际标准

FSAP 重视对银行、证券、保险业等领域核心原则遵守情况的评估，这有助于提升监管有效性和金融部门稳健性。这次危机后大家普遍认识到，更高的标准以及更好地执行对于降低微观和宏观层面的金融风险十分重要。例如，新近推出的巴塞尔Ⅲ提高了对资本质量、资本充足率和流动性比率的要求，提出了逆周期资本缓冲和全球系统重要性金融机构（G-SIFIs）额外资本要求。这就是说，一方面要在全球范围内严格执行巴塞尔Ⅲ，另一方面则需要适时对标准执行情况进行同行评估和专题评估，以促进标准的执行。通过设立更高的资本和流动性要求，巴塞尔Ⅲ将降低银行倒闭的可能性。当然，这并不是说会百分之百地避免这种可能性，尾部风险有可能减小，但仍会存在，仍需要予以考虑和重视，并规划相应的危机管理机制。

同时，我们认为，在标准制定过程中，应当注重一致性和公平性。在设立新标准或修订现有标准时，要考虑不同国家发展的特殊阶段和具体情况，避免将针对发达经济体"定制"的标准不加区分地用于全世界。

（二）中国实施国际标准的实践

近年来，中国注重引进并落实国际标准，受益匪浅。从本世纪初开始推进银行业改革以来，中国狠抓巴塞尔资本协议的落实和实施，特别强调提高资本充实率和资本质量。在亚洲金融危机期间，中国商业银行的处境比较艰难。当时很多评论认为，中国银行业已经在技术上资不抵债。为此我们下定决心推进改革，一方面大力推进市场化，另一方面在银行业和金融市场广泛推进实施相关国际标准，促使国内标准与国际标准趋同，推动金融业健康发展，维护金融稳定。

在此轮改革之前，中国银行业存在很多问题，如会计准则仍有计划经济色彩、贷款分类方法不准确、缺少外部审计、杠杆率和流动性管理不足、风险管理标准较低等，以至于各方对中国商业银行财务数据的真实性普遍持怀疑态度。因此，改革的一项重要内容是提高和落实标准并提升透明度，以保持国际社会对中国金融改革的信心。在 2003 年以来的改革过程中，我们始终坚持这一点，大大提高了资本要求、信息披露要求、会计与外部审计标准。特别是随着几家主要金融机构在香港等金融中心公开上市，进一步推动这些金融机构实施公众公司所需执行的更高的标准，如国际会计准则、公司治理和风险管理的相关原则等。

在此轮危机前，中国已基本完成了对大型商业银行、证券公司和保险公司的改制，为金融业应对国际金融危机打下了良好的微观基础，也使得金融体系有能力为经济复苏提供充足的信贷支持和金融服务。当然，总体而言中国现在还有一些差距，这也是为什么我们欢迎 FSAP 采用国际标准评估中国金融业的原因之一，这为我们继续努力指明了方向。

（三）危机应对及中央银行的作用

危机管理机制及应对危机、恢复经济可动用的资源也是一个重要的议题。在本轮危机中，尤其是在 2009 年和 2010 年，有一些批评意见认为使用纳税人的钱救助金融机构是不公平的。但当金融体系出现严重问题时，当局必须考虑如何应对危机、救助金融市场，避免经济出现衰退，这就要讨论政府拥有哪些可利用的资源，以及其中哪些可以用于救助。在此过程中，财政部门、中央银行或国际组织最终总是要使用一些资源来实施拯救，而且无法做到完全公平，在有人获益的同时总会有人蒙受损失。因此救助行动很可能会遭到批评，但从整体经济和多数民众的福祉考虑，我们必须采取行动来有效应对危机，防止危机失控而产生更大的负面效应。从这个意义上说，这是值得的。

可能有人提出权限问题，即谁授权你去运用资源实施救助？这在各国会情况不同，在中国是国务院授权的。遗憾的是，这个问题往往是不明确的，很难有预设的答案，尤其对中央银行而言更是如此。作为"最后贷款人"，中央银行当然可以提出，政府部门、财政当局或者国际组织更应该在"最后贷款人"之前采取行动。但问题是，如果没有任何人及时采取必要的行动，经济和金融市场即将陷入深渊，中央银行就应当及时采取行动。当然，救助行动和中央银行追求的低通胀目标之间可能会存在冲突，因此中央银行必须掌握好调节的艺术，使得救助行动对低通胀目标的负面冲击降到最小，同时尽量使其积极效果最大化。这也是金融稳定方面的重要议题之一。

三、加强宏观审慎和危机管理

微观层面的监管准则和微观领域的金融机构健康性并不足以完全避免金融机构的倒闭，更不用说能防范系统性危机。因此，应当在微观准则的基础上，加强宏观审慎管理、风险监测、早期预警以及危机应对能力。国际金融危机的教训表明，加强宏观审慎管理的重点是逆周期调控。

（一）中国在宏观审慎和逆周期管理方面的实践

2009 年春天，中国经济出现复苏迹象。此时，中国开始按宏观审慎政策框架的原理考虑设计新的逆周期措施。2010 年开始，央行实施了清晰的逆周期宏观审慎政策，以限制信贷过快增长、降低通胀。目前来看，结果是令人满意的，最近几个月通胀率呈逐步下降趋势。

中国的宏观审慎政策框架中给出了计算公式，使银行能根据资本充足率等要求自行计算确定需要建立什么样的缓冲。当然，计算时会包含多种因素，如是否属于系统重要性金融机构（D-SIFIs）、上一年度的信贷扩张速度、风险管理情况、审慎管理和拨备程度等。计算公式中还包括中央银行对景气周期的相机判断和激励、约束措施。这一框架的最终目的是维护金融稳定和对金融市场进行逆周期调节。

目前，很多国家都根据本国国情建立了自己的宏观审慎政策框架，其内容和形式也各有不同。对中国而言，我们已经采用这一框架且从中获益，并将"逆周期的宏观审慎政策"写入了中央文件。该框架是动态的，公式中的某些系数将根据具体情况按季进行调整。这种宏观审慎措施目前仍处于探索阶段，我们将不断加以改进。

（二）危机中采用区域货币互换安排

在危机中，美国与一些遭遇美元流动性困难的国家建立了货币互换安排，最近又与欧洲 6 个国家建立了货币互换安排。对于亚洲国家来说，如果出现美元流动性困难，也希望通过货币互换安排来解决问题，并可以通过两种渠道实现：一是与美联储建立货币互换安排；二是在亚洲建立区域内货币互换安排。后一种渠道又分两种形式：一种是本币互换，尽管区域内一些国家的本币尚未在国际上得到广泛使用，但是区域内的贸易和投资都很活跃，比如，东盟加东亚是中国目前最大的贸易伙伴，本币互换可作为摆脱外汇流动性困境的手段，有助于维护金融稳定。另一种是类似于《清迈倡议》那样的区域性多边安排。《清迈倡议》起源于应对亚洲金融危机，最早是多组双边安排，后来逐步扩大并多边化。总体而言，这些互换安排在一定程度上是对基金组织资源的有益补充。

四、结语

中国政府一贯重视金融稳定监测和风险防范。自 2005 年起，人民银行每年定期发布《中国金融稳定报告》，全面监测、评估金融体系的稳定状况。同时，人民银行会同其他金融监管部门不断加强对金融体系风险状况的及时监测和评估。我们充分借鉴国际经验，同时结合中国国情，不断推进金融改革，已取得很多积极成效。中国将 FSAP 看做是自身金融稳定评估的重要补充，是对中国金融体系的一次全面体检。今后，我们将一如既往地执行国际金融标准与准则，不断推动中国金融业深化改革，改进监管，完善金融稳定和危机管理框架。同时，我们愿意继续与基金组织合作，推动亚太地区对 FSAP 的参与程度，共同促进亚太地区的金融稳定、经济繁荣和可持续增长。

第二部分

最新国际监管标准
——在应对系统性风险方面的作用

- 本地区在执行巴塞尔协议Ⅲ、偿付能力Ⅱ和国际证监会组织（IOSCO）关于证券市场的最新指引以及在应对此次危机暴露出的市场基础设施缺陷等方面做了哪些工作？

- 如何确保上述监管改革和更严格审慎标准在各国保持一致，且不会对金融体系支持经济增长的能力产生严重影响？

- 还应采取哪些措施以提升地区金融监管的质量和有效性？

□ 宣昌能

中国人民银行金融稳定局局长

各位，下面我们将开始第二部分的有关议题，即"最新国际监管标准在应对系统性风险方面的作用"。根据今天下午的议程安排，四位发言人将就国际监管标准的有关方面发表评论，比如巴塞尔协议Ⅲ的主要内容。周行长刚才也就此发表了重要意见，包括更高标准的资本和流动性要求，尤其是具有宏观审慎特征的逆周期资本缓冲、对系统重要性机构的额外资本要求等，以及有关评估方法及强化的风险管理框架。

我们也谈到了基金组织关于巴塞尔协议Ⅲ框架的看法。有关专家和基金组织的官员提到巴塞尔协议Ⅲ的实施将对新兴经济体产生何种影响。我们知道，关于新协议对全球经济增长的影响以及协议的执行如何影响银行对实体经济提供服务的能力已经开展了大量的研究。但在新兴经济体，高质量资本的水平及其占比通常较高，正如周行长、刘副行长上午提到的关于中国的情况。在中国开展银行业改革时，我们非常重视高质量资本，即普通股的水平。特别是对金融机构实施政府注资、引入战略投资者以及公开上市等一系列重大改革以来，目前中国银行机构的资本中80%以上是普通股。因此，未来中国实施巴塞尔协议Ⅲ不存在困难，面临的挑战是如何持续保持如此高水准的资本充足率，我想这也是全球各国面临的共同挑战。

关于如何建立证券业和保险业系统重要性机构的评估和强化监管标准，上周金融稳定理事会（FSB）指导委员会邀请了国际保险监督官协会（IAIS）和国际证监会组织（IOSCO）的专家，讨论如何设计和实施有关全球系统重要性或系统重要性证券、保险机构的监管框架。这也将是今天的重要议题之一。实际上，我们注意到巴塞尔银行监管委员会（BCBS）、IOSCO、IAIS 成立的联合论坛在金融集团监管方面做了一系列工作。关于这方面，可能有代表会谈到这一问题，因为金融集团日益直接或间接控制、或投资于证券和保险部门。我认为，强化金融集团监管也会成为监管改革议题的一部分。

最后，我们还将讨论仅靠新国际监管标准就足够了吗？正如周行长所言，高标准和高资本充足率当然可以降低危机发生的可能性，但不可能将危机完全排除。因此，还需要宏观审慎政策框架、危机管理框架以及早期监测预警机制等来做补充。

在今天下午我们讨论这些议题甚至更广泛的议题时，希望在座所有专家踊跃发言，发表真知灼见。下面，有请第一位发言嘉宾。谢谢！

□ 维恩·拜尔斯（Wayne Byres）

巴塞尔银行监管委员会秘书长[①]

大家下午好！

首先我要感谢中国人民银行和国际货币基金组织（IMF）的邀请，让我有机会参加这次会议，就某些重要议题与大家一起交流。

我今天的报告主要谈论三个方面的问题：（1）亚洲地区如何应对新监管标准；（2）与这些新标准的实施的一致性相关的问题，我们如何确保它们有序实施而不会制造更多的混乱；（3）如何进一步提高监管质量。

我的发言主要集中于银行和银行监管方面，其中某些观点对其他类型的金融机构及其监管也同样适用。此外，需要声明的是，我以一个澳大利亚人的身份，而不是巴塞尔委员会代表的身份发言，尽管以我新的身份作下述发言也并无不可。

亚洲地区应对新监管标准

监管改革的目标很简单，也无可争议：我们致力于寻求一个更加稳定的金融体系，将其建立在更具适应性的金融机构基础之上。今天很多发言者已经触及到这个问题，我也认为，鉴于亚洲银行体系较好的起点，他们总体上已经做好准备实施改革。事实上，在许多情况下，他们可能已经开始推行改革。

一定程度上，有危就有机。目前其他地区正在吸取的经验教训，亚洲地区的银行业和监管机构早已吸取。毫无疑问，强有力的规章和监管所带来的好处在亚洲金融危机后已得到认同，因此，强化审慎标准的重要性在亚洲地区被广泛接受。普遍而言，相较于世界上的其他地方，该地区的银行业有着更高的资本缓冲和更好的融资策略。因此，新的改革对该地区带来的影响可能较小，转型成本相

[①] 在本次研讨会召开时，维恩·拜尔斯任澳大利亚审慎监管局执行总经理。

对较低。除此之外，巴塞尔银行监管委员会为改革提供了相当充分的过渡性安排。虽然 2013 年开始实施的巴塞尔协议Ⅲ框架引人注目，但 2013 年当年必须满足的新要求实际上是相当有限的。

由于新最低标准的过渡性影响较小，而且实际上亚洲地区的许多银行达到要求绰绰有余，因此我们看到很多国家已经瞄准更高的标准并加快执行也就不足为奇了。这反映出他们对银行系统潜在实力的信心。

执行中的一致性

新标准执行的一致性是一个有趣的问题，我认为，对不同的人，"一致性"就代表着不同的意思。如果你跟银行家交谈，他们希望所有国家执行一套共同的规则。而当你转向监管者时，一致性的意义将完全不同。监管部门所坚持的一致性意思是：最低标准能严格适用于所有国家和地区。

我认为这一点非常重要，在他们认为本地区可以比最低标准做得更好的情况下，我们没有因为对一致性的讨论而促使这些国家和地区不愿这么做。事实上，包括亚洲地区的许多国家已经表示，他们能够并将进行更多超出全球最低要求的改革。他们的行动有着一系列原因：为适应本地市场的具体特点，应对系统性重要金融机构造成的问题，以及更广泛的宏观审慎问题。但不管是什么原因，关键是在促进一致性方面，如果监管者认为有必要的话，我们不能限制他们采取应对措施的能力。

我认为每个国家在过渡速度和实施时间安排方面存在不一致是不可避免的。每个国家都需要考虑到自身情况，这必定需要平衡收益和过渡成本。正如我所言，相较于世界其他许多地方，亚洲地区具备以更快的速度、更低的成本实施改革的能力。巴塞尔协议Ⅲ的过渡计划在时间上是相当充裕的。这就是说，监管者应鼓励银行在切实可行的条件下尽快满足新标准。我猜测，我们也将看到不同程度的市场压力，这将促使在不同市场上银行采取不同的行为。

因此，总体来说，我们提出的问题就是，我们可以做什么，以促进执行的一致性。我的回答是，太多的一致性并不必然是一件好事，有些不一致是不可避免的，也是积极的。

提高监管质量和有效性

金融系统是复杂多变的，不可能通过简单设置一些规则进行管理。因此，在我讨论的三个问题中，最重要的就是如何提高监管的质量和有效性。危机后的许多改革工作一直侧重于修订原有的规则并建立新的规则，要求银行及其他机构在未来执行。显然，如果我们真的要实现我们的目标，也需要提高监管质量。

我们的目标就是在需要的时候，监管机构具备采取行动的意愿和能力。"行动的意愿和能力"这个提法曾被应用于美国的金融部门评估规划（FSAP）中。我是银行监管评估小组中的一员，我们在评估报告中提出这个概念，就是要强调美国监管制度中存在某些缺陷。这个观点也被国际货币基金组织关于"高质量监管所需条件"的报告采用。

在说到我们希望在需要的时候，监管机构具备采取行动的意愿和能力时，我想补充的是，"需要的时候"是会经常出现的。主动监管不是偶尔作为：它意味着经常行动。监管者必须能够影响银行的行为。要做到这一点，他们的干预必须是持久的。但我想要明确一点，我不是建议监管者去操纵银行。不过，监管者们需要定期质疑、督促和干预银行的行为，让银行证明他们知道自己正在做什么，知道自己承担着风险责任，以及在一个长期目标下以审慎的方式恰当地管理自身业务。

规则制定和监管之间存在重要关联。为寻求提高监管质量，我们需要确保在起草法规时，鼓励而不是限制积极监管。举一个例子来说明这一点，巴塞尔协议Ⅲ引入了资本留存缓冲要求。在座的许多人都知道，这是银行必须持有的最低资本充足要求之外的资本缓冲要求。如果银行的资本充足率下降，侵蚀该缓冲，其分配股东利润的能力将受到限制。

有两种方式可以对资本留存框架进行解释。第一种解释是，鼓励监管者早期干预。一旦达到资本留存范围的触发点时，监管者就必须进行干预。第二种解释是，所制定的规则允许银行自由经营，除非它们触及其中一个限制点，监管者开始实施干预。显然，这些规则的制定方式中，一种方式授权于监管者，而一种方式则严格限制监管者。我们在制定规则时，需要特别注意到，应确保我们设置的监管框架，能够促进积极监管。

巴塞尔协议框架的另一个例子是逆周期缓冲，它将宏观审慎理念引入到资本框架中。在这里，需要思考的是，面对系统中信贷增长过快时，什么是最好的应对方式？是以一种较为钝化的方式对所有银行使用宏观审慎工具，还是鼓励监管部门有针对性地进行监管，尤其是对于那些发展迅速、增长过快，从而更可能引发脆弱性的银行。在所有的可能中，对监管者来说，最理想的应对方式就是两者兼顾：既使用宏观审慎工具，也对机构进行单独处理。最重要的是确保不会出现这种局面：监管者不愿意对发生问题的机构采取行动，而只是简单地使用"钝化"的宏观审慎工具。

最后一点，出于个人爱好，我再谈一下提高监管质量方面的问题。在危机后的改革议程中已重点强调提高监管者信息共享和强化联合监管机制安排。我知道很多监管者，带着极大的诚意，在加大与他们的监管同行共享信息方面已经做了很多工作。联合监管机制较之于以前，已更加严格和频繁。但大多监管者仍被金融危机前写就的信息共享方面的法定权力所约束。对监管者之间更加自由的信息交流的期望和压力已大大增强，但坦率地说，配套基础设施建设并没有同步跟上：的确，许多监管机构所处的法律框架下仍然对信息共享存有重大障碍。这是一个需要解决的重要问题。

□ 苏哈迪（Suhaedi）

银行业研究和监管部顾问，印度尼西亚中央银行

最新国际监管标准在应对系统性风险中的作用
——印度尼西亚的经验

很高兴也很荣幸能在此发言。首先请允许我感谢国际货币基金组织和中国人民银行给我这次机会，可以与大家就最新国际监管标准在应对系统性风险和维护金融稳定中的作用进行交流。

一、三部曲：审慎标准、风险化解和危机防范

关于此议题的讨论很及时也很有意义。实际上，有关讨论通常与国家或国际层面的金融危机相关。众所周知，标准实施、风险化解和危机防范是相互联系的。此三者之间的关系可以表述为：标准执行得越好，风险化解工作越到位，发生的危机就越少。

我们目前讨论的最新国际监管标准是应对此次全球危机、增强金融部门稳健性的举措。在国家层面，印度尼西亚应对 1997—1998 年亚洲金融危机的经验表明，实施统一的法规和监管标准非常重要。导致 1997—1998 年银行危机的原因之一是对借鉴最佳做法实施银行业政策及监管的重要性缺乏认识，对监管标准作用的忽视导致印度尼西亚经济损失惨重。

鉴于上述痛苦的经验教训，印度尼西亚政府实施了全面经济金融改革，重点关注银行业重组、银行系统抗风险能力以及金融中介功能的恢复。印度尼西亚央行一直致力于完善法规和监管框架，推动实施良好公司治理和风险管理原则，以实现银行业稳健且具有抗风险能力的目标，使银行有效发挥金融中介的作用。

二、印度尼西亚 FSAP 评估结论

得益于亚洲金融危机后实施的全面经济金融改革，印度尼西亚经济在 2008 年国际金融危机中表现出较好的抗风险能力，保持了较强劲的增长。在消费和出口的基础上，投资成为主要增长引擎，增长更趋平衡。金融体系保持稳定，银行机构拥有大量的资本缓冲、充足的流动性、盈利能力良好。压力测试表明，极个别的银行在极端流动性冲击下将较为脆弱，其他一些大型银行存在集中度风险。汇率和传染风险可控。

2010 年 FSAP 评估结果也反映出印度尼西亚的良好状况。印度尼西亚很幸运地在危机期间接受了 FSAP 评估。危机体现出评估的诸多作用。换句话说，FSAP 评估发现了重要的风险隐患，从而帮助我们化解了有关风险，也采取必要措施为减轻危机影响做好了准备：比如制定了危机管理预案，包括关于金融安全网的法律。随着危机扩散，FSAP 评估团关注于一些重点领域，包括危机管理、流动性支持、跨境合作等。FSAP 评估团的建议有助于缓解危机的不利影响。

回顾印度尼西亚 FSAP 评估能获得许多有益发现。评估有助于印度尼西亚当局识别金融体系的脆弱性，并提出化解系统性风险的重要建议，包括宏观审慎政策等。在金融稳定评估方面，FSAP 评估团审查了银行和其他金融部门的稳健程度，开展压力测试；基于国际公认标准评价银行业、保险业和金融市场监管的质量，评估监管者、政策制定者以及金融安全网在应对系统性压力方面的能力。评估成功识别了主要的脆弱性。

三、最新监管标准的实施

关于国际金融改革，印度尼西亚作为 G20 成员承诺实施新的监管标准。我们根据本国实际经济金融环境努力实现维护金融稳定和促进经济增长之间的最佳平衡。印度尼西亚将于 2012 年实施巴塞尔协议 Ⅱ，目前正将巴塞尔协议 2.5 有关内容纳入监管框架。此外，我们正在就实施巴塞尔协议 Ⅲ 进行定量影响测算（QIS），将于 2013 年有选择地将巴塞尔协议 Ⅲ 有关内容纳入监管框架。关于系统重要性金融机构，我们正在就确定国内系统重要性银行（D-SIBs）的方法和模型进行研究。此外，印度尼西亚还研究了将有效处置机制主要内容纳入金融安全网机制的可能性。此外，印度尼西亚正在就 OTC 衍生品市场制定有关银行 OTC 衍

生品交易的监管政策。

关于宏观审慎监管，印度尼西亚央行过去几年提升了宏观审慎监管能力，包括识别内外部脆弱点，评估金融体系抗风险能力，预测金融稳定状况等。宏观审慎监管框架帮助印度尼西亚央行较好地应对了 2008 年 11 月的流动性风险。印度尼西亚央行将补充其现有的宏观监督工具，以履行好其宏观审慎监管职责。这些工具将有助于及早识别系统性风险在金融体系中的积累，这些风险会对整体经济造成不利影响。

四、国家层面改革的重点及面临的挑战

我们相信，新法规和监管标准将为未来全球经济的良好发展奠定坚实的基础。鉴于此，印度尼西亚承诺将及时一致地践行有关安排，以维护金融稳定，为实现经济的强劲、可持续和平衡增长奠定基础。值得注意的是，新标准的实施对印度尼西亚金融业的影响有限。印度尼西亚银行的资本充足水平大大高于巴塞尔协议Ⅲ的标准，流动性要求将对有些小银行构成挑战，不过对大机构的经营活动几乎没什么影响。而且，新标准对证券市场不会产生重大影响。

作为一个新兴经济体，印度尼西亚在法规和监管体制改革方面有亟须考虑的优先领域和挑战，这些领域与国际监管改革所涉及的有所不同。以下我举例说明我们所优先考虑的领域：

第一是发展挑战。印度尼西亚约一半人口无法享受到正规金融服务，这一群体包括最贫困人口。银行监管者面临的挑战是如何在设计监管制度时考虑到为这一群体提供金融服务，以推动减贫。为此，我们将重点提升国内金融体系的中介功能，促进金融包容性和金融教育来扩大存贷款基础，实现经济的强劲和包容性增长。

第二是通过采取宏观审慎措施管理好信贷扩张。目前，印度尼西亚的信贷总量与 GDP 之比约为 30%，大大低于周边国家。不过有些部门的信贷增长比较快（比如汽车、房地产业等），因此应予以认真监测。鉴于此，应制定建设性指引，指导针对特定部门问题的宏观审慎政策的设计及实施。

第三是监管能力及一致性。很多时候，银行倒闭不仅是因为缺乏合适的监管制度，而且是由于缺乏监管能力和一致性。因此，在完善监管标准的同时，还应努力提升监管能力。

第四是合作机制。正如上文中所提到的，金融稳定职责的日益交叉意味着我们需要设计有效的组织架构。根据国际最优做法制定指引大有益处。2011 年 11 月，印度尼西亚通过了关于建立"综合金融监管机构"（OJK）的法律。关键问题之一是如何实现宏观审慎监管和微观审慎监管之间的协调（相应职责由 OJK 和央行承担），以应对系统性风险，维护好过渡时期的金融稳定。在地区层面，区内国家应在母国——东道国监管、联合监管机制、地区监测、危机防范及风险处置等方面加强合作。

谢谢！

□ 陈家强

香港财经事务及库务局局长

非常高兴能够受邀在此发言。接下来的一小时我们将讨论本地区是否已经准备好实施巴塞尔协议Ⅲ、偿付能力Ⅱ（Solvency Ⅱ）的标准以及国际证监会组织（IOSCO）关于证券市场的最新指引。我们还将分享开始于 2008 年、至今仍未结束的国际金融危机带给我们的教训。

巴塞尔协议Ⅲ

首先，介绍一下香港地区未来实施新标准的计划。香港计划在巴塞尔银行监管委员会规定的时间框架内全面实施巴塞尔协议Ⅲ。根据目前的资本充足水平以及资本构成状况，香港银行在实施新标准上不会有太大问题。

偿付能力Ⅱ（Solvency Ⅱ）

关于保险业偿付能力监管，我们认为国际趋势是建立基于风险的资本监管框架。欧盟已经制定了偿付能力Ⅱ，设定了有关的定性、定量及披露要求，风险状况及风险管理水平等指标，来评估机构是否拥有充足的偿付能力。香港也在考虑本地现状的基础上朝此方向推进改革。

IOSCO 关于证券市场的最新指引

国际金融危机以来，监管者加强了对系统性风险的监测、化解和管理。香港对此并不陌生，实际上减少系统性风险一直是香港证券业监管者的法定目标。

证券及期货事务监察委员会（SFC）监测一系列指标来评估机构、市场及工具对证券市场有序和有效运行可能带来的风险。在很多方面，监测系统性风险融入 SFC 日常工作之中。

当然，无论监管能力强弱，任何监管者都无法预测到金融体系面临的所有风险。突发的未预期到的金融动荡或者某个重要外国金融机构的倒闭都将引发金融体系震动，当市场大幅波动、投资者和消费者信心低迷的时候尤其如此。

我们能做的是化解上述风险。

1. 对于交易所交易产品，监管者将监测其交易集中度、持仓分布及波动性。我们通过分析不同市场之间的关联性来评估相应的风险。尤其对交易所交易基金（ETF），我们已经设定了对手方风险敞口限额，并提出抵押品要求。

2. 企业信用评级机构及其分析师都受到较严格的监管，包括必须获得相应牌照并接受 SFC 监管。

清算所也接受严格监管，并且正按照 G20 的目标开展有关 OTC 衍生品监管改革。香港金管局正在筹建当地的交易托管库，香港证交所正在建立 OTC 衍生品中央对手方清算机制，二者均计划于 2012 年正式启动。

我们如何确保各国在实施监管改革及更高审慎标准时保持一致性，以及如何确保其实施不会给金融支持经济增长能力带来过大影响？

各国建立各自的监管机制固然很好，不过监管范围和实施上的差异将鼓励监管套利，从而增加系统性风险，加剧市场割裂。因此，要践行 G20 峰会上的承诺、确保新标准实施的一致性，就必须实现各国监管当局之间的协调。

国际货币基金组织和世界银行的 FSAP 项目对金融部门进行了最为全面深入的评估，评估各经济体执行金融部门标准和准则的情况，包括 IOSCO《证券监管目标与原则》、巴塞尔《有效银行监管核心原则》等。

FSB 建立了同行评估机制，对标准执行进程进行更具针对性的和更为详细的监测。其他标准制定机构包括巴塞尔银行监管委员会等也开展了各自的监测项目。

实际上，新标准能否成功顺利实施很大程度上取决于相关国家是否能有效参与最初的标准制定工作。为此，巴塞尔银行监管委员会于 2009 年扩大了成员，而且，FSB 最近建立的区域工作组也使得 6 个地区的非 FSB 成员经济体能够参与其中。同时，各地区经济体还可利用各种地区性机制，比如亚洲地区的东亚及太平洋央行行长会议组织（EMEAP），来讨论他们感兴趣的话题，并适时将其观点传达给国际标准制定机构。

长期来看，一个由资本充足、流动性充沛的金融机构构成的金融体系具有更强的抗风险能力，这将有助于降低未来发生危机的风险，促进经济长期可持续增长。不过，要确保监管改革自身不会给金融体系带来新的风险或增强其顺周期性。因此，要认真评估巴塞尔协议Ⅲ新资本和流动性监管标准的实施从宏观经济层面对市场运行和流动性产生的影响和效果。而且，要就新标准实施开展行业咨询，以确保正常的经济活动不会因改革而受到负面影响。此外，阶段性安排能够确保新标准的有序实施，实施巴塞尔协议Ⅲ的过渡性安排就是很好的做法：两个最新流动性监管指标，即流动性覆盖率和净稳定资金比例标准的实施已于 2011 年 1 月起进入观察期，并分别于 2015 年 1 月和 2018 年 1 月才开始实施。

如何进一步提升本地区监管的质量和有效性

国际金融危机暴露出金融监管方面存在的一些问题。我们认为 FSB 提出的有关金融监管的问题及建议有助于提升监管的力度和有效性。

改善金融监管的重要一点是尽量弥补数据方面的缺口。比如银行提供的信贷数据可能无法显示其对哪个经济部门的信贷敞口最大，监管当局可能无法获得银行存款来源的详细数据来分析其融资稳定性，因此弥补数据方面的缺口、完善银行和监管者的信息系统将有助于及早识别风险以及更好地掌握金融机构之间的关联性。

此外，监管者需要拥有履职的工具，包括清晰明确的职责、适当的权力和充足的资源。而且，监管者还应不断提升专业技能，更好地掌握市场最新发展，有意愿且有能力质疑银行的经营模式，并在必要时及时采取行动。

监管者还应采取更具前瞻性的监管方法，并能够使用适当的审慎工具来"逆风调节"。目前，大家越来越认识到应采用宏观审慎政策来减少金融体系的顺周期性。其中，巴塞尔协议Ⅲ框架下引入的逆周期资本缓冲是很好的做法。香港监管当局一直非常谨慎地防范资产泡沫和信贷过度扩张，为此我们积极使用各种审慎监管工具，包括提高银行准备金要求、降低抵押贷款的贷款价值比（LTV）以及严格管理贷款条件等。

考虑到金融体系的相互关联性以及系统重要性金融机构的全球化特征，有效的金融监管需要紧密的跨境合作。为此，国际社会已建立起针对国际业务较多的银行以及其他金融机构的联合监管机制和危机管理小组，旨在加强信息共享、监管合作以及提升危机处置效果。香港监管当局作为这些银行和金融机构的重要东道国监管者已积极参与以上联合监管机制和危机管理小组。

□ 赤松典孝（Noritaka Akamatsu）

亚洲开发银行地区经济一体化部门副主任

自 1997 年亚洲金融危机以来，亚洲的银行一直持续提高资本、拨备、流动性水平以及风险管理能力，同时减少不良资产。因此，即使根据巴塞尔协议Ⅲ的标准，亚洲的银行也是稳健的。现阶段，除日本外亚洲还没有全球系统重要性金融机构（G-SIFIs）。未来亚洲发展中经济体在实施更严格的审慎监管标准时面临的主要挑战是如何平衡好维护金融稳定与促进增长和发展之间的关系。在此方面与亚洲地区最为相关的是巴塞尔协议Ⅲ中关于如何处理贸易融资和回购交易的规定，巴塞尔银行监管委员会最近降低了旨在支持与发展中国家开展贸易的贸易融资的资本要求（通过杠杆率计算要求来体现）。不过巴塞尔银行监管委员会仍然认为需要保留针对贸易融资的资本要求。在计算杠杆率时还要求纳入回购交易，从而使得回购交易的成本上升。而亚洲经济体正在发展债券市场，其中回购对债券市场的发展至关重要。因此，亚洲经济体在实施上述准则时面临两难选择。另外，关于以财政赤字严重和公共债务沉重经济体的政府债券作抵押的回购交易，有关指引正在制定中。[①]

在国际层面，巴塞尔协议Ⅲ或者偿付能力Ⅱ等微观审慎举措并不足以确保金融稳定。欧洲实施的较严格的审慎要求与巴塞尔协议Ⅲ的精神一致，而欧洲正在实施的新审慎要求连同公允价值会计准则导致了银行的去杠杆化。去杠杆化有的是以资产清算的形式，有的则是从包括亚洲在内的全球其他地区撤资，从而引发了亚洲地区的资本外流。[②] 而之前美欧采取的量化宽松政策曾使亚洲地区遭受了大规模资本流入的冲击。[③] 如果在某地区按照国际最优做法采取加强金融稳定的举措会使资本流入其他地区，那么有关国家必须具备处理相应问题的能力。否则，仅靠微观审慎措施难以实现真正的金融稳定。

---

① 作为"亚洲债券市场倡议"（ABMI）的一部分，东盟＋3 正在考虑推动跨境抵押品的使用。在这方面，对财政赤字严重和公共债务沉重经济体的政府债券予以适当考虑将很关键。

② 在这种情况下，即使《维也纳倡议》似乎也帮不了亚洲。

③ 更早之前，由次贷问题和雷曼倒闭等因素导致的外部需求收缩对亚洲的出口产生了不利影响。

目前，东盟国家正在推动其银行等金融部门实现一体化，这是 2015 年实现东盟经济共同体的内容之一。东盟国家致力于建立共同的银行框架，在此框架下符合条件的银行可以在所有的东盟国家开展业务。虽然此举可能会给东盟国家带来很大的益处，但也可能会带来风险。尤其是考虑到这将导致系统重要性金融机构的产生。目前，巴塞尔银行监管委员会明确了国内及全球系统重要性金融机构的概念。亚洲开发银行考虑是否还应该明确地区性系统重要性金融机构的概念，并提供相应的监管指引。如果不能在国际层面解决这一问题，东盟国家需要在地区层面来解决。这将要求该地区各国当局实现更为紧密的监管合作。

有些亚洲国家是 APEC 成员，APEC 强调 OTC 衍生品中央清算机制以及在此方面实现公平竞争的重要性。[①] 不过，亚洲发展中经济体总体上在发展衍生品市场方面处于落后地位。除了高收入国家，亚洲地区的其他国家缺乏在国内建立 OTC 衍生品中央清算机制的能力。即使建立了有关清算机制，通常也是作为证券交易所的一部分。因此，在清算所内进行 OTC 衍生品清算的要求会导致有关清算所从证券交易所中独立出来，促进交易所之间的竞争。这将有助于东盟国家实现资本市场的融合，但是有些东盟成员国似乎不太愿意 OTC 衍生品集中在地区内少数几个清算所进行清算。因此，尚不清楚上述考量将会加快还是会放慢该地区实施 OTC 衍生品集中清算以及按照巴塞尔协议 III 对未集中清算的 OTC 衍生品执行更高资本要求的步伐。

---

① 根据《多德—弗兰克法案》。

第三部分

防范与应对

——如何为下次危机做好准备？

- 当前识别系统脆弱性（包括主权风险、或有债务以及剧烈资本流动）的机制是否有效？

- 采取哪些具体措施将风险监测范围从银行部门扩大到整个金融体系？

- 如何确保应急预案和跨部门合作在国家和国际层面更为有效？

- 现有全球金融安全网是否完善？地区性或跨地区工作能起到何种辅助作用？

□ 申齐润（Je Yoon Shin）

韩国财政部副部长

韩国已经经历了 1997 年、2008 年和当前的三次危机。幸运的是，每次我都站在最前线，因此，关于如何应对下一场危机，我想和大家分享一些经验。

我认为危机的甄别主要包括四个要点：一是危机的早期甄别；二是无漏洞金融监管；三是称职的监管机构；最后一点，也是最重要的一点就是建立全面的金融安全网。在本文中，我将更多地探讨最后一点。

一、系统性风险识别

没有人能够准确地预测到美国次级抵押贷款会引发一场国际金融危机。次级抵押贷款对全球金融市场造成了严重影响，甚至对实体经济也产生了影响。因此，及早甄别这类风险非常重要。我认为这包括两个层次的风险识别，一是国际层面，二是国家层面。在今天上午的会议上，许多人谈到二十国集团（G20）发起的早期预警演练和雷曼兄弟公司倒闭造成的外溢影响，而我更想关注国家层面的问题。

正如 G20、金融稳定理事会（FSB）和国际货币基金组织（IMF）所建议的那样，我们需要建立一些机制以提前甄别风险，这些组织还建议对银行进行压力测试。然而，正如大家所看到的，欧元区爆发了主权债务危机。尽管二十国集团领导人宣称，他们认为未来不会再次发生类似 2008 年那样的危机，但 2010 年 4 月，希腊却爆发了主权债务危机。虽然我们无法准确地预测或甄别出系统性风险，但我们应尽力提前发现。

关于早期预警演练，已经有了很多讨论，但我希望国际货币基金组织能够更多地致力于设计出一些宏观经济模型以提前准确地甄别风险。目前，他们正专注于评估关键风险，但这仍远远不够。我们还应该加强国际层面的双边监督，并建立国家层面的预警框架，这非常重要。

如今，主权风险是全球经济的热点问题。重点是如何舒缓市场情绪，尤其是关于公共债务的可持续性。在这里，我想介绍一下韩国的情况。1997 年亚洲金融危机后，我们修订了监管标准，这也是我们战胜 2008 年国际金融危机的原因之一。我们已经建立起"早期预警系统"，并主要对外部稳定、金融稳定、原材料、房地产和劳动力市场等五个方面进行监测。随着具体部门的模型量化，在"早期预警系统"中，我们已经引入了一些定性的方法来评估危机的可能性。为了更好地化解和管理财政风险，最近我们还建立了财政风险管理委员会（Fiscal Risk Management Committee）。幸运的是，韩国政府的债务与国内生产总值（GDP）比值非常稳定，仅有 34%。但韩国仍存在许多潜在的风险因素，如人口老龄化等问题，我们将密切关注新的福利体系对我们财政状况的影响。

二、影子银行

第二个需要关注的是无漏洞金融监管。到目前为止，已经有很多人论及影子银行，我不想再具体谈及。但我想强调的是，在某种意义上，对影子银行的监测与监管以及影子银行与传统银行之间的协调，是非常重要的。

就韩国而言，2003 年曾发生了一场小规模的信用卡危机。当时，许多人认为，没有必要对信用卡行业进行监管，因为它不吸收存款，并且是基于市场原则运行的。但资本市场突然陷入窘局，随后强烈地影响了整个金融市场、实体经济以及信用卡行业，以致当时消费迅速下降。我不想将话题局限于影子银行。但是，即使一个很小的领域也是非常重要的。如今的韩国，互助储蓄银行（MSBs）在金融部门具有一定代表性。某些问题，甚至很小的一部分，也可能撼动整体。这是我们从最近经历中得到的教训。在韩国，互助储蓄银行所占份额只有 1.7%。但它能以一些社会问题的方式，撼动整个经济体。

金融部门的风险是如何传导到实体经济的？有可能通过信心渠道。当问题发生在一个很小领域内时，如互助储蓄银行，它可能会因为严重打击市场参与者的信心而被传导到整个市场。为舒缓市场情绪，我们做出了很多努力。根据金融稳定理事会（FSB）的报告，影子银行的交易量达 20 万亿美元，而传统银行交易量只有 10 万亿美元。金融稳定理事会和其他标准制定机构应努力加快步伐，以解决这些问题。

三、称职的监管者

在国际层面，自 2008 年 G20 华盛顿峰会以来，G20 和标准制定机构已经形成了一些机制性成果，进展良好。在国家层面，上午的会议中，中国同行提到他们已经建立起 3 "C" 机制，包括沟通（Communication）、合作（Cooperation）和协调（Coordination），并且也取得了良好进展。

我认为在制度建设方面，我们应该加紧努力。沟通非常重要。银行、证券以及保险业监管者都不想将自身掌握的真实情况告诉给他人。我们应该建议他们要更加开明，只有这样他们之间的沟通和协调才会得到进一步改善。我想强调的是，我们需要关注一些小的领域。监管机构的许多员工热衷于参与到一些重点行业的监管中，例如银行业。但他们不愿意积极参与到某些小领域，如互助储蓄银行和信用社的监管中，因为这类工作非常艰苦，又不太受监管机构重视。他们要求在银行业监管部门，而不是信用社监管部门工作。这是单一机构存在的监管漏洞。就韩国而言，我们成立了单一监管机构，即金融监管局（FSA），监管所有的银行业、证券业以及保险业部门。在我担任金融监管局副主席时，我要求不同部门之间的工作人员定期轮换。我建议，金融稳定理事会应该设法解决这些问题，以填补市场中的监管漏洞和人力资源缺口。

与其他许多国家一样，韩国也设置了一些监督委员会。我担任这些监管机构的主席，这些机构包括中央银行、金融监管局，金融监督院（FSS）和韩国存款保险公司（KDIC）。如有必要，我们经常互相沟通并共同制定政策。我们共同宣布政策措施，以此向市场表明，监管机构之间没有任何冲突。我认为这是舒缓市场情绪的一个很好的例子。

四、金融安全网

最后需要谈及的是金融安全网，实际上它包括三个层次，即国家、地区和全球。关于国家安全网和外汇储备积累，存有一些争论。许多新兴国家认同这样一个经验，即拥有的外汇储备越多，对国家越有利，尤其是在危机时刻。但它却加剧了全球经济失衡，这在 G20 和其他国际论坛上引起了极大的争论。什么是外汇储备的最佳水平？这是一个两难问题。从新兴市场的角度看，我们的国内利率近乎 4%，但我们外汇储备对美国国债的投资收益率低于 2%。那么，为什么新兴市场仍然试图积累外汇储备？如果每一个国家都积累外汇储备以防范未来的危机，这将是一个两难的囚徒困境。因此，解决这个问题的唯一办法是建立一个地区性的金融安全网。

最近，韩国与日本、中国签署协议增加了货币互换额度，分别是与日本700亿美元、与中国560亿美元。这是出于预防的考虑。我们不必仅仅为防范未来的危机而大肆积累外汇储备。就清迈倡议多边化协议（CMIM）而言，其安全网资金仅1200亿美元，但它很快会增加，也许会达到2000亿美元。所以第一步是建立国家安全网，第二步是建立地区安全网作为补充，第三步也是最后一步是建立全球性安全网。

每当我们讨论全球安全网，总会涉及道德风险问题。2010年，韩国在G20层面提出了一些安全网问题。当时有一个争论热点就是如何防范道德风险。最近，IMF已改善了一些新的贷款工具的条件。我们需要不断加强全球安全网建设，并应有一些防止道德风险的方法。

没有人知道我们该如何预知未来。我们应不遗余力地努力甄别未来的风险因素。前行的道路仍然漫长。

□ 小内斯特·埃斯佩尼拉（Nestor A. Espenilla，Jr.）

菲律宾中央银行副行长

谈到金融危机，我们实际上对此知之甚少，难以准确地预测出其爆发时间、爆发地点和危机的情况。金融市场本身在发展，不断有复杂的金融工具问世，这些都可能给将来造成意想不到的麻烦。从根本上看，在下次危机爆发之前，我们根本不知道我们是否已经做好应对的准备。

无法对危机进行准确预判并不能成为我们对金融体系进行积极主动改革的障碍。但是，我们不应为进行改革而改革，我们需要对市场形势和特征进行更深入的了解，了解市场是否最大限度地保护公众利益、是否能有效地运行。这就是我们面临的挑战之所在：考虑到金融市场的不可预见性、内在的风险性以及其中的利益冲突，因此，在危机发生之前我们就应预先设定审慎政策变量。

1. 是否存在一套有效识别金融体系脆弱性的机制，能识别出包括主权风险、或有债务以及大量资本流动等风险？

答案是：不太可能。我们不知道风险可能通过什么交易/产品/过程/机构等渠道演化成系统风险，即无法根据微观领域的风险确定宏观风险，也无法知道风险在各个体系中的传递渠道。此外，由于各国的金融市场结构都具有自身特色，各国的金融市场之间存在较大差异，风险的传递机制也各不相同。

实际情况是，同样的外部主权风险对两个不同国家的影响是不同的。我们可以鉴别出一些风险产生影响的基本原理，但由于风险的传递渠道不同，我们不可能预测出风险影响的大小、溢出效应的范围及可能产生的后果。同样的道理，或有债务的风险以及大量资本流动风险也无法预料。

2. 如何监测银行体系之外庞大金融体系的风险？

银行体系内的风险本身就十分复杂，而且，当银行体系风险扩散至银行体系之外时，风险必将更加复杂且种类繁多。然而，这种划分比较牵强，尽管风险的升级十分相似。当银行体系的风险溢出到证券或保险市场时，银行监管者不可能无动于衷。事实上，银行体系风险之所以能扩散到其他部门，正说明这些部门在抵御这些风险方面具有的脆弱性。

从这个角度看，我们可以认为，风险缓释实际上是降低了风险的预期冲击，而不是消除了风险的根源。由于金融市场本质上就具有风险性，我们需要真正关注的不是是否产生了风险，而是风险的大小、传递及其所产生的冲击。因此，不管金融稳定的目的是减少不稳定因素还是维持金融体系平稳运行，金融稳定都应该是所有金融监管者共同的职责。

既然目标是监管合作，需要解决的实际问题就是：界定银行、证券、保险市场监管职责的边界；产品（如衍生品）如何监管；以及金融机构的市场行为如何监管等。当货币政策、银行监管和市场基础设施分属不同的部门管理时，中央银行面临监管合作问题。

3. 如何在国际和国内两个层面上更有效地进行应急规划和部门合作？

在国内层面，事先建立一套应急框架十分有用，这样在危机发生时能做到有据可依。应急框架至少应包括以下内容：明确各个监管机构的职责、危机时的工作机制。这样可以让各部门在危机出现时能及时参与、避免混乱。

另外，由于我们不可能总提前预测危机，因此对危机的模拟演练更显得重要，我们可已通过这种模拟演练发现存在的漏洞和目前政策工具的不足。

在国际层面，危机的模拟演练就不再实用，而计量和模型则发挥了更大作用，但模型只有基于真实的数据，才可能推测出危机的广度和传染路径，从而对现实做出正确的指导。

基于国内情况建立的模型只有与全球模型相关联才能反映出真实的情况，网络分析对于全球模型较为合适。但关键是要全面开放全球网络模型，所有的利益相关者都能理解这种国际间风险敞口、达成共识并接受国际方面的技术援助才能真正改善国内模型。

4. 全球金融安全网是否有效？何种地区及跨地区的动议能够有助于金融安全网络的建立和维护？

目前对全球金融安全网的理解有两种观点，一种就是凡是有风险的业务一律禁止，另外一种是基于不同国家的风险设立业务限制。但前者可能不符合全球总体利益，而后者则需要对可接受风险设定上限。目前面临的挑战是：可接受风险的上限是否具有足够的适应性，能适用各个不同国家及各种不同情况。

以风险为基础的业务限制提供了一个可行的相对标准，对本国市场上的各种业务进行确认并限定了一个共同的风险上限。这种方法的可行性在很大程度上取决于利益相关者是否遵守国际最佳实践，这又引发了如下问题："国际最佳实践"是否对所有情形都是"最佳"的？

因此，第一种观点的绝对标准可能更能为各国所接受。我认为只要一国的审慎管理做到以下两点，就不必依赖于全球金融安全网：一是一国必须能清楚地阐明本国的政策框架，并说明此框架如何能与全球现存的秩序相一致；二是一国必须建立一个可信的监管框架，能及时纠正本国市场的不当行为，化解金融风险。我的主要观点是：在金融安全网方面，一国做好本国的审慎监管工作比单纯依赖全球金融安全网更有效。因为前者讨论的是如何在风险扩大前化解风险，而后者则是被动地应对风险。但是我们相信，把两者结合起来更理想，但这种结合必须是真正的融合并适合一国的国情。这一点很重要。

□ 山冈浩实（Hiromi Yamaoka）
日本中央银行金融体系和银行检查局局长助理

危机防范与应对——日本的经验

前言

首先，我想向中国人民银行和国际货币基金组织表达最真挚的感谢，感谢他们举办了如此成功的研讨会。特别感谢中国人民银行员工不辞辛劳，将我的演讲稿翻译成中文！

汉字很久以前便传入日本，于我们是非常珍贵的礼物，但有时却成为学童们的梦魇。他们在小学就要学习约 1000 个汉字！正是由于艰苦的学习，日本人能理解绝大多数汉字的意思。尽管我不知道汉语发音，我肯定幻灯片的中文版很棒。

金融危机——无止境的"轮回"

全球政策制定者显然面临着挑战。全球经济当前仍在面对危机，即欧洲主权债务问题。如今，即使政策制定者对如何防范未来危机高谈阔论，人们会说，"如果你是好医生，现在就给我治胃疼的良药。如果有效，我以后会再听听你对防止体重超重和高血压的建议"。因此，在此次演讲中，我将尽可能针对当前危机提出意见。

图 1 是著名的太极图，功夫熊猫的标志。（毫无疑问，对日本的孩童，熊猫是最好的中国进口品！）这一标志在亚洲广泛使用，具有多种解释。最广为流传的解释是阴暗面（阴）起源于明亮面（阳），反之亦然，阴面和阳面不断变换彼此互换，并永久持续下去。

63

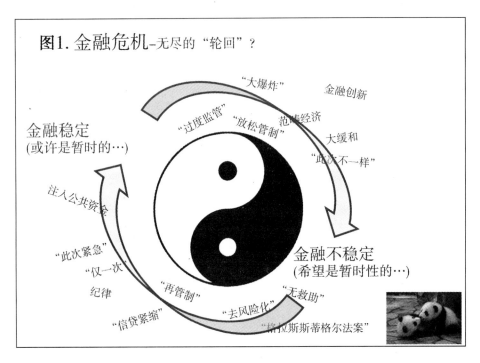

图1. 金融危机–无尽的"轮回"?

让我们通过这标志来理解金融危机。首先，部分经济学家在其模型中假定金融稳定是常态而金融不稳定是例外情况。但如果我们坦率地回归历史，将金融稳定和金融不稳定作为永恒循环的两个阶段似乎更为恰当。我敢说，金融稳定本身甚至是另一次危机的起源。

最好的防范未必是最佳应对

我也想强调，对于危机而言，最好的防范也许不是最佳应对。早晨慢跑有益健康，但医生不会建议一个得了重感冒卧床休息的人去这么做。相似地，更多资本将使银行在中期具有更强的抗风险能力，但在去杠杆化过程中提高资本限制可能引发灾难性的信贷紧缩。显而易见，公共资本注入和一揽子存款担保会引发道德风险，但这些措施对于抑制当时的危机却是必要的。诸如此类，所有政策工具都有阳面和阴面，因此对政策制定者而言，最困难的是在准确评估病人状况的基础上在两者之间寻求平衡。

日本的经验

此次国际金融危机后，公众反对使用纳税人的钱进行救助。在日本，尽管公共资本注入设想早在 1992 年就由当时的宫泽首相提出，但三年后才进行大规模注资。回头看，去杠杆化和经济下滑所带来的损失远大于纳税人的直接损失，事实上，大部分注入的公共资金如今已得到偿还。

推绳子？——宏观审慎宽松

金融危机后，政策制定者面临的又一挑战是如何"推绳子"。在讨论宏观审慎政策时，经济学家往往考虑"紧缩"，例如提高逆周期资本缓冲，而非宏观审慎"宽松"。事实上，亚洲发展中经济体成功经受住了此次危机考验，迄今为止却始终在考虑宏观审慎紧缩问题。而对于近期遭受危机的经济体而言，去杠杆化导致银行贷款与 GDP 比率下降，金融功能失灵使经济下行压力加大。此外，危机国家的政策制定者往往已经用尽"宏观"工具，财政状况恶化，货币政策位于"零利率区"。因此，对于这些国家的政策制定者而言，真正的挑战是寻找方法来缓解金融状况以及阻止因政策工具的严格限制而产生的去杠杆化，而不是提高逆周期缓冲或降低贷款价值比（LTV）。

事实上，在日本金融危机后，日本央行的宏观审慎政策（如 2002 年的股票回购计划）目标都是阻止去杠杆化和缓解金融状况，而欧洲政策制定者现在面临相同的问题。毫无疑问，拥有审慎工具是重要的，但更重要的是何时使用这些工具。

相互作用和反馈环——风险游戏

图 2 说明了政策制定者的另一大挑战。由于任何经济活动均伴随着风险承担，风险承担的适度很大程度上取决于总体经济规模（如幻灯片所示气垫中的空气总量守恒）。如果微观审慎政策试图将银行部门的风险"挤出"，可能仅仅将风险转移到其他部门，如影子银行、家庭以及主权财富基金（SWF）和中央银行等公共部门。因此，我们必须就适当的风险共担制定全面战略以促进可持续的经济增长。

因此，图 3 上是在亚洲很有名的另一个符号图。这标志表明包括水、土壤、植物、火等在内的大自然各种元素是如何密切地联系在一起，彼此之间发生复杂的反馈关系。而金融体系、市场和经济之间复杂的反馈关系正是宏观审慎政策所

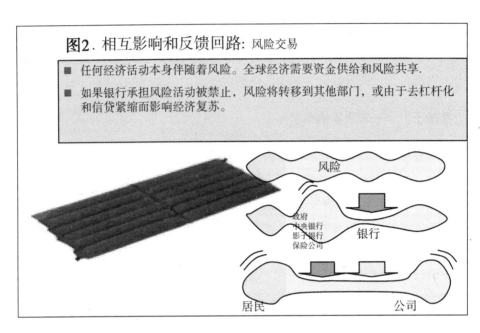

图2. 相互影响和反馈回路: 风险交易

■ 任何经济活动本身伴随着风险。全球经济需要资金供给和风险共享.

■ 如果银行承担风险活动被禁止，风险将转移到其他部门，或由于去杠杆化和信贷紧缩而影响经济复苏。

要重点关注的。

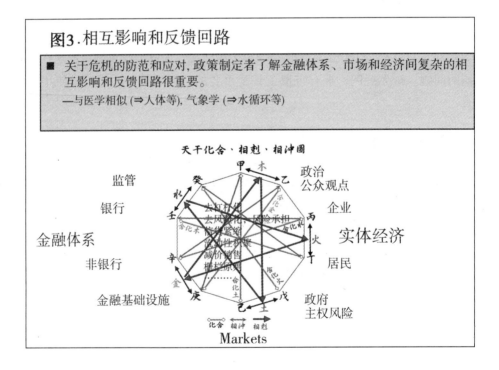

图3. 相互影响和反馈回路

■ 关于危机的防范和应对, 政策制定者了解金融体系、市场和经济间复杂的相互影响和反馈回路很重要。
    ——与医学相似 (⇒人体等), 气象学 (⇒水循环等)

防范和应对：需要做些什么？

最后，根据日本的经验，我想谈谈对危机防范和应对都非常重要的问题。

首先，必须防范"信心过度"。

以往的危机中，风险总在各种类型的"信心过度"中积累，"信心过度"包括生产率增长、政策框架和风险管理技巧等，正如太极图中阴面起源于阳面。事实上，日本资产价格泡沫源自高增长和低通胀。

第二，我想强调良好"做法"在危机防范和应对中的重要性。

图 4 的标题（"危机发生在现场，不是在会议室"）是日本著名侦探电影"Bayside Shakedown"的经典台词。其实，电影中年轻干警说的是"犯罪"而非"危机"。这个故事里，高层官僚总在会议室讨论组织架构和预算分配问题。由于他们从未到过犯罪现场，总是发出没用的指令。这部电影表明年轻干警不仅要与犯罪作斗争，同时还要与警察局的官僚作斗争。事实上，这部电影对危机管理和应对还有另外一层含义，危机管理其实是诸如不让存款者在大街上排队的一系列行动。除非我们能在紧急情况下一个周末就做出决策，否则即使有看上去很好的制度框架，也是毫无作用的。

东日本大地震

图 5 是我们从悲惨的东日本大地震中获得的经验。其实，日本人为防范海啸采取了各种措施，釜石港有世界最大的防波堤，长 1960 米，深 63 米。然而，海啸的实际规模远超过人们想象，防波堤被完全摧毁。但我也想强调无数良好做法和各类机构的奉献在灾后重建中发挥了极其重要的作用。

对金融稳定而言，宏观审慎政策、全球系统重要性金融机构政策框架或高层委员会就是防波堤。任何情况下，过于依赖特定方法，例如相信宏观审慎政策总能有效，可能成为未来另一场危机的起源。

对于 FSAP，我相信 FSAP 能够也应该在维护金融稳定方面发挥重要作用。与此同时，从亚洲的角度看，IMF 第四条款磋商和 FSAP 常常积极推荐某些发达经

图4. "危机发生在现场,不是在会议室!"
　　　　　–来自"封锁彩虹桥"(日本一部轰动的警匪片)

■ **日本经验表明危机管理措施很重要。**
　—法律和制度框架仅是危机管理的一部分。
　— 看似好的制度框架可能是无用的,除非能保证快速决策和执行(例如,周末之内),
　　因为市场发展迅速,应对的任何延迟都会遭到投资者攻击。

（防范危机的做法）

✓永远不要让存款者在街上排队。

　—如果人们在街上或电视上,看到排队,他们也会加入。

　—如果存款者一大早来到银行,让他们进来!

✓永远不要发生现金短缺。

　—央行需要迅速地提供足够的流动性（现金）!

✓当局有效的沟通策略很重要。

✓央行有必要每天监测银行流动资金。

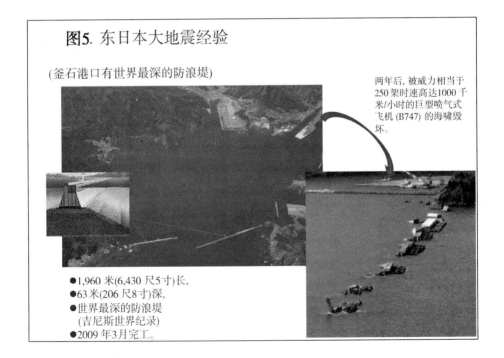

图5. 东日本大地震经验

(釜石港口有世界最深的防浪堤)

两年后,被威力相当于250架时速高达1000千米/小时的巨型喷气式飞机 (B747) 的海啸毁坏。

●1,960 米(6,430 尺5寸)长.
●63 米(206 尺8寸)深.
●世界最深的防浪堤
　(吉尼斯世界纪录)
●2009 年3月完工.

济体的全新政策和框架，如"金融大爆炸"以及不进行"逆风调节"的通胀目标制。尽管我尊重西方文化，但我想重申日本在近两千年从亚洲国家引入了许多理念和框架（正如我的演讲稿所提到的），并从中受益良多。我相信 FSAP 定会极其重视公平性和灵活性，使包括亚洲经济体在内的所有成员国受益。

希望 IMF 的 FSAP 越办越好，谢谢！

□ 赤松典孝（Noritaka Akamatsu）

亚洲开发银行地区经济一体化部门副主任

　　近年来亚洲国家在完善包括国内跨部门协调在内的金融监管框架方面成效显著，特别是遭受 1997 年亚洲金融危机冲击的国家都建立起了较完善和全方位的金融监管框架。亚洲开发银行特别赞赏亚洲国家普遍重视房地产和资产泡沫风险，并利用债务收入比（DTI）和贷款价值比（LTV）等指标进行分析和监测。从金融法规和监管看，这些国家在应对未来金融不稳定和冲击方面已有较好准备，但此判断是基于亚洲国家在可预测的将来不太可能出现主权债务危机这种假设之上的，而主权债务危机一旦出现将影响和破坏金融部门稳定，有如当今欧洲国家所面对的情况。

　　但是，亚洲国家在加强跨市场关联性方面的监管仍有待加强。陷入次贷和资产证券化问题的单一险种保险业务和 AIG 等案例使人们普遍认识到银行业和保险业之间的关联性。另外，房地产市场出现泡沫时，市场根据未实现的资本利得进行估价，从而导致大量持有房产的企业股票上涨，而这些企业可能包括拥有大量分支机构的银行。同时，地区内部分国家的银行①又会向投资者提供融资购买股票，产生证券市场泡沫的敞口。出于稳定考虑，显然应禁止银行开展这些业务。但亚洲发展中经济体由于缺乏功能完善的回购市场，证券公司无法进入市场获得流动性，因而通常面临别无选择的两难局面。另一方面，有效运行的房地产信托投资基金（REIT）市场即使无法稳定房地产市场价格，也能通过参照标的资产租金现金流使市场价格合理化。

　　此外，亚洲开发银行认为亚洲国家面对大量跨境资本流入，普遍陷入货币超发、通货膨胀以及汇率大幅波动的困境。过多资本流入导致金融机构及其员工过度放贷和刺激投资等不审慎行为，当员工收入基于金融机构的短期业绩时，不审慎行为将加剧。这损害了金融机构公司治理的完整性，对金融监管者提出重大挑战。亚洲开发银行认为包括资本流动管理在内的货币管理对于金融监管的有效性

---

　　① 如中国和越南。

至关重要。部分国家已经采取宏观审慎管理措施，如设定信贷规模增长目标遏制银行过度放贷，并取得一定成效。[1]

为有效管理跨境资本流动，首先应有效监测流入资本的性质。韩国提出了很好的模型，可供地区和全球借鉴（尽管申齐润先生没有明确的在其发言中提及）。

---

[1] 如中国和越南。

主旨发言

国际金融体系的未来：亚洲视角

金仲秀（Choongsoo Kim）

韩国中央银行

□ 金仲秀（Choongsoo Kim）
韩国中央银行行长

国际金融体系的未来：亚洲视角

女士们，先生们，晚上好！

非常高兴、也很荣幸在这一高层地区研讨会上、在上海这么高贵的城市发表主旨演讲，上海是当今中国开放和繁荣的标志。对中国人民银行周行长、IMF 副总裁朱民先生和金融顾问和货币与资本市场部主任 José Viñals 先生，我深表感谢。

国际金融危机给世界经济蒙上了一层厚厚的阴影。发达经济体因房地产泡沫破裂引发的金融动荡外溢到实体经济，并通过跨境效应影响了许多新兴经济体，其中很多都是无辜的旁观者。包括韩国在内的亚洲国家，由于经济基础十分健康，较好地应对了此次国际金融危机。

回顾过去，亚洲稳健的经济基础，是在 1997 年亚洲金融危机后经过痛苦的结构性改革才取得的。当时地区中许多国家采取了开放金融市场、加强审慎监管、增强财政稳健性、增加外汇储备缓冲等措施。总之，亚洲没有白经历这场危机，而是从中吸取了许多深刻的教训。我希望我们的欧洲伙伴也能这样做。

如果说重视经济基础的稳健性是 1997 年危机的主要教训的话，那么亚洲从此次国际金融危机中能够吸取哪些重要教训呢？我认为是要面对现实：亚洲虽然被誉为世界经济增长的引擎，但不可逃离国际金融体系重大缺陷的影响而独自在国际金融体系重构中发挥更加积极的作用。

众所周知，过去三年来，国际金融体系改革备受争论。目前国际金融监管改革已取得了一些进展，巴塞尔协议Ⅲ已经出台。即便如此，仍有许多方面有待于改进，包括全球流动性周期的反复无常、有效的全球金融安全网的缺失。

在构建新的国际金融体系中，我们面临哪些挑战？亚洲能作出什么贡献？下面我想就此谈谈自己的看法。

监管改革：实现平衡

先谈谈金融监管改革面临的政策挑战。

监管失败是此次国际金融危机的一个主要原因，这一点已有共识（IMF 2009，Truman 2009）。因此无疑应加强审慎监管，从多角度重点关注系统性风险。然而，值得注意的是，我们不能将钟摆向另一个方向偏得太远了，因为过度监管将会阻碍哪怕是有益的风险承担行为，进而损害长期增长潜力。

有关经济发展的文献认为，金融中介的质量和数量对长期增长很重要。现有的研究也认为，放松金融监管无疑是把双刃剑：一方面可通过促进金融创新提高经济增长，另一方面也会因为增加了金融危机的可能性而扼杀经济增长（Ranciere et al.，2008）。综合来看，实践提示我们应当有一个良好的监管框架，从而在金融稳定和经济增长或效率之间实现平衡。当然，金融危机往往会导致长期增长明显放慢，而经济增长放缓或停滞无疑也为金融危机的爆发提供了温床。

在推进监管改革的过程中还应考虑另一个平衡，即审慎监管政策和货币政策之间的平衡。国际金融危机清晰地告诉我们，价格稳定不足以保证金融稳定，金融稳定对价格稳定也很重要。当然，就政策目标、传导机制和政策效果而言，货币政策与宏观审慎政策有区别。然而，价格稳定与金融稳定的内在联系说明，需要在这些政策之间进行适当的协调。因此，我认为，现在正是摒弃丁伯根原则、转而寻求货币政策和宏观审慎政策最佳组合的时候了（Committee on International Economic Policy Reform 2011）。

然而，要在宏观审慎政策和货币政策之间实现平衡，这事说起来容易做起来难。理论上，宏观审慎政策可以在一个封闭的金融市场中较好地处理资产价格泡沫，货币政策在控制信贷供给总量并稳定宏观经济方面较为有效。但在实践中，很难区分什么是由于生产率的提高而导致的信贷需求激增，什么是由于非理性繁荣而产生的信贷泡沫。目前关于这方面的实践指导几乎没有。我认为最好的办法是，通过交流并汇集各国经验来建立最优做法。我期待着国际货币基金组织发挥主导作用。

溢出效应：全球治理

下面来谈谈全球溢出效应对政策制定带来的挑战。

在全球一体化不断加深的今天，金融部门和实体部门的跨境溢出效应成为各种金融危机的关键因素，尤其是当金融危机是全球性的时候。这也正是使得 2008 年的金融危机和目前正在发酵的欧洲债务危机，无论在影响范围上还在影响程度上，演变成全球性危机的因素。

在这方面，全球流动性受到人们的特别关注，不仅因为它是危机的潜在触发器，还因为它是跨境传染的途径。全球流动性通过许多参与者间的复杂交易而产生和消失，这些参与者既有私营的也有官方的，既有发达经济体的也有新兴经济体的。影响全球流动性的因素很多，从储备货币国的货币政策和监管政策到金融市场的风险偏好和创新，甚至全球性银行的顺周期行为。

实践表明，金融危机发生频率居高不下常常与全球流动性过剩有联系，而且当全球流动性大部分通过不稳定的短期融资工具来筹集时，这种联系将更强烈，所导致危机的成本往往更高。更重要的是，最近有研究表明，2008 年的国际金融危机，与其说是全球储蓄过剩或净资本流动失衡的结果，倒不如说是"全球性金融过剩"或"以总融资流动（gross financial flow）度量的全球流动性失衡"的结果（Shin 2011，Gourinchas 2011）。

因此，将全球流动性保持在一个稳定且可持续的水平，对全球金融稳定至关重要。然而，在目前的国际金融体系架构下，尚无有效机制对此问题给出一个全球性的解决方案。简而言之，各国不协调政策的简单加总，远远不能实现全球金融稳定。这就是为什么需要一个能有效监测并控制全球流动性的全球治理框架。

同样的道理，要想彻底解决欧洲债务危机，也需要一个全球性的解决方案。渐进式或延迟的政策应对，都不能阻止危机从边缘向中心传染，只会使问题变得更糟糕。我相信，我们的欧洲伙伴的解决方法是有问题的，因为那只是局部的、着眼于国内层面的方法，没有考虑到债务危机向新兴经济体和其他发达经济体的溢出效应。一个全球性解决方案，可以控制这种外部性，在解决不稳定的债务问题方面将要有效得多。例如，新兴经济体的强劲增长和稳定的融资环境，将有利于欧元区和其他地区有序地去杠杆化。

在这方面，我期待着二十国集团（G20）发挥更大的作用和更强的领导力，同时国际货币基金组织和其他国际组织不断提高监督能力。G20尤其适合于进行全球性政策协调，在应对2008年国际金融危机中，G20在协调制定宏观经济政策方面发挥了突出的作用。这种在危机管理方面的作用可以也应当延伸到危机预防政策方面，包括全球流动性管理。此外，G20还为亚洲提供了一个高级别的平台，使亚洲国家可以在解决全球流动性问题、更重要的是在重构国际金融体系的过程中，主张自己的战略性利益。

加强全球金融安全网（GFSNs）

第三个政策挑战与全球金融安全网有关。

在此次国际金融危机之前，大多数新兴市场经济体的危机是"国产的"，很少有例外。但是本轮国际金融危机却与源自发达经济体的全球流动性过剩有关，并进而波及新兴经济体。迄今为止，基本的政策建议总是说新兴经济体应该做什么，却很少讨论发达经济体为稳定全球流动性能做什么或应该做什么。而且，自国际金融危机以来，许多国际性的政策讨论也与全球流动性议题有关，但其重点仍然是"由北向北"的资本流动，而非"由北向南"的资本流动。

当前以及将来，对新兴经济体来说最紧迫的一个问题，是如何保护好自己免受外汇流动性短缺的或有风险，防范发达经济体的负面溢出效应。加强资本流动监测和宏观审慎监管，将有助于防范全球流动性过剩的风险和随之而来的资产价格泡沫风险。但是，面对全球流动性的突然逆转或混乱，新兴经济体仍然显得很脆弱。

全球流动性混乱一直是单向性的，从发达经济体开始，然后向新兴市场经济体外溢。但其实际结果却不是单向性的。新兴经济体的经济增长放缓和汇率贬值最终会影响发达经济体，使其经济下滑。因此，我们有理由认为，主要中央银行和国际货币基金组织应该在加强全球金融安全网方面承担更大的责任。的确，在国际金融危机期间，美联储向部分新兴经济体提供的货币互换，在安抚市场情绪和稳定汇率方面相当有效。我相信，最近续签的中韩、日韩货币互换，代表着金融安全网向全球性方案迈出了重要一步。我也十分赞赏国际货币基金组织为此提供的预防性信贷额度（Precautionary Credit Line）。

运作良好的全球金融安全网，还有助于降低新兴经济体积累大量外汇储备的意图，进而缓解全球失衡问题。也许有人会说，为了防止道德风险，在中央银行互换安排的准入方面保持建设性模糊是必要的。我同意建设性模糊的优点，但我也有理由认为，道德风险被夸大了。我们应该敏锐地意识到，全球金融安全网旨在解决全球性的流动性混乱，而不是特定的或"国产"的流动性危机。而且，对一国而言，金融危机的成本太高了，不仅有经济成本，还有政治成本。金融危机的这种高昂成本，本身就是对债务方道德风险的有效威慑。

亚洲金融发展策略

最后我想强调亚洲金融发展的策略问题。

如果按 GDP 和贸易量计，亚洲在世界经济中所占比例相当高，而且这个比例还在持续上升。然而，如果以金融计，亚洲所占比例与其在世界贸易和收入中所占比例根本不相称。亚洲贸易以少数储备货币记账和结算，其中以美元为主。亚洲的跨境资本交易也是这种情况。

在贸易和金融中对外汇的过度依赖被认为是亚洲金融脆弱性的根源。如此高度的依赖性也说明，亚洲在创造安全资产方面的能力有限或欠发达。如能将金融业发展到与其经济影响相当的水平，亚洲应该有能力提供足够规模的、来自本地区的安全资产。这不仅有利于亚洲金融稳定，也有助于通过缓解特里芬难题促进全球金融稳定。

金融发展是一个复杂的过程，涉及方方面面，需要有良好的金融监管、高端的人力资源和技术，甚至还要有文化作为支持。在当前情况下，对亚洲来说最为重要的是再接再厉，继续学习如何搞好金融。而学习的关键是金融自由化和市场开放。亚洲国家不应该放弃在开放资本账户方面的努力，即使是在国际金融危机爆发后全世界都在讨论如何加强金融监管的时候。事实上，发达国家的监管改革，为亚洲国家进一步开放资本账户提供了一个最佳机会窗口，在此时间窗口资本流动突然终止或异常波动的风险较低。

我坚信，资本账户开放的第一步应该是允许汇率有更大的弹性。在向浮动汇率制和资本账户开放过渡的过程中，要合理安排好顺序，这将有助于增强金融业的抗风险能力，使高成本危机发生的可能性降至最低。历史经验表明，处于"中间地带"的汇率机制易于引发危机（Ghosh 2010，Bubula and Otker - Robe 2003）。当前的欧元区财政危机清晰地表明，即使是单一货币联盟，最硬的盯住制度，在面对外部冲击时也是脆弱的。

结语

国际金融危机从许多方面改变了全球金融格局。新的监管规则将得到实施以防范危机，而负债累累的国家将努力有序地去杠杆化，以恢复金融稳定和经济增长。然而，未来充满挑战。全球溢出将继续，贸易和金融保护主义的风险不会轻易消逝。在这个相互关联的世界中，我们需要一个全球性的解决方案。我们需要一个全球性的司法管辖，以使全球性的解决方案成为真正的可能。

在过去的半个世纪里，亚洲的繁荣和增长主要得益于其政策的开放性和前瞻性。如果贸易和金融市场是封闭的或自给自足的，那就没有什么学习可言了。通过不断地推进金融自由化，亚洲应当增强其金融业，纠正金融和实体部门之间的失衡。唯有如此，亚洲才能成长为世界经济增长持续稳定的引擎。我相信，现在是为此行动的时候了。

谢谢！

参考文献

Bubula, Andrea and Inci Otker - Robe. 2003, "Are Pegged and Intermediate Exchange Rate Regimes More Crisis Prone? IMF

Committee on the Global Financial System. 2011, "Global Liquidity - Concept,

Measurement and Policy Implications," BIS

Committee on International Economic Policy Reform. 2011, "Rethinking Central Banking"

Ghosh, Atish, Jonathan Ostry, and Charalambos Tsangarides. 2010, "Exchange Rate Regimes and the Stability of the International Monetary System," IMF

Gourinchas, Pierre – Oliver. 2011, "Global Imbalances and Global Liquidity"

IMF. 2009, "Lessons of the Financial Crisis for Future Regulation of Financial Institutions and Markets and for Liquidity Management"

Ranciere, Romain, Aaron Tornell, and Frank Westermann. 2008, "Systemic Crises and Growth," *Quarterly Journal of Economics*

Shin, Hyun Song. 2011, "Global Banking Glut and Loan Risk Premium"

Truman, Edwin. 2009, "The Global Financial Crisis: Lessons Learned and Challenges for Developing Countries"

专题发言

宏观审慎监管的挑战

巴里·艾森格林（Barry Eichengreen）

加州大学伯克利分校

□ 巴里·艾森格林（Barry Eichengreen）

加州大学伯克利分校经济和政治学教授

宏观审慎监管的挑战

很高兴被邀请参加此次研讨会并就"中央银行在宏观审慎监管中的作用"发表演讲，这使我有机会宣传、介绍国际经济和政策改革委员会（Committee on International Policy and Reform）的首份报告《中央银行再思考》。该报告最近已由布鲁金斯研究所出版①，我的演讲引用了其中的一些结论。不过随后我所要讲的无疑是我个人的观点，这些观点得益于该委员会同事的启发，他们是：Mohamed El – Erian，Arminio Fraga，Takatoshi Ito，Jean Pisani – Ferry，Eswar Prasad，Raghu Rajan，Maria Ramos，Carmen Reinhart，Helene Rey，Dani Rodrik，Ken Rogoff，Hyun Shin，Andres Velasco，Beatrice Weder di Mauro，and Yongding Yu（余永定）。

国际金融危机动摇了将微观审慎监管作为维护金融稳定主要工具的信心。但我认为，许多中央银行仍然认同将货币政策和金融稳定看成是两个不同领域这一传统的两分观点，只不过微观审慎工具已经让位于宏观审慎工具（如逆周期资本要求）。这些工具是由金融稳定领域的专家，而不是负责货币政策的中央银行家们设计出来以备实施的。

做出这种区分是基于这样的认识，即在有效维护金融稳定方面，利率是一个非常生硬的工具。这通常引出这样一个的问题，即中央银行是否应当通过提升利率来应对资产价格泡沫。在 20 世纪 90 年代和 21 世纪初，关于是否要针对资产市场发展做出反应以及如何反应，中央银行家们展开了充分的讨论，得出结论的

---

① Committee on International Economic Policy and Reform, *Rethinking Central Banking*, Washington, D. C.：Brookings Institution（2011）.

是，中央银行有责任对资产价格泡沫做出反应，但不以资产价格为目标。

不赞同刺破泡沫的理由有两点：

一是很难识别资产价格泡沫。

二是即使出现了资产价格泡沫，货币政策不是解决问题的最佳办法。因为小幅调整利率不会对资产价格产生影响，只有大幅调整利率才足以刺破泡沫。然而，大幅调整利率又会对经济产生负面影响，加大了产出的波动性，得不偿失。

上述两个理由中，第一个理由无疑是肯定。但第二个理由仍有待商榷。认为小幅调整利率不会对资产价格产生影响，这一点对股市来讲似乎是很有道理。如果股市一年的涨幅达到 20%，那么小幅调整利率对快速上涨的股票价格的确影响不大。但是，股票市场也许不是讨论货币政策在维护金融稳定方面的作用的最佳领域。房地产市场（其对杠杆和信贷的影响更明显）和其他与房地产投资有关的金融市场对金融稳定的意义更重要。就房地产贷款而言，货币政策对银行和其他金融中介的杠杆决策影响很大。在这方面，即使融资成本的微小变动也会对风险承担行为和融资条件产生影响。毕竟，金融中介借钱是为了放贷。因此，借款和贷款之间的利差是金融中介使用杠杆的一个关键性决定因素，并对银行贷款、风险溢价以及正在繁荣的房地产市场之间的相互关系产生非常重要的影响。

关注银行和其他金融中介的风险承担行为自然会使政策制定者提出另一个关于经济稳定风险的问题。例如，政策制定者可以问，良好的融资环境会不会突然逆转并对经济产生负面影响，而不是等房地产泡沫"证据"（无论是什么样的证据）出现了才采取行动。即使人口、住户规模以及生活水平等长期因素基本上能够解释房地产价格的上涨，但如果政策制定者也认为，宽松的货币政策环境将导致房价和融资环境的骤然逆转，并对金融体系以及经济产生不利影响，那么就有必要进行政策干预。

因此，不反应导致了危险的不对称反应。即中央银行允许信贷自由增长，助涨了资产价格；而在泡沫破裂后，中央银行为救助金融机构和债券持有人又向市场大量注入流动性。这种不对称导致资产负债表过度扩张，体现为：当风险溢价水平较低时信贷增长速度更快，杠杆率更高；但当风险溢价上升时，去杠杆化过程会更加猛烈，并经常伴有泡沫破裂。

由此可见，中央银行应防止信贷市场过度膨胀。实行通胀目标制的中央银行也许会认为，他们这样做是自动而为，因为较高的资产价格会通过财富效应刺激总需求，进而产生通货膨胀压力。然而，即使总需求效应没有出现，但一旦发现融资环境和降低了的风险溢价预示着信贷扩张的开始，额外采取"逆风行动"是可取的。但是另一方面，当市场环境出现"繁荣迹象"时——即资产价格迅速上涨并伴随着信贷大幅扩张——实行通胀目标制的中央银行也许想保持在较低的目标水平，因为否则的话政策会变得不对称，并加大宏观经济的波动性。

"逆风行动"政策的一个后果就是"不同的工具有不同的目标"这一丁伯根分类在实践中很难执行。我们知道，利率政策会影响金融稳定，进而影响实体经济。同理，宏观审慎政策也会影响信贷增长和外部均衡，并对宏观经济和价格稳定产生影响。例如，当消费信贷迅速上升同时住户部门债务率较高时，根据景气周期调整贷款价值比或债务收入比以限制贷款增速，将对宏观经济金融稳定产生非常重要的影响。

因此，我们不能将丁伯根分类看做是困境中的不得已之举，认为一个工具完全针对一个目标。我认为，宏观经济金融稳定是货币政策和监管政策通过最优组合而实现的目标。

当然，丁伯根分类的信仰者会担心，认为一旦模糊了针对目标而分配工具的界限将会损害中央银行的操作自主权，中央银行的法定职责会因此变得不够清晰，其行动将更难有法律依据。

我认为这些担心是有道理的，因为当货币政策目标主要是维护价格稳定时，中央银行所承受的压力将会小一些。然而，需要记住的是，中央银行的独立性是实现目标的手段，而不是目标本身。如果限制货币政策范围仅仅是为了维护中央银行的独立性，那么中央银行的合法性将会受到质疑，因为这使得中央银行看起来有点"遥不可及"，其所追求的目标是狭隘的、深奥的，与其平民化职责不相称。

最终，政治现实将维护金融稳定的职责赋予了中央银行。正如英国北岩银行倒闭后所发生的情况，中央银行将因金融体系的问题而遭到谴责，无论其是否被正式赋予了监管的职责。金融体系一旦出了问题，作为"最后贷款人"，中央银行将承担收拾残局的责任。因此，与其在危机后采取措施，还不如在危机前分配更多资源加以预防，尽管有了美妙的丁伯根原则。

宏观审慎工具

那么，作为宏观审慎监管者，中央银行应当具体做点什么呢？我认为可以从两个风险维度来考虑这个问题，一个是纵向维度（即时间维度），另一个是横向维度（即跨部门维度）。

关于纵向维度，宏观审慎监管者应当针对金融体系的顺周期性而开发一系列政策工具。逆周期资本缓冲就是一个这样的工具，不过这还不够，因为逆周期资本缓冲只限于银行体系。可以考虑采取补充措施，如像 IMF 所提议的，针对所有金融机构征收系统性风险税，即对金融机构不稳定（非核心）融资头寸额外收费。这种税可根据经济周期而做适当调整。

限制银行贷款的措施，如关于贷款价值比或债务收入比的规定，将对传统的银行监管措施如资本要求起到很好的补充作用。资本要求本身可以以长期股权或股权类工具作为核心资本，并补充以额外的应急资本缓冲。

有些措施（如资本金要求）可能会对跨境竞争产生影响，所以需要进行跨境协调。其他措施（如贷款价值比规定）无须进行跨境协调，因此可以因经济周期变化而有很大的不同。

关于横向维度，有关政策需着重考虑系统重要性金融机构（SIFIs）。在处理倒闭金融机构时，一个好的处置机制将有助于降低对事先缓冲（如资本）的依赖程度。问题的复杂性在于许多系统重要性机构都积极开展跨区域或跨产品业务，而这些新的规定还没有得到很好的协调，因而可能不足以应对大型的跨境或跨市场机构失败问题。因此，新的处置机制并没有解决"大而不能倒"（TBTF）机构所蕴含的道德风险问题。也就是说，对这类机构的隐性的、用公共资源进行补贴问题没有得到解决。这也说明了事前采取措施的必要性。

总之，宏观审慎工具的目的应包括降低机构变得"大而不能倒"的动机，征收系统性风险税可以起到这样的作用。当然，这样做的前提是要量化系统性风险敞口，并明确征税主体、征收对象以及征收条件。

此外，还可以针对 SIFIs 的系统性风险状况施加额外资本要求。在这方面，瑞士已采取了行动。瑞士政府针对"大而不能倒"机构成立了专门的委员会。据我理解，除了将资本缓冲要求提高至接近巴塞尔协议Ⅲ要求的两倍外，该委员会还根据机构的系统性风险（其计算公式为该机构的资产负债规模和市场份额的函数）来计算额外资本要求。

其他措施包括禁止 SIFIs 的某些业务范围（如不允许从事财产性交易），或限制某些业务（如零售银行的业务等，正如英国维克斯委员会所议），或者甚至分拆 SIFIs。我个人不太支持这些措施。这些措施可能只是将风险转移至限制范围之处，但并没有解决"大而不能倒"问题。

机构责任

下面，我想谈谈应该由谁承担金融稳定职责这个问题。答案有二，一是由多个机构（中央银行、系统性风险委员会、微观和宏观审慎监管者）共同承担，赋予其工具，并规定其协作履职；二是由单一机构来承担，可能是中央银行，并赋予其多重职责和工具。

在此次国际金融危机爆发前，金融稳定职责由多个机构分担的模式处于主导地位，尽管这种模式并不成功。因此一些国家如印度、美国等，纷纷设立了新的协调机构，虽然这些机构似乎还缺乏执行力。在欧洲，推进区内协调的难度更大，因为在欧洲又额外增加了一层监管机构，而且其自身的权力还很有限。联合监管机制就是跨国协调的一种方式，该委员会汇集了大型跨国机构的母国和东道国监管者。但总体来看，跨国协调不充分的问题仍然存在，尤其是在欧洲。

虽然人们对究竟哪种模式最优尚未达成共识，但关于金融稳定应当作为中央银行的一个主要目标的讨论，使得从监管的角度看将该职责赋予中央银行的重要性日益增加。如果中央银行有维护金融稳定的职责，同时也拥有使用宏观审慎校正工具的权力，那么中央银行可在利率工具和宏观审慎政策工具间进行很好的取舍。此外，中央银行应当通过其货币政策操作来参与金融市场。中央银行拥有宏观经济领域的专家职员，同时其资产负债表能力使其成为可以发挥最后贷款人作用的一个机构。

反对单一机构模式的声音也很强烈，理由之一是这种模式使得中央银行更容易受到政治干预。当金融稳定所受威胁的特点和中央银行采取的行动得不到公众的理解时，中央银行不得不努力证明其行动的合法性。公众及其推选的代表也许有意见，例如，当中央银行控制信贷增长并导致资产价格下跌时，他们可能会迫使当局采取措施扭转形势。

单一模式还有可能导致中央银行的利益冲突。例如，中央银行可能会人为地维持低利率，目的是帮助陷入困境的金融机构，或处理面临清偿能力不足（一个可能由财政当局或其代理出面处理更为合适的问题）的银行，就像处理出现流动性困难的机构一样。

总的来说，如果决定由中央银行承担宏观审慎监管职责，那就应当同时考虑采取措施以加强中央银行的独立性，避免政治干预。同时，中央银行要积极参与公众讨论，对其绩效进行评价，这一点很重要。此外，中央银行还应就其政策的合理性加强与公众的定期沟通机制，关于这一点的重要性也正在日益显著提高。

总之，两种模式各有所长，各国的制度特点和政治安排决定了究竟哪种模式最合适。但是，无论选择哪种模型，有一点是明确的，那就是货币政策与金融监管政策的有效协调将是金融稳定的关键。

第四部分

宏观审慎政策
——如何具体实施？

- 系统性风险的识别和监测——哪些模型和指标最为有效？

- 宏观审慎工具——哪些工具能发挥作用？原因是什么？

- 制度设计——各机构应履行何种职责？确保问责和协调的最佳机制是什么？

- 国际协调——宏观审慎政策的国际协调有作用吗？对亚洲而言，可能和可行的协调方式是什么？

□ 基思·霍尔（Keith Hall）
澳大利亚储备银行行长助理

　　首先，感谢中国人民银行和国际货币基金组织（IMF）给我这个机会，使我有幸来上海参加本次研讨会。

　　与在座的各位央行同事们不同，我本人并没有运用宏观审慎工具的直接经验，因为在澳大利亚我们没有实施过宏观审慎工具。但最近，金融稳定理事会（FSB）在同行评估报告中这样评价澳大利亚："澳大利亚具有进行系统性监管的隐性宏观审慎目标，通过每天对单个机构进行监管，来监测系统性风险"。下面，我讲一下澳大利亚的制度安排和政策实施特点。我们的许多政策措施是最近才建立起来的，这些政策措施同治理结构特别是制度安排和委托代理关系的适当性存在密切联系，同时它们也同金融监管和金融稳定分析所能利用资源的数量和质量密切相关。

　　澳大利亚目前的监管体系是 20 世纪 90 年代末形成的。当时，出于对金融集团加强监管的考虑，所有澳大利亚金融监管部门联合建立了"金融体系问询（FSI）"制度，澳大利亚政府接受了金融体系问询制度提出的建议：剥离中央银行的监管职能，将其移交给新成立的专门的审慎监管机构——澳大利亚审慎监管局（APRA）。对此，当时也有一些担忧，主要是担心中央银行一旦丧失监管权，会对中央银行履行金融稳定职能产生负面影响，且政府在决定设立澳大利亚审慎监管局时特别强调央行具有维护长期金融稳定的职能。因为监管者会掌握大量关于金融风险的信息，央行只有在履行监管权的同时才能更好地履行金融稳定职能。

　　尽管如此，澳大利亚储备银行和审慎监管局从一开始就根据新的制度安排履行自身职责。我们共同的目标是：确保审慎监管局对单个金融机构进行更有效的监管、更好地保护存款人和投保人利益；同时，确保该制度安排不会削弱澳大利亚央行对系统性风险的监控能力。

　　我认为下面两种做法对实现上述目标起到了关键作用。

一是建立有效的部门间合作安排。我们知道，澳大利亚央行可以参与审慎监管局的政策工具，同时审慎监管局也可以参与央行的政策工具，特别是在危机期间更是如此。同样关键的是：央行和审慎监管局一起，会同证券监管部门——证券投资委员会（ASIC）、政府金融政策制定者——财政部协同一致，共同制定金融政策措施，这些政策措施跟得上金融创新的步伐并能够监控相关系统性风险。

我们认为加强协作的最有效办法是建立金融监管委员会（Council of Financial Regulaors）并赋予其如下职责：

- 识别金融体系中的重大发展趋势，包括影响整体金融稳定的各种因素；

- 确保现有的协作机制能够对实际或潜在的导致金融不稳定的因素做出准确反应，并有效解决各监管部门的职责重叠问题。

值得注意的是，从设立之初，金融监管委员会就是一个不具备独立法人资格和独立权力的非正式合作组织。委员会在新监管体系的重要性体现在其成员单位身上。委员会的主席由澳大利亚储备银行行长担任，其成员包括各金融部门的首脑。由于澳大利亚储备银行具有金融稳定分析的特殊优势，委员会秘书处设在储备银行。委员会以联合谅解备忘录的形式确定各成员单位的职责和角色，同时各成员单位之间还通过签署双边谅解备忘录的形式确保有效的信息沟通并保证各个政策目标的顺利实现。

值得强调的是，我并不认为澳大利亚的金融监管委员会是部门有效合作的"最优模式"，各国可以根据实际情况建立各自的合作机制。此外，定期召开非正式工作会议的做法也同样重要。但委员会确实在达成风险共识、防止宏观审慎政策和微观审慎政策错位方面起到了十分关键的作用。在一些国家，建立部门间合作机制的需要可能并不是很迫切，特别是对于金融监管权还在央行手中、央行可以完全行使监管权的国家更是如此。在昨天的会议上，我了解到许多具有金融监管权的央行也正在努力完善其金融稳定方面的制度安排。

二是赋予澳大利亚审慎监管局明确的金融稳定职责。这种做法对控制系统性风险十分关键。这样，审慎监管局在制定政策措施时，既要维护金融体系的整体稳定，又要确保单个金融机构的安全和稳健。这种做法的潜在含义是：系统性风险是损害存款人和投保人利益的头号杀手。为行使其维护金融稳定职责，澳大利亚审慎监管局行使日常监管职能时，要考虑到一系列系统性因素。换句话说，监管时要重点关注对金融体系具有重大影响的金融机构，即系统重要性的金融机构（SIFIs）。通过将概率论和评级影响模型纳入监管和反馈系统，被监管金融机构的系统性影响越大，其被监管的力度也就越大；在某些情况下，可能对金融机构采取额外的审慎监管措施，如更高的资本充足要求。

澳大利亚审慎监管局一直认为，采取积极主动的监管方式是其对维护金融稳定作出的最大贡献。在积极主动的监管方式下，审慎监管局能够阻止有问题的金融机构向有问题的借款人发放高额贷款，这种监管方式可能对控制美国次贷危机的爆发具有重要防范作用，对其他与房地产相关的信贷危机也可能具有重要的防范作用。也就是说，对单个金融机构最有效的微观监管工具才是最好的监管。同时，最好的监管也体现在宏观层面上：通过控制家庭、企业甚至是主权的杠杆的过度累积来控制系统性风险。但是，如果只是金融部门的资产负债表十分漂亮，而其他经济部门步履维艰，这也不是我们想要的结果。

我刚才提到的都是宏观审慎监管方法，而不是宏观审慎规制政策。二者的区别在于：宏观审慎监管明确地针对金融不平衡问题，如果对金融不平衡不加以修正，可能会影响金融稳定。在这方面，澳大利亚审慎监管局所采取的做法值得称道，它宣布将在 2016 年实施逆周期资本缓冲要求，作为巴塞尔协议Ⅲ改革的一部分。逆周期资本缓冲的实施细则还需要进一步研究制定，我们认为，要测定资本缓冲要求与特定变量（如信贷规模）之间的变动关系，同时又要保证适度的短期灵活性十分困难。你们也许知道，在货币政策方面存在制定规则与自由裁量权的争论，在逆周期资本缓冲方面也同样存在。存在这样一种可能性，逆周期资本也以制定规则为主，同时赋予政策实施者一定的自由裁量权，但短期内难以得出最终结论，因为就货币政策而言，实现这种平衡就耗费了几十年或者更长的时间。

货币政策在宏观审慎框架中应扮演什么样的角色？韩国中央银行行长 Kim 在昨天晚上和加州大学伯克利分校经济和政治学教授 Barry Eichengreen 在今天上午都提到了这个十分熟悉的政策难题。换句话说，如何用一种政策工具实现两种重要的政策目标：既控制通货膨胀又维护金融稳定？同大多数央行的观点一样，我们认为稳定的物价环境就是对维护金融稳定最大的贡献。但与此同时，过去十年给我们最大的政策教训是：除非你十分小心，价格稳定、通胀可控的大环境下可能蕴含着风险严重积累，这种情形可能导致资产价格大幅上涨，然后资产价格泡沫破裂。我们认为，这并不说明运用货币政策工具可以积极扭转资产泡沫，也不意味着只是消极地接受资产泡沫。我们不能消极地接受资产泡沫，未来的货币政策需要改革，至少要针对资产泡沫做出积极响应。

最后，我想强调的是，不管我们选择何种制度安排，我们都面临着实施有效宏观审慎政策的实际挑战：就是如何进行系统性风险监测，如早期预警等，使我们能更好地鉴别出金融体系的风险和脆弱性。我相信今天来参会的央行都已经在最近几年大幅增加了对金融稳定分析的投入，或者将在未来增加投入。

不幸的是，重视系统性风险监测并不能保证我们能更好地控制系统性风险，Mr. Yamaoka 昨天就已经总结了原因，在金融领域，"早诊断，早治疗"的规律同样适用。在这方面，我们的目标同国际货币基金组织（IMF），尤其是货币与资本市场部是一致的，国际货币基金组织在系统性风险监测和金融稳定分析方面的研究是全球领先的，因此，虽然需要阅读的东西很多，但花时间去读一下国际货币基金组织的《全球金融稳定报告》是十分值得的，尽管读报告的过程有时会十分枯燥。我的报告到此为止，谢谢大家！

□ 安德鲁·邱（Andrew Khoo）
新加坡金管局总裁助理

今天，我想与大家分享新加坡关于宏观审慎政策方面的做法。我想强调的是，在宏观审慎成为通用的监管术语之前，一些工具就已经被广泛地应用于审慎管理目的了。

我的发言将集中于我们关于房地产市场的措施，但我们的宏观审慎的工作大大超出了房地产市场的范围。来自新加坡境内外的脆弱性和风险都被密切监测。我们致力于了解风险是如何传递至我们的金融体系和机构的，以及评估我们金融体系的抗风险能力。

宏观审慎政策框架下有几个要素。包括：监测揭示风险累积程度的指标，如信贷增长、资产价格上涨、资本流动、融资趋紧、货币错配等，以确定我们对新出现的趋势和问题是否采取措施以及如何解决问题。银行通过压力测试来检测其抗风险能力。考虑到对国内的系统重要性，我们对本国注册的银行提出额外资本要求。对影子银行部门的监测，则有助于揭示其风险及其与银行体系的关联。

目前，我们已经着手跟踪整个系统对欧盟的风险敞口情况，并确定风险敞口最大的金融机构。明确欧盟银行在国内信贷提供中的作用，特别是确认这些银行是否在特定借款市场占有很大的市场份额，以便我们评估其去杠杆化影响。一些欧盟的银行在贸易融资领域占有很大份额，因此，我们一直在密切注视着在这方面的进展，尤其是在欧盟银行退出时其他银行填补的能力。

在机构设置方面，金管局内设有宏观审慎管理司，隶属于我们的金融监管组。该部有两个处。金融监督处致力于识别风险及其传输渠道，并由金融研究处的研究工作予以紧密支持。

后者负责研究宏观金融联系，以便设计适当的逆周期资本缓冲机制来满足巴塞尔协议Ⅲ的要求。我们支持逆周期资本缓冲，因为它可以解决金融体系的顺周期性问题。但在设计该机制方面还需要做更多的工作，以确保能够对已采取的房地产措施起到补充作用。

新加坡的房地产市场是一个主要的风险来源，对家庭和银行的资产负债表的潜在影响很大。购房者和建筑业合计占非银行贷款总额的四分之一强。从宏观审慎的角度看，有必要确保家庭没有过度杠杆贷款，同时银行维持良好的信贷标准以及足够的缓冲来应对房地产价格调整。

房地产价格的调整可能会对家庭和银行造成严重影响。由于资产价格下降会导致银行的资产质量恶化，给予家庭和开发商的授信额度也可能下降。这又会对资产价格造成负面影响，形成螺旋式下降，最后对实体经济产生负面影响。

下面谈一下我们所采取的政策措施，这些措施主要针对市场的供需双方。

贷款的按揭比率（LTV Ratio）上限已经过一系列的向下调整。全国的按揭比率上限从 90% 降低至 80%。对于第二套房的按揭，按揭成数上限进一步由 80% 下调至 70%，然后到 60%，该政策主要针对投资目的的买房者。对非个人的借款人而言，比如基金，按揭成数更低至 50%，因为我们假定这些都是投资者。

简单的数学计算就可以揭示按揭成数上限是如何运作的。90% 按揭成数上限，意味着只要银行愿意，借款人可以凭借自身拥有的 1 元，最高可借入 9 元。按揭成数不超过 80% 意味着，借款人可以凭借自身拥有的 1 元，最高只能借入 4 元。因此，按揭成数上限限制了家庭的贷款杠杆。按揭成数一个看似微小的变化则可以对借款产生较大的影响。此外，较低的按揭成数上限，也意味着当楼价下跌时，银行有较大的缓冲。

采取其他措施包括最低现金支付比例（首付比例），我们从 5% 提高到了 10%。新加坡的购房者允许使用其在国营退休金计划（中央公积金）中的储蓄来支付购房款。通过增加首付比例，购买者必须更少地依赖退休金储蓄和银行贷款来购买房地产。

为遏制投机，"创新贷款"计划已被叫停。允许买家以最少的现金支出在竣工前购置物业的延期付款计划也已被叫停。交易成本也已增加。政府出台了卖方印花税①，规定买家在购买房屋后特定时间内就出售的需缴税。连同已经存在 3% 的买方印花税一道，短期投机者面临的抑制税率大增。

政府最近还推出了附加买方印花税（ABSD）。外国人必须支付 10% 的附加买方印花税，永久居民购买第二套和公民购买第三套均需支付 3% 的附加买方印花税。这是针对特定小部分买方市场的一个政策，从而抑制对房地产的投资需求。

目前的低利率环境刺激借款人借入超过其偿还能力的款项的情况已经引起了注意。作为提高消费者风险意识的一部分，从 2012 年初开始，银行将被要求向借款人提供住房贷款情况表。银行将用两页纸以简单的英语提醒潜在的借款人关于利率上升对其还款义务的影响。

最后，结合需求措施，政府已扩大其卖地计划，以增加新加坡私人物业的供应。

我们的政策措施成效如何？

整体交易活动下降。预售②，一种代理投机业务活动，也下降了。房地产价格指数增速已经放缓，虽然增长率在不同的细分市场是不同的。但增长仍然是正的。楼价仍在增长，目前已达到创纪录的水平。

然而，住房贷款余额增长放缓。按揭贷款中按揭成数在 80% 以上的只占 5% 左右。这意味着，只有在楼价发生 30% 以上的下跌时，银行才会面临资产质量的压力。事实上，当市场在 2007—2009 年期间大幅下降时，银行并没有受到很大影响。国际货币基金组织第四条款磋商小组当时表示，新加坡通过了一个真正的压力测试。

我们的宏观审慎政策方法为新出现的风险提供了一系列有针对性的工具。

---

① 目前，如果购房者在购房后第一年内出售其房产，税率为 16%；在第二年内出售，税率为 12%，在第三年和第四年内出售，其税率分别为 8% 和 4%。

② 预售是指发生在竣工之前的销售。

房地产市场被认定为一个风险源，多种工具被用来缓释其风险。我们的做法相当简单且无一定之规。我们相信，针对风险源所采取的措施会产生直接且更快的效果。宽泛的措施对所有信贷部门所产生的意想不到的后果得以避免，特别是在没有证据表明其他部门存在过度信贷增长的情况下。

我们针对不同类型的买家采取了不同的措施。对首次置业的按揭成数的规定是最宽松的，尽管仍然鼓励审慎放贷。对于那些购买后续置业的，按揭成数上限则更加严格。对于短期投机者，则提高其交易成本以阻止他们参与楼市。

当然我们也面临挑战。我们每个措施的阈值或步长的设置以及实施的时间都是一个需要判断的问题。这是在实施方面的挑战。

更严格的决策方式需要对金融部门和实体经济部门之间的联系进行更好地理解和建模。最近一期的《全球金融稳定报告》标题为"可操作的宏观审慎政策：何时开始行动"的第3章已经开始了这方面的尝试。报告承认，这项工作仍然任重道远。我们欢迎国际货币基金组织对这一领域进行更深入的研究。

宏观审慎政策的另一个挑战是缺乏一个清晰的目标。我们如何衡量金融稳定？政策制定者不能证明自己是正确的。一旦我们选择采取行动，我们将永远不会知道反事实。我们永远不会知道，如果我们的行动先于价格上涨，那么随后的不稳定校正会发生什么情况。

政策的执行也是一个挑战。让我举一个例子。我们打算对投资者规定较低的按揭成数上限。但是，这很难执行，因为银行没有办法确定借款人的真实意图。银行想要为资信良好的借款人提供更高的按揭贷款。我们最终实行的政策是：对于已有按揭的借款人规定较低的按揭成数上限。银行需要事先向信贷局调查，以确认借款人是否已有住房贷款。但这会影响那些只有一套住房并希望改善居住条件的人，因为这意味着他们要么必须先出售现有的房产，要么将面临较低的按揭成数上限。

最后，成功地实施宏观审慎政策需要相关各部门之间的协调合作。

新加坡金融监管局（MAS）既是中央银行又是综合的金融监管者，所以我们没有一些其他国家或地区所面临的部门间协调的问题。MAS 负有维护金融稳定的法定责任。在金管局，"金融稳定例会"汇集了金管局的监管和中央银行职能。我们与财政部之间也有定期会议机制。虽然金管局是最后贷款人，但如果银行需要注资，这笔钱必须来自财政部。

在对房地产市场实行的措施中，我们采取的是"整体政府"方针，有一个跨部门的工作组，由财政部（其可以提高或征收交易费用）和国家发展部（其负责土地供应政策）组成。

在我的演讲结束之际做一个总结。房地产市场的措施很重要，但不是我们的宏观审慎政策框架的唯一方面。我们的政策仅仅反映了我们认为需要采取的措施，但这些可能无法在其他国家或地区适用。谢谢！

□ 通谷来·琳丕泰（Tongurai Limpiti）

泰国中央银行行长助理

宏观审慎政策：泰国的经验

　　早上好！首先，感谢国际货币基金组织和中国人民银行邀请我参加此次研讨会并做发言。宏观审慎政策的具体实施一直是学术界和政策制定者的关注焦点，危机后尤其如此。为便于大家对我的发言进行讨论，我将发言分为以下三部分：（1）国际金融危机的教训，（2）泰国实施宏观审慎政策的经验，（3）泰国银行宏观审慎政策的制定过程。在概括国际金融危机教训之前，我先简要介绍一下危机的原因以及危机后的一些情况。

次贷危机的主要原因

　　宽松的货币政策：发达国家持续宽松的货币政策导致资产泡沫。

　　金融监管不足：由于竞争激烈，金融机构放松了信贷投放标准，同时家庭的财务约束薄弱；金融创新扭曲了信贷审批过程的相关责任和管理。金融机构对金融创新产品（如 CDOs 和 ABS）的投资缺乏足够的风险管理能力；对影子银行（如投资银行、养老基金、保险公司和对冲基金）的监管不足，且影子银行由于监管套利而发展迅速。

国际金融危机

　　资产泡沫破裂后，房价急剧下降，不良贷款率迅速上升；流动性短缺和美国金融机构的巨额损失和资不抵债相继出现。雷曼兄弟以及其他知名银行的破产最终导致风险传播，引起了全球金融危机；为应对危机，各国采取了一系列果断措施，体现了各国政府的意愿和能力。

国际金融危机的教训

刚刚发生的国际金融危机凸显了公共政策中合理的微观审慎政策的必要性。微观审慎政策对建立充分的审慎监管，解决系统性金融风险积聚，预防金融危机，维护金融稳定具有至关重要的作用。与此同时，宏观审慎监管应在增强金融体系稳健性和风险吸收能力方面起到更重要的作用。

后危机时代，国际上对宏观审慎政策不仅仅是一个特殊时期的政策工具，而且是维护金融稳定的一个常态政策工具越来越有共识。

一个典型的例子是：巴塞尔协议Ⅲ中关于逆周期资本缓冲的规定是应对逆周期的一个宏观审慎工具，并对系统重要性金融机构实行更严格的资本要求和监管。

此外，金融稳定理事会（FSB）、国际货币基金组织（IMF）和国际清算银行（BIS）强调宏观审慎政策框架的三个重要方面：识别和监测系统性金融风险、制定和校准宏观审慎工具、建立国内和地区范围内的制度和治理安排。

泰国实施宏观审慎政策的基本原则

1. 宏观审慎政策通过直接消除根本原因而起到防止系统性风险的作用，而不是危机发生后再针对症状进行应对。对泰国银行而言，这需要尽早采取措施来解决宏观经济不平衡或金融脆弱性，如杠杆率过高、部分经济部门负债率过高或不同类型的资产泡沫。

2. 将宏观审慎政策作为"逆风而动"的措施，来防止系统性风险的积聚，增强金融体系的抗风险能力。

3. 实施宏观审慎政策时要具有一定的判断力，要灵活对待宏观经济和金融形势的变化。例如，由于洪灾，泰国银行最近推迟了针对低层住宅的按揭成数政策。

4. 宏观审慎政策的实施要与货币政策和微观审慎监管政策相协调。这对于保持政策的一致性，进而有效地维护整体金融和经济的稳定至关重要。

概括来讲，在实施宏观审慎政策时，我们应向自己提出以下三个问题：（1）政策自身是否合理？（2）对所有股东来讲，政策是否实际？（3）政策的实施时间是否合适？在我下面阐述的泰国银行经验中，以上原则也会经常出现。

泰国银行长期将宏观审慎政策和微观审慎监管作为金融稳定政策工具。上述政策工具与通胀目标制一起有助于增强金融体系抗风险能力、抵御国际金融危机和国内动荡。

泰国实施的宏观审慎政策

（1）2002 年实施外汇净资本头寸；

（2）2003 年、2009 年和 2010 年对按揭贷款实施贷款成数规定；

（3）2002 年、2004 年和 2005 年收紧信用卡贷款和个人贷款；

（4）2006 年和 2007 年实行贷款损失拨备。

2002 年的外汇净资本头寸政策

对外汇净头寸的监管有助于抑制泰国银行业的外汇风险。作为对超买、超卖外汇头寸政策的补充，泰国银行对单个币种持汇量和外汇总量都实行了净头寸管理。这一举措与 BIS 的相关举措一致。

事实表明，金融机构的单个币种持汇量和持汇总量都大大低于监管要求。特别是，外汇净头寸在 2008 年金融危机期间大幅下降，反映了金融机构根据环境变化管理外汇风险、调整风险敞口的能力。

2003 年、2009 年和 2010 年对按揭贷款的贷款成数规定

泰国的贷款成数政策以前面提到的几个宏观审慎原则为基础。对贷款成数政策的使用和随后的调整表明该政策具有预防性质。更重要的是，泰国当局灵活调整这一政策，以适应不断变化的经济形势。

2003 年，1000 万泰铢以上按揭贷款的贷款成数最高为 7 成，以预防豪华住

宅投机。2009 年国际金融危机期间，取消 7 成贷款上限，取而代之的是对贷款成数超过 8 成的抵押贷款施以较高的风险权重资本要求。

由于贷款成数政策比较有效，2010 年晚些时候，对 1000 万泰铢以下的按揭贷款额度也实施了成数限制。实施这一政策主要有以下两点考虑：首先，防止银行在竞争激烈的按揭贷款市场中过度冒险，虽然当时尚未出现资产价格泡沫迹象；其次，考虑到高层住宅的竞争比低层住宅竞争更为激烈，高层住宅市场比低层住宅市场早一年执行较严厉的贷款政策。

高层住宅市场的贷款成数政策已于 2011 年初执行。但考虑到泰国最近的洪水状况，泰国央行决定将针对低层住宅市场的执行日期从最初设定的 2012 年 1 月 1 日向后推迟一年。

2002 年、2004 年和 2005 年收紧信用卡贷款和个人贷款

以下例子将表明如何综合使用宏观审慎政策、货币政策和微观审慎政策来解决行业不平衡问题。

本世纪初快速增长的消费信贷以及一些发展中经济体出现的家庭部门不平衡促使我们收紧信用卡贷款和个人贷款。主要措施是将非银行信用卡公司纳入监管范围、对信用卡持有人设定最低要求、设定最高信用额度和最低还款额。针对个人贷款也出台了相关规定。

以上措施有一定效果，这些市场的信贷增长迅速下滑。这表明，合理运用宏观审慎政策能直接解决行业不平衡问题。相反，运用传统的紧缩货币政策影响面比较大，会对其他部门产生难以预料的严重后果。

2006 年和 2007 年实施贷款损失拨备

最后讲一下泰国银行在"逆风行动"的大环境下实施宏观审慎政策的经验。

在泰国银行业于 21 世纪第一个十年中期持续盈利的大背景下，根据国际会计准则（IAS）第 39 号，泰国银行实施了更为严厉的贷款损失拨备政策。银行的不良贷款覆盖率上升，增强了抵御资产减值的缓冲。

在讲述泰国银行宏观审慎政策制定过程之前，我想介绍一下金融稳定的工作程序：（1）识别关键部门的脆弱性；（2）监督系统性风险并对其影响进行评估；（3）适当的政策反映；（4）危机处置和管理。

宏观审慎政策横跨很多部门，金融稳定委员会的主席是泰国银行行长，成员包括所有的副行长，和负责审慎监管、货币政策和货币市场操作的行长助理。委员会主要负责全面监督和风险评估。这一治理结构有助于对系统性风险进行全面评估，并协调制定预防措施。一旦达成政策建议，金融稳定委员会将向相关委员会提交建议以最后制定政策。

金融稳定报告在定期会议上提交金融稳定委员会，会上讨论金融系统的各种脆弱性和风险。金融稳定委员会不仅讨论特定部门的问题，也讨论不同金融市场、资本市场、金融机构和宏观经济的联系。泰国银行目前正在研究欧债危机对泰国金融体系的影响。研究既关注金融体系间的联系也关注贸易联系。这里我们用到了网络模型，以更好地理解金融机构间的关联性。我们发现，通过泰国金融体系而产生的直接影响是比较有限的，因为泰国对欧洲国家的风险敞口较低。然而，由于泰国比较依赖出口，我们的主要担心是通过贸易渠道带来的间接影响。委员会还通过泰国银行的每日宏观监测来关注危机的发展以及其对金融市场和金融机构的影响。此外，委员会已经拥有了一些政策工具来稳定金融体系。

此外，我们的政策协调主要包括以下两个层面：

国内政策协调。作为主要监管者，泰国银行主要负责银行业监管，同时也是保险业和证券业监管委员会的组成成员。而证券交易委员会和保险委员会的负责人也同时是金融机构政策委员会（Financial Institutions Policy Committee，FIPC）的成员。这种交叉任职能有效避免金融集团的监管套利。

跨境协调。作为东亚及太平洋地区中央银行行长会议组织银行监管工作组（EMEAP WGBS）的一员，泰国银行定期和其他成员交换宏观审慎政策的执行经验，以及对国际监管规则的看法。

为完成上述金融稳定工作程序，下面我将讲一下危机处理过程。泰国银行作为最后贷款人，依据《泰国银行法》向银行提供流动性。针对清偿能力问题，不良贷款和不良资产由曼谷商业资产管理公司（BAM）购买，随后进行私有化处理。额外的资本注入需泰国银行先向金融机构政策委员会提出，随后递交金融机构发展基金（FIDF），由金融机构发展基金向内阁寻求财政化解决方案。一旦内阁同意，金融机构发展基金将进行资本注入。但是，如果要关闭任何一家金融机构，存款保险局将发挥作用，依法对每个存款人赔付的额度为一百万泰铢。

谢谢！

□ 亚历克斯·吉布斯（Alex Gibbs）

英国驻国际货币基金组织执行董事

概述

我主要就本部分第三个议题，即关于制度建立的问题阐述英国的具体做法——这并不是说我们已找到了解决方案，事实上我们还未找到。我认为我们应吸取英国自身以及其他国家的经验教训，与时俱进逐步完善制度。我还将谈谈第四个议题，即关于国际协调的问题。

首先，英国很早就开始制定宏观审慎政策。英国 FSAP 评估提示英国对宏观审慎政策在执行初期所能起到的作用应抱更为现实的态度，事实确实如此。

挑战是巨大的。如果将货币政策和宏观审慎政策作比较，在英国，英格兰银行拥有一个单一对称、量化的政策目标，一个至少在正常时期可以运用的政策工具，同时拥有丰富的专业知识和能够详细评估内在联系的模型，以及完善的决策投票程序和沟通行动信息的跟踪记录。

我们正要求金融政策委员会（FPC）研究制定（期望达成一致）一项政策目标，该目标并不以数量化指标来定义，可能与其他政策重叠甚至冲突，具有多种政策手段，而针对这些政策之间关系的研究目前还较少。

正如 IMF 所述，有充分理由证明需保持谨慎。危机过后，政策制定者很自然地希望采取新的政策措施，在英国相关讨论正在激烈地进行中。但与此同时，不要忽视完善传统的宏观政策和监管政策，因为危机证明这些政策也存在问题。

制度设计

制度设计方面，英国正向着"三峰"（triple peak）模式转变，其中包括英格兰银行下的金融政策委员会，它具有明确的宏观审慎职责，识别和处置系统性风险。自 6 月以来，该机构运行正处于过渡阶段。明年底前，该机构将获得法律基础和法定权力。

基本机制设计

我们认为，一个单独设立、具有独立性的宏观审慎机构是非常重要的。如果不采取这样的机制，可能无法明确将系统性稳定问题作为关注重点，这是我们从危机中得到的教训。微观审慎监管者很自然地将关注重点落在针对单个机构的问题上。归根结底，这是其职责所在。因此，尽管微观审慎部门需要完全参与其中，并提供很多支持系统性问题研究的相关信息，我们仍认为这种机构分设是非常重要的。

关于如何设定新机构的目标、职能、成员组成和问责机制，英国在这方面已开展了大量工作。

目标方面，我们认为机构的目标是监测系统性金融风险，并采取措施消除和降低相关风险，以确保金融体系的抗风险能力。但随之而来的挑战是如何确保金融稳定和经济增长之间的平衡，因为两者之间存在权衡问题，这甚至在长期内都会存在。某一经济体的金融体系受到抑制可能会避免金融不稳定的发生，但也会遇到许多其他问题。一定程度上，由于部分市场参与者资产负债表具有脆弱性，且相互关联的网络颇为复杂，我们不得不接受金融体系很容易陷入不稳定状况的现实。

针对上述挑战，我们应将目标定为确保金融体系具有充足的抗风险能力，能够在不损害经济大部分功能的前提下应对潜在的尾部事件。金融政策委员会将开展一次测试，评估其干预措施能否避免对中长期经济增长造成损害。

但当全球状况变得更为严峻时，我们应更进一步，提升关于抗风险能力的标准。这并非对商业周期进行微调，而是在周期的不同阶段需要对提升抗风险能力的政策进行重新校准。

因此，可能会运用到两类政策，一类应对金融体系的结构性问题，另一类应对周期性问题。正如我们在此次危机中看到的那样，我们应认识到周期本身会受到金融部门结构的影响，这一点非常重要。

这就是英国设立新的宏观审慎机构的主要考量。

金融政策委员会将向微观审慎和市场监管者提供建议，并在少数领域在经过深入讨论后向这些监管者发出指令。关于对于监管者的指导权力是此次立法的重要部分，有待进一步讨论。但无论讨论结果如何，有一点是明确的，那就是金融政策委员会将根据风险的性质和规模，拥有一系列政策工具和手段。

问责机制

鉴于新机构的政策手段将远超过通常独立机构职责范围的政策手段，例如限制个人和企业获得信贷，因此问责机制显得尤为重要。

核心机制是透明度

如要求金融政策委员会明确使用政策工具的方式和原因，并对工具的效果进行评估。金融政策委员会还应适当和公开透明地使用工具，并将国际法考虑在内。这些要求都包含在政府建议中。

金融政策委员会每年需向财政部和议会提交两次《金融稳定报告》，披露金融政策委员会季度会议记录，所有向微观审慎部门发出的指令将在议会留档。

议会起到的作用主要是在立法过程中参与讨论。

专业知识/成员组成

另一个问题是机构设在哪里以及由谁承担此项工作。

所需专业人士主要来自中央银行和微观审慎监管者。金融政策委员会由 11 位成员组成，包括 6 名英格兰银行代表以及各微观审慎监管者的负责人。

此外还需要考虑咨询和质疑职责以及与政府的联系。英国金融政策委员会其他成员还包括 4 名经验丰富的独立外部人士和 1 名无投票权的财政部人员。

最后谈谈机构之间的协调问题

鉴于政策之间存在重叠，一个重要的问题是如何在该架构下实现与其他机构的有效协调。

核心问题是与微观审慎监管者的联系。在英国，由于两个机构均是同一机构——英格兰银行的下设机构，协调相对容易。但金融政策委员会在政策制定上与财政部的协调并非如此顺畅。

此外，还有其他可能出现的复杂问题，如与货币政策的相互关系，不难想象清晰界定职责问题说起来容易，但实际操作中并非易事。

我们从以下几个方面解决上述问题。第一，允许宏观审慎政策和货币政策委员会成员有所交叉。第二，委员会会议的顺序安排不同。鉴于金融政策委员会不会频繁地对政策工具进行微调，会议的频率相对较低。而货币政策委员会（MPC）作为"最后行动者"，根据不太频繁调整的宏观审慎政策来进行决策。具体实践中如何操作仍有待研究。

国际协调

最后，谈谈国际合作和协调问题，这对于确保宏观审慎政策取得成功至关重要。对于高度的全球金融一体化而言，这一点是显而易见的。

鉴于英国金融服务的性质，我们非常关注这一问题。作为许多重要全球性机构子公司和分支机构的东道国，英国的监管部门在共同加强对系统重要性金融机构的并表监管方面起到重要作用。与此同时，许多机构以分支机构的形式开展业务，在英国当局的管辖范围之外，这也是伦敦金融城的性质决定的。

合作对于周期性政策工具的实施尤为重要。当一国提高资本要求时，如果有不受其监管的信贷机构进入市场填补信贷空缺，则政策就会失效。可能的解决方案是由各国监管者签订对等协议，承诺确保本国所监管的机构不会影响对方政策的实施。这一问题较为复杂却非常重要，需要进一步分析研究。结合与会各方的经验，我很想听听对上述做法是否可行的意见。

关于昨天讨论的巴塞尔协议框架，各国法律制定者和监管者在宏观审慎政策方面应拥有裁量权，可按照本国国情的需要，实施高于最低要求的标准，以维护金融稳定。不能用"一刀切"的做法。我们认为，考虑到行业的规模和性质，无论从本国还是全球金融稳定的利益出发，英国应有权实施比欧洲更高的标准，这对于英国非常重要。

最后，还有一个关键领域需要相互协调——信息共享。IMF 双边和多边监督机制在积累相关经验方面起到关键作用。不要因为是全新领域就低估其重要性。

第五部分

会议总结和主要收获

□ 刘士余

中国人民银行副行长

首先非常感谢国际货币基金组织在中国上海召开这次重要的亚太经验交流会，也感谢来自亚太地区的各位同事以及国际货币基金组织、金融稳定理事会（FSB）、国际保险监督官协会（IAIS）的监管官员和专家远道来参加会议。各位的到来正值上海天气由阴转晴，但愿这种天气的变化能够代表世界经济的走势，希望欧洲主权债务危机走向也能像这两天上海的天气变化一样令人愉快。

人民银行作为此次会议的承办方，受益良多。各位代表在会上介绍了很多好的经验，值得中国借鉴和吸收。在一天半的会议讨论中，大家对原定的讨论主题作了非常广泛的延伸和拓展，已经从金融稳定评估扩展到金融风险监测、风险预警、风险处置、国际合作、央行职能以及宏观审慎的技术和方法等议题。我的体会是，各位专家的讨论可能留有一定空间，但是没有分歧，也没有激烈的争论，这说明本次会议非常务实，大家对维护金融稳定的看法日趋一致。结合中国的情况来看，会议主题的广泛延伸恰好说明了 FSAP 本身的复杂性、系统性和必要性。实际上，做好 FSAP 评估需要多方面人才、专业以及制度的集成，是一项系统工程。中国的实践说明，FSAP 在识别、防范和管理风险方面的重要性是非常突出的。这几年来我们明显感觉到，国际货币基金组织在推动 FSAP 方面所做的艰巨努力和取得的成绩，评估方法不断趋于完善。虽然由于各国情况不同，大家可能对 FSAP 评估有不同的看法和建议，但是对这项制度安排已经没有大的分歧。

刚刚完成的中国 FSAP 评估不仅让各个国家和国际组织加深了对中国金融体系稳健程度和风险状况的了解，更加让我们自己清醒地看到金融体系中存在的一些问题，并将有关改革建议列入了中国《国民经济和社会发展第十二个五年规划纲要》。国务院领导高度重视评估团指出的中国金融体系面临的突出问题和对中国政府的政策建议，而且在明年初由中央政府主持召开的全国金融工作会议中，我们也将对这些问题进行更加深入的分析，并制定改进的时间表和目标要求。

下面，我想结合各位代表的讨论提出一点看法：

一是重视 FSAP 评估结论，持续发挥 FSAP 机制的作用。各国的金融体系、金融市场毫无疑问都带有一国经济、社会、历史和文化的特点。在评估过程中，评估团应尊重这种历史和格局，关键要看这种制度能不能解决一国经济、金融所面临的实际问题，而不能套用某一固定模式。如果没有确切迹象表明某项制度安排将引发风险，那就要承认该国这一制度的存在有其合理之处。

从中国的实践来看，任何改革既需要内部的认真准备，也需要在全球化过程中集中各方面智慧来加以推动。对于评估团的改革建议，尤其是政府和金融监管部门做出承诺的，受评国应当履行诺言不断推进改革。中国有句古话叫"行胜于言"。FSAP 是五年一次循环的评估，这期间可能发生很多意想不到的问题，对于评估团的建议尤其是与受评国达成一致的改革建议可以列入国际货币基金组织第四条款年度磋商，这将有利于进一步提升一国金融体系的稳健程度。也就是说，要把货币政策、财政政策和金融稳定政策同时作为国际货币基金组织第四条款年度磋商的重点。这是对下一步持续发挥 FSAP 作用的建议。

二是各国要把自己的事情做好。在经济金融全球化进程中，一国金融风险的外部影响，即溢出效应非常明显。同时，一国内部某一金融领域的风险甚至非金融领域的风险也可能引发整个金融体系的动荡。这实际上是交叉性产品和跨市场经营带来的必然结果。无论是从历史角度还是从现实的复杂程度来看，任何国家和经济体关键是要把自己的事情办好。同时，在一国内部，无论金融市场如何发展，金融制度如何安排，微观金融机构的财务基础以及良好的公司治理结构仍是关键。再好的制度，如果离开微观金融机构的财务健康，将无法落到实处。因此，各国把微观金融机构的财务稳健性抓好，保持自身金融体系的稳定，是对国际金融稳定的最大贡献。

三是注意防范风险母国对被传染国的溢出风险。国际经济金融全球化是不可避免的趋势。在此过程中，金融机构的跨国经营、包括跨国设立分支机构和跨国代理业务已成为常态。这就需要此类金融机构的母国和业务分支机构的东道国之间真正加强合作。这一问题早在国际商业信贷银行倒闭时，就已摆在各国监管当局面前。回过头看，过去几十年中发生的各类金融案件在涉及跨市场情况时，在母国和东道国信息共享及协调行动方面均或多或少存在缺陷。我们在金融监管中往往警告市场要防范道德风险，其实在金融全球化的今天，在一国金融风险存在全球溢出效应的情况下，也应当突出强调母国和东道国之间的责任，要防范由于监管不力和个别利益引发的道德风险，这将把全球危机成本降到最低，并促进全球经济复苏。因此，建议将金融监管当局之间的信息共享，特别是关于高风险机构和高风险业务信息的及时通报纳入国际货币基金组织评估框架，作为对受评国在维护国际金融稳定、防范金融风险方面的一项重要职能加以评价。

四是加强对影子银行的监管。中国作为新兴市场经济体和发展中国家，其金融体系还有相当不完善的地方。我们要立足于中国实际情况来深化金融改革，包括加快推进资产证券化以促进货币市场和资本市场的协调发展。商业银行依赖资本市场融资的模式不实际也不可持续，并会使实体经济融资受到很大限制。因此，银行资产必须进行证券化，这将有利于银行业务的多元化，也有利于债券市场和信贷市场的协调发展。同时，中国地方政府融资平台的风险说到底是财政风险，这一问题产生于中国发展过程中，无法再用传统的计划经济办法来解决，唯一可行的办法可能就是发展市政债市场。这需要我们有改革、创新的勇气，借鉴成熟市场的模式来推动中国市政债的发展。

关于影子银行体系问题，从中国的实践来讲，由于监管范围较宽，遗留在监管体系之外的不多。维护金融稳定是中央银行的基本职能，通过支付清算、账户管理、金融市场监测以及回购交易资格准入制度，可以适当限制影子银行体系的融资能力，并对银行体系各类机构的市场行为加以监测，防范潜在风险。同时，中央银行应事先掌握金融市场产品情况，不能盲目信任市场，要对各种产品的功能及可能产生的风险做出清醒判断，严格限制或禁止带有污染性的金融衍生产品进入市场。

五是完善金融风险早期预警和处置机制。无论是国内微观金融机构的风险，还是一国的金融溢出风险、区域性风险，都是处置得越早、越快，成本将越小。这一点中国有很多的经验和教训。如果我们早两年进行国有银行改革的话，可能财务成本会更小。因为不良资产在表内时有互相传染的趋势，这好比一筐桃子，其中一个烂了，如果不及时拿出来，可能第二天会烂五个，再过一天可能一筐全烂了。因此处理危机无论是市场退出、倒闭清算还是破产重组，都应该越快越好。

维护金融稳定，需要我们用热情和智慧，更需要用行动和实践，来履行中央银行和监管当局的职责。会议结束之际，我代表人民银行总行，再次感谢国际货币基金组织与人民银行共同举办此次研讨会，感谢各位同仁来上海参会并提出非常好的评论和建议，特别感谢国际货币基金组织工作人员和人民银行上海总部工作人员为筹备会议付出的辛勤努力和高质量的服务！

最后，祝大家工作顺利。祝远道而来的客人在上海逗留愉快，返程一路平安！中国央行始终愿意同亚洲各国同仁在维护金融稳定、推进 FSAP 评估等方面作出更多的合作及贡献。

谢谢大家！

□ 何塞·比亚斯（José Viñals）

国际货币基金组织金融顾问和货币与资本市场部主任

大家下午好！在经历一天半紧张而富有成果的讨论之后，请允许我对研讨会的主要内容做个简要总结，归纳关键信息，并提出自己的观点。

首先，我要感谢与会嘉宾为我们的讨论作出的积极贡献。FSAP 已成为 IMF 工作的重要组成部分，你们的观点和建议将帮助我们提高 FSAP 的质量和相关性。我还想对此次研讨会的慷慨的主办者——周行长和他的同事们——表示诚挚的谢意。此次会议的成功召开与他们艰苦的工作、奉献精神和对所讨论题目的浓厚兴趣是分不开的。

昨天，朱民先生在开场发言中提到，提高 FSAP 的质量是一个双赢的结果。我非常赞同。该项目不仅大幅度地提高了 IMF 监督机制的能力和效率，而且还极大地提高了监管当局监测和维护金融稳定的能力。

下面我简要总结一下在四个部分讨论中的主要话题：

（1）首先，与会嘉宾普遍认同 FSAP 能够从独立的视角发挥作用。比如，它能帮助国家监管当局识别金融部门的潜在脆弱性，能够帮助他们设计长期政策和改革，以确保金融稳定。

（2）新的国际标准如何解决系统性风险？

（3）我们做好应对下一次危机的准备了吗？

（4）宏观审慎政策。

根据讨论情况，请允许我提出以下两方面的关键问题：

（1）国际金融改革和国际货币基金组织的作用。

（2）进行中的亚洲金融改革：国际货币基金组织能提供怎样的帮助？

1. 国际金融改革和国际货币基金组织的作用

（1）修复和重构国际金融体系已取得进展。这项工作正朝着正确的方向迈进，但需要做的事还很多。着眼长远，政策制定者需要采取结构性的办法以解决金融领域长期存在的问题，重点关注以下目标：

国内：

• 加强微观审慎监管，包括对系统重要性银行的监管。这需要增加监管机构的权力、资源和能力，并注重早期干预。

• 检视并辅助薄弱的金融机构。当发现资本不足时，银行必须有可靠的和及时的再融资渠道，否则将被接管。该项措施并未成熟，因此在现阶段未发挥作用，从而增加了道德风险。

• 将宏观审慎监管纳入政策框架。宏观审慎政策需要识别和关注系统性金融风险的累积。

• 形成可信的中期财政整固策略以防范主权风险并确保金融稳定。

多边：

• 就如何限制全球系统重要性金融机构风险达成协议。

• 通过制定协调一致的危机管理框架和明确的跨境银行处置指导原则，确保跨境危机处置方案的可行性。

• 更加关注影子银行体系，并适当扩展监管范围。

• 构建全面的宏观审慎政策框架和一整套政策工具，加强国际合作以确保执行的一致性。

（2）金融稳定框架——国际货币基金组织的作用是什么？

• 为重新思考全球市场的规则和监管提供建议，与 BIS、FSB 和各成员国合作，完善改革日程表。

- 继续与 FSB 共同推进早期预警演练，分析跨境的金融关联度以及金融和经济政策的跨境溢出效应，不断提升风险分析水平。

- 在构建宏观审慎政策框架方面发挥主导作用。

- 通过双边和多边监督机制以及其他国际组织，与各国当局密切合作，努力防范未来危机的发生。

2. 进行中的亚洲金融部门改革：国际货币基金组织能提供怎样的帮助

- 与各国当局密切合作，通过改善数据收集和分析方法，利用技术援助（TA）和监督机制，提高风险识别、评估和监测能力。

- 强化微观审慎监管，包括加强对系统重要性金融机构的监管和提高风险管理能力。

- 就管理主权风险的宏观金融影响及其与金融稳定的关联性，形成可信的战略。

- 通过宏观审慎政策措施，识别和管理系统性风险及其金融稳定溢出效应。

- 检视并辅助薄弱的金融机构。当发现资本不足时，银行必须有可靠的和及时的再融资渠道，否则将被接管。该项措施并未成熟，因此在现阶段未发挥作用，从而增加了道德风险。

Monitoring and Managing
Financial Stability
Lessons from and for the FSAP

Welcoming Remarks

Zhou Xiaochuan

Governor, PBC

Good morning, Ladies and Gentlemen,

It is my pleasure to welcome you in Shanghai, to share our experiences in the exercise of the Financial Sector Assessment Program (FSAP), and exchange views on how to sustain financial stability. At the invitation of the International Monetary Fund (IMF) and the People's Bank of China (PBC), the Symposium has brought together distinguished participants from major international financial organizations, central banks, finance ministries and regulatory agencies, as well as market participants in the Asia Pacific region. We also have an academic, Prof. Eichengreen as our special guest.

The recent global financial crisis has highlighted the importance of monitoring and assessing financial stability. Since the outbreak of the crisis, maintaining financial stability and promoting economic recovery have become the top priority for policymakers. Naturally, the FSAP initiated by IMF and the World Bank (WB) has become a well accepted framework for financial stability assessment. At the first Summit in Washington, the G20 leaders committed to undertake FSAP exercise.

The China FSAP was launched in August 2009. To facilitate the process, PBC, together with 11 other government agencies, set up specific work mechanisms and principles. Over the past two years, the joint Fund-Bank FSAP team conducted a thorough assessment of China's financial system and financial institutional framework, and made many useful recommendations. Here again I would like to thank them for their professionalism and dedication.

The Chinese government attaches great importance to the FSAP exercise. Our Premier Wen Jiabao and Vice Premier Wang Qishan paid attention to FSAP assessment including vulnerabilities identified and the policy recommendations. Under their leadership, PBC and regulatory commissions will strengthen China's financial stability, regulatory and supervisory framework by incorporating the FSAP findings as appropriate.

The FSAP exercise for China was in general successful and fruitful. The China FSAP reports, namely the *China Financial System Stability Assessment* (*FSSA*) and the *China Financial Sector Assessment* (*FSA*), have been published on November 15 by the Fund and the Bank respectively. Generally speaking, the assessments in these reports were objective and positive, and the proposals on further reform were constructive. I believe the exercise will contribute to China financial sector reform and financial stability.

As highlighted by the recent global financial crisis, traditional regulatory arrangements that focus on the soundness of individual financial institutions failed to capture the evolution of financial market and associated risks. In this connection, building a stronger macro-prudential policy framework has become a common policy option for international organizations and national authorities. Along this line, since the crisis, many international financial organizations, for instance the Financial Stability Board (FSB), the Fund, the Basel Committee on Banking Supervision (BCBS), have been working to reshape the regulatory philosophy and restructure the regulatory system, supporting a stronger macro-prudential policy framework, encouraging cross-border regulatory cooperation, and updating and implementing international financial standards and rules. These organizations play an essential role in the reform of global financial system and financial regulation, and are indispensable for enhancing financial stability framework.

As the global financial crisis is still with us today, we need to keep in mind how vulnerable and complex the economic and financial situations remain as we strengthen regulations and enforce other corrective actions. And this would require stronger coordination and cooperation. Today, gathering here at the initiative of the IMF, and building on our experiences with the FSAP, we will discuss in depth financial stability monitoring and management, and analyze the latest international regulatory standards and the impact of the recent international financial regulatory reform. We will also exchange ideas on how to enhance the financial stability framework, improve the identification and monitoring of systemic risks, and build a macro-prudential policy framework. These topics are rather challenging, relevant as well as timely, and thus merit our intensive reflection.

I wish the symposium a complete success.

— Thank you!

Opening Remarks

Min Zhu

Deputy Managing Director, IMF

Good morning, distinguished guests, and welcome to our symposium on the Financial Sector Assessment Program. I am so pleased that you are able to join us here in Shanghai. It is a rare opportunity for us to gather senior decision makers in the region to exchange views on efforts to respond to the global crisis and on the IMF's role in promoting financial stability. This meeting would not have been possible without the collaboration of the People's Bank of China. I would like to express my sincere gratitude to Governor Zhou and his staff for their hard work and generous hospitality.

We are gathered here today as policymakers around the globe are switching back into firefighting mode. What had begun as a financial sector crisis turned into a sovereign debt crisis and has now morphed into a fully-fledged crisis of confidence. Markets are particularly worried about the continuing adverse feedback loop between sovereign risk and financial sector weaknesses. Big and bold political decisions are needed to reduce sovereign risk. But we also need increased efforts to bolster the financial systems both in advanced and emerging economies. We believe that our improved FSAP can play an essential role in this process. And your views and recommendations will help us to further develop the FSAP into an effective surveillance and crisis prevention tool.

Before I delve into the details of the FSAP, I would like to say a few words about the impact of the current crisis on both advanced and emerging economies. Major advanced economies seem to have entered a vicious cycle of weak economic activity, financial distress, and high public debt and deficits. Emerging economies, by contrast, show stronger fundamentals that have underpinned global economic growth so far. But these economies are not immune. In fact, vulnerabilities are increasing, and potential spillovers from advanced economies are weakening their economic outlook. It is not surprising that many Asian policymakers have publicly warned about growing downside risks and have begun to adjust their policy stances.

Financial markets have been weighed down by the combination of weaknesses in major advanced economies and cyclical cooling in emerging economies—even though investor fears have somewhat eased due to the coordinated action last week by the world's top central banks to provide dollar liquidity to the global financial system. The Euro Stoxx 50 index has dropped by more than 15 percent since the beginning of this year. Even those investors who diversified by "buying the world", as measured by the MSCI world equity index, are down nearly 7 percent for the year. And markets have become increasingly volatile, as seen in the sharp increase in the VIX—the so-called "fear index" —since June[1]. Some are even beginning to wonder whether the global economy is heading for a bust that is greater than the one in 2008 – 09.

At the heart of the problem is the euro area crisis. Core European countries are now coming under pressure. Foreign investors are fleeing Europe's sovereign debt markets, pushing up long-term yields on Spanish and Italian debt to 6 percent—near levels that are normally considered sustainable. German bund asset swap spreads have recently reached levels not seen since the aftermath of the Lehman Brothers collapse.

With conditions deteriorating in the sovereign debt market, Europe's banks are finding it increasingly difficult and expensive to borrow money in the wholesale market. At the same time, they are facing a wall of maturing debt—which some analysts estimate at over € 600 billion for next year. [2] This has meant that Europe's banks are increasingly reliant on the European Central Bank for short-term liquidity, with latest estimates suggesting that ECB funding has increased by about € 125 billion since June and by about € 50 billion since September.

---

[1] VIX Index: Pre-crisis, 7/1/08: 23. 65; Peak, 11/20/08: 80. 86; [Today, 12/8/11]: 30. 6

[2] Market estimates suggest that of the € 600 billion falling due, Germany accounts for € 157 billion; Italy € 206 billion; France € 99 billion; and Spain 50 € billion, with Netherlands, Belgium, Austria, Finland, Portugal and Ireland making up the rest.

Under these circumstances, it will be difficult for Europe's banks to meet the European Banking Authority's new 9 percent core tier 1 capital targets. The scope for tapping equity markets is very limited, given that European financial stocks have dropped by nearly a fifth since the beginning of this year[①]. The risk is that banks will be more likely to cut lending or sell assets. Because of this deleveraging trend, there is a serious risk of intensifying adverse feedback loops between the financial sector, the real economy, and fiscal positions within and beyond the euro area.

These real economy strains are already evident. Europe's broad Economic Sentiment Indicator has deteriorated in recent months, as has the Business Climate Indicator, while capacity utilization is expected to fall in the fourth quarter. And we have seen significant marking down of growth forecasts both by governments and, most recently, by the OECD to levels that are nearly recessionary.

The euro area crisis is threatening to spill over to the rest of the world through financial and trade linkages.

In the United States, the revised estimate of third-quarter GDP growth of 2 percent was below expectations. Even this level may be difficult to sustain in the fourth quarter, given weak income growth, high unemployment, declining house prices, and the fact that higher consumption was financed primarily through reduced savings. Continuing political disagreement over fiscal policy is weighing on market sentiment in the U. S. The recent failure of the U. S. super-committee to reach an agreement on reducing the fiscal deficit has raised the prospect of across-the-board spending cuts of $1. 2 trillion— a massive fiscal adjustment that would hit economic growth. This has prompted further warnings by rating agencies of a downgrade.

Other major developed economies—notably Japan and the UK—are facing equally challenging conditions. Japanese industrial production fell sharply in September, and while October's PMI suggests moderate expansion in the fourth quarter, growth prospects are not strong. In the UK, the forecast for economic growth in 2012 has been revised

---

① Financial sector equity declines YTD (Dec 1): World (-21%); Europe (-19%); USA (-28%); Japan (-21%); Hong Kong (-25%); Korea (-22%).

down to less than 1 percent, and it may be hard to avoid a recession if the euro area contracts.

One message I would like to underscore is that, while Asia has been relatively unscathed by the crisis so far, there is no room for complacency. We do not think that emerging Asia has "decoupled" . If anything, weaker global demand and more difficult international financial conditions could expose underlying vulnerabilities—often driven by rapid credit growth. There are already signs that economic growth in emerging Asia is slowing. PMI manufacturing reports from China and India point to moderating activity relative to earlier in the year. Weak trade numbers in other, smaller economies confirm signals that the weakening external outlook may dampen otherwise strong growth in the region.

Recent IMF spillover reports have shown that Asia is still highly vulnerable to shocks through the trade channel. Europe is one of the largest export markets for a number of Asian countries, including China, India, and the Philippines. While intra-regional trade is gaining importance, part of this intra-regional trade is on the same supply chain as trade with Europe. The experience of the 2008 crisis shows that a disruption in trade with Europe and America would also likely disrupt intra-regional trade.

And, of course, Asia is also affected through the financial channel. Foreign investors have traditionally played a significant role in Asian equity and bond markets, and many countries in the region have sizeable exposures to European banks through trade credit lines, loan syndication and other wholesale funding. [1] There is growing evidence of disengagement by some major European banks that are active in emerging markets that could have a substantial impact on credit supply through these channels. Meanwhile, banks in emerging Asia continue their recent pace of deleveraging as they are seeking to build liquidity buffers.

---

[1] Euro zone bank claims are greater than or just under 10 percent of GDP in 3 countries: Australia, New Zealand and Vietnam. For the NIEs, ASEAN countries, Japan and India the ratio is close to 5 percent. Euro zone bank claims on China are relatively small. Euro zone banks also supply almost 50% of Asia's trade credit.

As you know, the IMF is heavily involved in the current crisis management. This is the firefighting part of our work. At the same time, we have been increasing our efforts to prevent future financial crises through improved surveillance tools such as the FSAP.

Allow me to expand on the role of the FSAP[①], which we believe will become an essential underpinning of global financial stability. Launched in 1999, in response to the Asian financial crisis, the FSAP is aimed at helping national authorities to identify financial sector vulnerabilities and design longer-term policies and reforms. For advanced economies, FSAPs represent a unique opportunity to strengthen and reshape their financial sectors, based on the lessons from the current crisis. In emerging economies, FSAPs can help national authorities to prevent future crises.

Typically, the FSAP focuses on three core areas:

1. First, it assesses the effectiveness of financial supervision against broadly accepted international standards. The global crisis has underscored the need for improved standards and codes to address systemic risk. These regulatory changes present challenges for both national authorities and the Fund. The question is: "Are we prepared to implement new, tougher standards, including Basel III?"

2. Second, the FSAP assesses the source, probability, and potential impact of key risks to macro-financial stability. It takes a comprehensive view of the financial system and its linkages with the real economy. This involves quantitative stress testing of banks and the broader financial system. In addition to its quantitative findings, the FSAP provides a qualitative assessment of the authorities' ability to monitor and identify systemic risks. In this context, the FSAP can be used to develop and refine macroprudential policies to limit the buildup of financial imbalances and prevent systemic risks.

3. Third, the FSAP assesses the authorities' ability to manage and resolve financial crises. It provides a framework to assess the adequacy of contingency planning and

---

① The FSAP is conducted jointly with the World Bank for emerging market and developing economies, with two components: a financial stability assessment by the Fund, and a financial development assessment by the Bank. For advanced economies, assessments are conducted by the Fund and focus on financial stability.

financial safety nets, including cross border issues, and defines action plans to deal with insolvent financial institutions.

Participation in the FSAP had been voluntary until last year, when G20 leaders decided to make it mandatory for jurisdictions with financial sectors that are deemed "systemically important". Mandatory FSAPs, which take place every five years, allow the Fund to monitor more closely those members that are likely to have the most impact on systemic stability in the event of a crisis.

The decision to make the FSAP mandatory for systemically important economies is one of the key outcomes of the year-long debate on modernizing the Fund's surveillance mandate following the global crisis. It is a landmark decision that formally brings financial sector issues to the core of the Fund's bilateral surveillance, bridging the gap between the Fund's two key surveillance tools: the Article IV consultation and the FSAP.

Since the creation of the FSAP, 138 countries have volunteered to participate in the program (many more than once), and about 35 FSAPs are currently under way or in the pipeline. Demand for FSAPs has risen sharply since the beginning of the 2007 - 08 financial crisis. In a recent survey, three-quarters of respondents indicated that they were satisfied, or very satisfied, with the overall usefulness of the FSAP.

Our recent internal analysis shows that the program has played a useful role as an independent review. Before the onset of the recent global financial crisis, FSAP assessments were able to pinpoint the main sources of risk. As the crisis unfolded, FSAP teams have also been quick to adapt the scope of assessments to focus on such critical issues as crisis management, liquidity support arrangements, and cross-border contagion. FSAP recommendations have been helpful in mitigating some of the consequences of the crisis.

And of course, there are lessons to be learned. The experience of the past five years has shown that assessments need to pay more attention to liquidity risks and cross-border, or cross-market, linkages. And even when risks were accurately identified, our recent review concluded that the warnings given in FSAPs can be even more loud and clear.

I am glad to say that we are adapting the FSAP to take into account these lessons and to strengthen its effectiveness, in several dimensions:

● First, the FSAP has become more flexible, taking into account country-specific circumstances.

● Second, the FSAP includes an improved analytical toolkit, covering a broader array of risks, macro-financial feedbacks, and cross-border spillovers.

● And third, "off-site" work is being strengthened to enhance the continuity of assessments and the effectiveness of "on-site" reviews.

We believe that the improved FSAP could play a particularly important role in the Asia Pacific region. Although the FSAP was created in the aftermath of the Asian financial crisis, Asia appears to have embraced it with less enthusiasm than other regions. Only half of the Asian IMF members have completed an FSAP so far—compared with all European member countries, 68 percent of countries in the Western Hemisphere, 81 percent of countries in the Middle East and Central Asia, and 59 percent of countries in Sub-Saharan Africa.

But this situation is changing. Since the onset of the financial crisis, most Asian members with large financial sectors have completed the FSAP, or have it in the pipeline. This is consistent with the increased leadership role that Asia is playing in multilateral bodies such as the IMF and the G-20. And we at the Fund are pleased—and proud—to be able to work more intensively with our Asian members.

A case in point is our first ever FSAP of China and Indonesia in the last two years. In both countries, the FSAP praised the remarkable progress that had been achieved over the last decade in reforming their financial systems. This had helped them weather the worst effects of the 2008 crisis. But gaps still remain. China should broaden and deepen its financial markets and services to create a more diversified and innovative financial sector that is based on commercial principles, while in Indonesia, enforcing the rule of law and addressing weaknesses in transparency and governance issues are priority.

To conclude, I am convinced that the improved FSAP represents a "win-win" situation. Not only has the program significantly strengthened the capacity and effectiveness of the IMF's surveillance function. But it has also greatly enhanced the authorities' ability to monitor and manage financial stability.

We believe that the FSAP will continue to evolve, especially in response to the needs of authorities in this region, and some of its future FSAPs are likely to become a source of best practices that others would want to follow.

There are many questions that we have yet to address. For example:

- Should the IMF encourage its members to conduct more FSAPs and FSAP updates?

- What about the resource constraints facing the IMF and the authorities?

- What is the best way to improve the FSAP (bottom-up versus top-down approach)?

- How can we tailor FSAPs to the needs of fast-growing emerging economies?

- Are we prepared for the major regulatory changes, including Basel III?

During the forthcoming sessions, you will have a chance to discuss these, and many other, issues. I am confident that we—individually and collectively—will come away with valuable lessons. I hope your discussions will be both productive and enjoyable. Thank you!

Session I

The Financial Sector Assessment Program —The Role of an Independent Review

- In what way can the FSAP be more effective in (i) identifying key systemic risks and triggering improvements in systemic oversight; (ii) identifying gaps in microprudential supervision; and (iii) addressing weaknesses and strengths in crisis management frameworks?

- What can be done to improve the traction of FSAP policy recommendations, both at the time of the conclusion of the assessment and in the context of the ongoing dialogue between the Fund and the jurisdiction in question?

- What aspects of the FSAP could be strengthened to improve its relevance to the region?

□ José Viñals

Financial Counsellor and Director, IMF

Current and Future Roles of the FSAP

The FSAP was started in 1999 after the Asian Crisis as a tool to help the authorities in the following 3 dimensions: (1) To assess the effectiveness of financial supervision against broadly accepted standards; (2) To identify the sources, probability and impacts of key risks to macrofinancial stability; (3) To assist country authorities in managing and resolving financial crisis. The basic idea is to engage in a very frank dialogue with countries' financial authorities, not only to find financial vulnerabilities but also to come up with a set of recommendations that will help them address the vulnerabilities and improve the stability of the financial system, both in the short-term and in the medium term.

We have recently conducted an internal review of the effectiveness of the FSAPs in order to see what they are actually doing for member countries. What we have discovered is a mixture of good news and some bad news. The good news is that we found, in the run-up to the recent global financial crisis, the FSAPs in many cases were able to point out the main sources of risks and, in general, the recommendations of the FSAPs were helpful in mitigating the worst consequences of the crisis. But we also found that the pre-crisis FSAP was far from a perfect tool and had shortcomings. The key shortcoming was the under appreciation of liquidity risks, systemic liquidity risks, and the FSAP probably failed to take into account crucial issues such as cross-boarder and cross-market linkages and systemic interactions between products, markets and institutions. So we missed systemic risk assessment in many cases. This is why we have introduced some changes recently in order to make sure the FSAPs keep the benefits of the past without the shortcomings they had.

134

The FSAP has now become a more flexible tool by better taking into account country specific circumstances. It also has benefited from the improved analytical tool kit which now covers a wide range of risks, cross-boarder spillovers and the interactions between the financial sector and the broader economy. Things like systemic risks, macro-prudential policy frameworks, the connection between sovereign risk and the financial system or the systemic implications of sudden stops of capital flows all figure prominently in the FSAP now. Moreover, we have sought to make crisis management more candid and transparent. If I had to summarize the key elements of the new FSAPs, it will be the following: the FSAPs are tough but fair and they are delivered in a very clear manner to authorities. Perhaps the most important recent change to the FSAP process is the decision taken last year by the G20 leaders to make the FSAP mandatory for jurisdictions with financial markets deemed to be systemically important. Every 5 years, 25 national financial systems which are deemed to be of systemic importance would be examined through an FSAP and FSAP update. The Fund needs to monitor, in its surveillance function, the systemic stability of these countries in order to have a better idea of what are the risks to global financial instability and where they may come from, and to issue policy recommendations to better maintain global stability. So this is something that really brings the core of the Fund's surveillance to our financial world.

The improved FSAP is particularly useful in the context of the Asia-Pacific region, where we have seen significantly increasing demand for FSAPs since the onset of the financial crisis. The Fund has conducted its first FSAP of China and Indonesia. We had fantastic cooperation from the respective countries.

The evolving nature of the FSAP and the evolving nature of the global financial system mean that we have a lot to learn. This is a learning-by-doing exercise, and we have a lot of learning to do to make sure the FSAP is always one step ahead of the curve but not behind the curve. This is why we really appreciate your candid suggestions.

☐ **Liu Shiyu**

Deputy Governor, PBC

Toward A Broader Role of FSAP through Strengthened Cooperation

Deputy Managing Director Zhu Min, Dear colleagues, Ladies and Gentlemen:

Good morning!

In his welcoming remarks, Governor Zhou Xiaochuan touched on China's experiences in the exercise of the Financial Sector Assessment Program (FSAP). As a participant in China's FSAP exercise, I'd like to share with you some of my thoughts.

Since its launch in 1999, the FSAP, as an effective international assessment program, has been widely recognized by the international community, and has contributed to the monitoring and management of financial stability globally, progress of financial reform and development in the economies under the program. China started self-assessment in 2003 based on the FSAP framework and other related international standards. The results show that good progress has been made in the financial reform, financial market development, and financial regulation. At the G20 Summit in Washington D. C. in November 2008, President Hu Jintao committed that China would undertake an FSAP exercise. The exercise began in August 2009, and was concluded in November 2011. I wish to thank the joint team of IMF and WB experts, whose expertise, professionalism and team spirit helped conclude the mission successfully and left a deep impression on us.

The FSAP exercise has helped the world to gain a better understanding of China's financial system, and help China's financial sector to better understand the challenges that it is faced. On this occasion, I'd like to share our experience in promoting sustained, healthy and stable development of the financial sector through advancing reform, strengthening regulation and encouraging innovation. There are basically three points:

First, we continually deepen the financial reform in accordance with market principles.

An important experience of China in this aspect is to preserve micro-level financial health of financial institutions. After the Asian financial crisis, we felt the urgency and importance of financial reform. In the reform process, we attached great significance to financial resilience of individual financial institutions. Under the leadership of the central government, we started the financial restructuring of the major financial institutions in 2003. This process has been basically completed now with the state-owned financial institutions transformed into listed public companies. In the joint stock reform, the government recapitalized US $80 billion to the four state-owned banks. The recent years have witnessed improved corporate governance, enhanced risk control mechanisms, and better financial indicators in the largest banks. These measures have helped overhaul China's financial system and strengthened its overall resilience, thus providing a solid foundation for China to preserve financial stability during the storms of the 2008 financial crisis.

Mr. Zhu Min oversaw the shareholding reform of the Bank of China when he was with the bank at that time. I believe he has a deep understanding of the difficulty of financial restructuring at the micro level. Later on he became the deputy governor of the PBC, the difficulty of advancing financial restructuring from a macroeconomic perspective must have a deeper resonance in his heart.

Second, we have strengthened macro-prudential management.

The Asian financial crisis in 1997 and the global financial crisis in 2008 pointed to the fact. that, important as micro-level financial soundness is, preventing risks of systemically important financial institutions is of greater importance to macroeconomic stability. China's 12th Five-Year Plan has outlined the establishment of a counter-cyclical macro-prudential framework and a mechanism for early warning, assessment and resolution of systemic risks. We face daunting tasks in macro-financial management this year. Management of inflation is the top priority in addition to preserving financial stability and advancing financial reform. Macro-prudential instrument and measures have been applied in this round of macro-economic management measures, with good results. For example, differentiated reserve requirement ratio and loan loss provisioning requirements have been applied to financial institutions with rapid capital depletion and fast loan growth, which helped improve prudential regulation of financial institutions on micro level and contribute to macro-prudential management of the whole system. Moreover, China is committed to implementing the Basel III by augmenting accounting standards and disclosure requirements, speeding up the establishment of a deposit insurance scheme, and improving mechanism and measures to resolve systemic risks, as suggested by the FSAP mission.

Third, we encourage financial innovation and enhance the efficiency of financial market in resources allocation.

China's industrialization and market-based reform are well underway, accompanied by accelerated application of information technology and urbanization. This results in demand for diversified financial products and services. In recent years, innovation in institutional arrangements and financial products based on international experiences have promoted development of the financial market, especially the bond market, narrowing the bond market's gap compared with other segments of the capital market in China and also with foreign bond markets. The BIS estimated that China's aggregate and annual new issuance of bonds rank among the top five worldwide. This cannot be achieved without the innovation of institutional arrangements and financial products.

Meanwhile, the FSAP mission highlighted the absence of a competitive financial market for small and micro enterprises, rural areas, agriculture and rural residents. This is an objective conclusion, and we highly value it. Since 2001, and more so since 2003, the PBC and other financial regulators have made concerted efforts in fostering a competitive financial service system for micro and small enterprises, rural areas, agriculture and rural residents, but so far without desirable results. The efforts are still ongoing. We encourage all kinds of capital, including that from the overseas market, the private sector and the large-sized enterprises to be channeled to small and medium-sized financial institution, to enhance their quantity and accessibility.

Moreover, I would like to share our FSAP experience from an operational perspective.

First, the assessment mission and the assessed country should be willing to communicate and exchange views. Just like someone seeking health check at a clinic, the assessed is obliged to give an objective and frank introduction of the development trajectory, history and cultural background of its economy and financial sector during the assessment.

Second, strong coordination and leadership is indispensable. Soon after making the commitment to join the FSAP program, we set up an inter-agency steering group chaired by Governor Zhou Xiaochuan to enhance coordination at three levels: ministers, deputies, and director-generals. This has been essential in helping us complete the meticulous work of data calibration and ensure data consistency with new definitions, since many technical concepts and operations in the Chinese financial system are different from those in other market economies. Moreover, working groups were also established to facilitate coordination by the CBRC, CSRC and CIRC respectively.

Third, it is important to have a full-time office at the working level. At the PBC, we have established an FSAP office within the Financial Sability Bureau, with the mandate of coordinating with the Fund and the Bank during the assessment. The office continues to operate after the assessment, to study the conclusions of the assessment and learn from the experiences of other countries and regions, thereby helping us promote the reform and prepare for the next round of assessment.

Fourth, budgetary support and arrangements are needed. In this regard, the Ministry of Finance made special budgetary arrangements for the FSAP, reflecting our serious commitment to the process.

For countries that have not joined the FSAP yet, I hope you will find these four operational points helpful. I also believe that, as the Fund and the Bank continue to expand and improve the program, the FSAP will gain greater traction as a widely accepted mechanism in the international financial system. For this purpose, I would like to make three suggestions.

First, national circumstances should be respected. In the assessment, stage of economic development in a country or region needs to be taken into account to fully appreciate the history, culture and current situation of the financial system and market landscape, instead of using the traditional approach to assess market development and management. This will also enhance the appeal of the assessment to make sure it is more widely accepted and its conclusions are more relevant.

Second, it can become more focused through strengthening monitoring and management of systemic risks in major economies. Risks in economies with systemic significance carry enormous spillover effects, as we can see from the global financial crisis and the European sovereign debt crisis, which are still weighing on global recovery and having an impact on growth in China and other emerging market economies. As a lesson from these crises, closer monitoring and stronger management of risks in systemically important economies through the FSAP is necessary, and higher standards and requirements should be set for these economies.

Third, there should be stronger cooperation. Cooperation between the FSAP mission and member countries is extremely important. To do so, member countries should present its financial system in a comprehensive and objective manner, while the FSAP mission needs to listen to the views from member countries.

Ladies and Gentlemen, dear colleagues,

This symposium provides a great opportunity to share experience and insights among friends from central banks, regulatory authorities, as well as the IMF, FSB and other international organizations. We at the PBC will be happy to learn from you, and are ready to work with you to advance the FSAP process, to the benefit of financial sector development globally, and as a support for our mission of financial stability.

Thank you.

□ Meg Lundsager

Executive Director (USA), IMF

Introduction

I'm very pleased to be able to speak with you today. Drawing on the experience of the United States with the 2010 FSAP, and my experience as an Executive Board member, I would like to share my thoughts on the value-added of the FSAP, what has gone well, and what perhaps could still be improved.

The experience of the past few years has taught us a great deal about macro-financial linkages. The Fund is familiar with a vast array of country experiences, and it should use this knowledge to convince its members of the importance of reform. After all, we have had plenty of negative experience, especially over the last few years, with the consequences of failing to act to stem financial vulnerabilities. The IMF's focus on the linkages between the real economy and financial sectors is critically important to helping us all improve prospects for economic growth and job creation.

Thoughts on the general value of the FSAP

The FSAP is really unique in that it focuses on systemic risk, taking a holistic view of the financial system and the context in which it operates. The FSAP seeks to shed light on the "big picture" vulnerabilities in a country's financial system, including those which could come from home or abroad. These types of vulnerabilities can be overlooked and the crisis highlighted to all of us the importance of addressing them.

The IMF's surveillance of the U. S. economy and financial system has seen the development of new tools for assessing "spillovers" on other countries that could result from domestic vulnerabilities. The Fund should extend this practice to other countries, both large and small——after all, even small countries can impact their neighbors through financial sector linkages.

An additional strength of the FSAP is its focus on finding gaps in regulation.

Importantly, the Fund recognizes that regulatory gaps may be of a legal nature or an enforcement nature, in which regulators have legal powers but neglect to exercise them.

The FSAP also includes an assessment of a country's compliance with international standards and codes for financial supervision. One important benefit of this assessment for domestic regulators is that they receive up-to-date information on best practices around the world and an arm's-length outside assessment of how they might improve.

Benefits of the U. S. FSAP

The U. S. FSAP in 2010 provided a systematic, independent assessment and verification of the root causes of the financial crisis. This was valuable to the U. S. authorities because it can be difficult to step back and see the big picture in the midst of a crisis, but the FSAP team was able to do so. The FSAP identified the major issues with the U. S. financial system and potential solutions. While much of this coincided with our own internal assessments, the FSAP was helpful in organizing our thinking.

The FSAP team performed stress tests of U. S. banks. These tests followed those done by U. S. regulators in the Supervisory Capital Assessment Program (SCAP) undertaken in 2009, which was seen by markets as a highly successful and credible exercise. The FSAP's own stress test work was useful in that it provided support for the SCAP results, coming from an independent and credible source. This helped to build further confidence in U. S. financial institutions.

Another benefit of the FSAP assessment was the coordination and communication that it promoted among U. S. regulators and supervisors. The U. S. authorities formed an FSAP Coordinating Committee, and this was almost a precursor to the Financial Stability Oversight Council (FSOC), the new U. S. macroprudential policy coordinating body.

Going through the FSAP together also helped U. S. regulators think of themselves as a system, rather than as separate parts. This helped lead to significant interagency cooperation, while respecting individual agency mandates and independence, and helped instill a sense of collective responsibility for financial stability. The idea of collective responsibility for financial stability is now the essence of the FSOC, as regulators can use peer pressure to spur each other to act when necessary to address a potential vulnerability.

In addition, the U. S. FSAP seemed to "raise the bar" in the assessment against the Standards and Codes. We hope that this rigor continues.

How the FSAP could still be improved

I'm sure that today we will discuss the issue of "traction" of IMF surveillance, including the FSAP. In general, getting traction with country authorities on the IMF's recommendations can be difficult. In defense of country authorities, while the FSAP assessment is good at identifying underlying problems and provides a number of possible solutions, it is often less clear *how* the authorities can translate these ideas into specific policy solutions particular to a country's circumstances.

I'd like to offer a few ideas on how traction might be improved.

First, it may be helpful if the FSAP team were to recognize that the effectiveness of regulation is more important than any particular structure. In the U. S. case, for example, the insurance sector supervisory structure looks very cumbersome, with state-level regulators, but in practice the system works well, with the NAIC (National Association of Insurance Commissioners) promoting dialogue at the national level.

Second, the IMF should make sure that assessors and the team are well briefed, well before discussions begin, on the country's institutional structures and enforcement mechanisms. This could help improve traction by giving the authorities the confidence that possible solutions proposed would be more workable within their particular national context.

Third, the IMF team's recommendations for changes to be made should be accompanied by a convincing rationale as to *why* the IMF believes the changes are crucial. To say that "others do it this way" is not always enough. The team needs to explain how a particular action worked or did not work in another country. To do this, the team needs to understand the historical and political context of existing structures.

Fourth, the IMF could better tap into its institutional memory to provide convincing solutions. IMF staff have accumulated significant knowledge of countries' political economies. A policy solution may look good on paper but be difficult to implement in a particular national context. Fund staff's experience in how countries were able to implement required reforms could be tapped more effectively. In particular, the FSAP team should try to tap knowledge of how the benefits of reform have persuaded vested interests to join a national consensus for addressing weaknesses in financial sector oversight.

Beyond the idea of traction, the IMF should be more willing to use cross-country examples to help country authorities with the issues they are facing. For example, Fund staff might recall that another country faced a similar issue, and they could recommend that the authorities engage with the other country to discuss their policy response and how it worked (or did not work).

Another way the FSAP could be improved is the work of the assessors. The Fund relies on external assessors to complete the Review of Standards and Codes (the ROSCs). This makes sense, but the Fund needs to monitor the *consistency* and *quality* of the ROSCs across countries. The Fund should also be sure to take ownership of the standards assessments. In the end, they should be the IMF's evaluation, not just the evaluation of a group of assessors.

A final way in which the FSAP could be improved is the follow-up process. While this is improving, we still feel that Fund staff could keep better track, in Article IV consultations, of whether FSAP recommendations have been adopted. In addition, the Fund should look back at the *effectiveness* of reforms adopted as it fashions its future advice. Of greatest importance is whether a particular regulatory structure works, regardless of its specific form, and the Fund should be willing to acknowledge that differing structures can be equally effective.

☐ Deepak Mohanty

Executive Director, Reserve Bank of India

Good Morning, First of all I would like to thank the organisers, the Peoples Bank of China (PBC) and the International Monetary Fund (IMF) for inviting me to be a part of such a distinguished panel on this important issue of financial stability. The Financial Sector Assessment Program (FSAP), conducted jointly by the IMF and the World Bank, assumes further importance as the eurozone financial problems threaten to spillover. The FSAP was launched in May 1999 in the wake of the Asian financial crisis, and it was revamped in September 2009 following the recent financial crisis. The revamped program has been made a mandatory part of the bilateral Article IV surveillance to be conducted every five years in 25 jurisdictions with systemically important financial sectors. India, being member of the G20 and belonging to the list of systemically important countries, is actively participating in the program.

Mr. Chairman, I propose to first talk about our experience in dealing with financial stability before I turn to the Fund-Bank FSAP. We were one of the few countries to participate in FSAP pilot programme way back in 2001. Following which we conducted a series of self assessments in the past decade. Such self-assessment followed a forward-looking and holistic approach. It was based on three mutually reinforcing pillars:

One, financial stability and stress testing; two, legal infrastructural and market development; and three, implementation of international financial standards and codes. It was a process of great learning and entailed strong commitment by all concerned.

Apart from the self-assessments, we have examined issues in the financial sector by setting up of a number of high-level Committees and Groups and implementing their recommendations as appropriate. The global financial crisis did not deter us to introduce credit default swaps for corporate bonds. We also addressed the regulatory issues arising out of the functioning of micro-finance institutions. The reform in Indian financial sector has thus been gradual, non-disruptive and a continuous process, though, I must admit, we have had our fair share of critics for being slow.

The current global debate is on making financial stability an explicit objective of central banks. However, in India we have recognised financial stability as an objective of monetary policy much before the unraveling of the current crisis. Since the early 2000, maintaining financial stability has been a part of the stated policy objectives, with both monetary and regulatory policy measures being employed to achieve that goal. The fact that Reserve Bank is also the regulator and supervisor of the financial system, helped in better coordination between macro and microprudential regulation. Much before the crisis in the advanced economies, the Reserve Bank had taken a number of prudential measures for limiting the exposure of the banking system to sensitive sectors and appropriately rebalancing the risk weights of different assets. While there may be some conflicts in the multiple responsibilities entrusted with central banks, there are significant synergies and confluence of interests which far outweigh the apparent conflict of interest.

Currently India is undergoing FSAP exercise. In this context I would like to highlight a few issues.

First, based on our own self-assessments, we have been trying to plug in the loopholes. The progress has been good in some areas, while a lot remains to be done with respect to a few other areas. While we have made good progress in several supervisory and regulatory issues, our progress has particularly been tardy with respect to timely implementation of bankruptcy proceedings, enforcement of creditor rights and insolvency systems, which has legal as well political aspects to deal with.

Second, India has been participating in the current initiatives in international financial regulatory reforms being undertaken by the IMF, the BCBS, the FSB and the G20. We have initiated several measures towards this direction. We feel that the progress made by us on G20 regulatory agenda is satisfactory as reflected in our efforts towards adoption of Basel III, effective supervision of financial conglomerates (a popular term for SIFIs in India), issuing guidelines on sound compensation policy, and strengthening the anti-money laundering measures.

With respect to the ongoing FSAP assessment in India, we have sent our comments on the reports/technical notes as well as the consolidated *Aide Memoire*.

While we look forward to work on the key recommendations, I offer a few suggestions with a view to improving the effectiveness of the FSAP exercise. To put it differently, what more can be done?

First, standard assessments for all jurisdictions should not be compromised for the over emphasis on a more risk-based approach by focusing surveillance resources on systemically important financial sectors. As the recent events from peripheral Europe have demonstrated that sovereign debt crisis in a small and so called systemically-not-so-important country can also have significant destabilizing spillovers. In view of this and for the sake of global and regional financial stability, it is important to give due weightage to standard assessments for all jurisdictions.

Second, there is a need to streamline the several assessment mechanisms that have been instituted in the post crisis period. Illustratively, the ongoing global regulatory reforms under the aegis of G20 places high importance on peer reviews and assessments. The agenda of reforms includes a wide variety of issues ranging from compensation reforms to shadow banking. The FSB (Financial Stability Board) makes a separate assessment of the progress in global adherence to international standards on every individual issue.

Thus there is the pressure of a sudden deluge of assessments and peer reviews. It would be a good idea for the FSAP to draw from the FSB assessments so as to avoid overlaps.

Third, we would like the FSAP to be a two-way learning process. We look forward to receiving technical inputs on such issues as stress testing, which we feel will help us in building a more robust analytical framework. On the other hand, we would expect the FSAP team pick up good practices from our financial system. For example, the use of macroprudential regulation as a countercyclical policy tool has also met with considerable success in India. With a view to monitor the contagion risk, we have started to make use of network analysis which is an excellent tool to study interconnectedness and systemic risk. The IMF could look into these Indian experiences and share them with others.

Fourth, we feel that the traction of FSAP policy recommendations can be enhanced by making the policy recommendations more country-specific. We feel that the IMF needs to extend its work towards more flexible modular assessments tailored to country needs rather than one-size-fits-all approach based on best practices to make it more acceptable to the jurisdictions. Here, it is necessary to broaden our approach on how we define the best practices——it should be such that we recognize that best practices could emanate from any part of the world. The recommendations from FSAP are also more likely to get greater acceptability if the country-specific concerns are addressed more effectively.

Fifth, the development dimension of the financial sector needs a special mention. In the revamped FSAP, apart from gauging the stability of the financial sector, the other important objective of the exercise is to assess its potential contribution to growth and development. In India, we are pursuing the development objective through a greater thrust on financially inclusive growth. This implies penetration of financial intermediation and formal channels to cater to the requirements of a large continental economy with diverse population and demographic characteristics.

Additionally, the thrust of the development strategy gives emphasis on closing the gaps in the physical and social infrastructure. Thus, we would expect some flexibility and additional efforts on the part of the IMF and the World Bank with respect to emerging market economies.

Before I conclude, let me mention that in addition to steps taken to improve prudential regulations, customer service, and enhance supervision, we have initiated policy discussions with regard to providing new bank licenses; designing the roadmap for the presence of foreign banks; holding company structure for large financial entities and review of supervisory process. We have made a significant change in the financial regulatory architecture with the setting up of the Financial Stability and Development Council (FSDC). To address legal reforms Financial Sector Legislative Reforms Commission (FSLRC) has been set up. Nevertheless, we expect the FSAP exercise to play a significant role in shaping our post-crisis initiatives to strengthen the regulatory and supervisory architecture based on the evolving international consensus as well as careful examination of their relevance to the India-specific context.

Thank you for your kind attention.

☐ Xuan Changneng

Director General, Financial Stability Bureau of the PBC

Thank you, Mr. Chair, for allowing me this opportunity to make a very brief remark.

First of all, I want to thank the Fund and the Bank, China FSAP team, especially those who are sitting around the table today. I know Jonathan Fiechter, Udaibir Das, Keith Hall, among others, contributed significantly to the successful execution of China's FSAP.

Deputy Governor Liu just gave a very excellent summary of China's FSAP experience. As he mentioned, we coordinated with all the other agencies, especially the three regulatory commissions, in making sure the mechanism work effectively.

I want to make a brief remark about what Meg just talked about, on how to enhance the traction of FSAP findings and recommendations. Deputy Governor Liu also mentioned that in our experience, there're some parallel feelings or experience, particularly in terms of these important lessons. I think it's much easier to agree on what should be done, what actions should be taken, what should take place, however, it's much harder to agree on the timing and sequencing of action plan. In this particular respect, I think the China FSAP team had done a very good job in terms of being sensitive about China's specific situation as they did in the US case.

For example, we talked about their involvement, the influence of the US FSAP process on Dodd-Frank legislation. They told us while the process of US FSAP has some bearing on the legislative process that led up to the Dodd-Frank Act, but they deliberately and wisely, stayed away from making specific prescription for how to go about, say, whether they should have a unified banking regulator or whether they should have a federal charter for the insurance industry. I think that's very wise, because to get into that detail, as probably, would require a much harder implementation in terms of the complex legislative process. Also, for the regulation of the futures business, for example, if you want to say you have to merge the CFTC with SEC, that would get into a very complex, maybe messy, tough issue with respect to the Finance Committee of Senate or its counterpart in the Congress, in the House, I mean.

In the case of China, we had many rounds of discussion between us and the FSAP team about the timing and sequencing of the reform. I think all the recommendations that they put in the reports have a very high correlation with wordings the China's 12th Five-Year Plan has. And all the major elements are there. They captured very well what needs to be done for China's financial system going forward. The issue is more about when and how. And that's where we have some divergent views, and regarding the regulatory framework, there are some slight issues as well. But in overall, China FSAP team have done an excellent job in terms of striking a balance between what needs to be done and how they can be implemented and the timing and sequencing.

I strongly echo what Meg said in her remark about the US FSAP experience. That's very important. Going forward, it's critical to improve the effectiveness of the FSAP process and make it more widely accepted. FSAP methodology probably needs to think about how to make it become a more effective traction in terms of focusing on the how. And I echo some of the speakers from other countries. I think that is very very important. Thank you.

□ Noritaka Akamatsu

Deputy Head, Office of Regional Economic Integration, ADB

FSAP started with a focus on microprudential regulation and supervision of financial institutions but is now understood to have improved on the macroprudential assessment of the financial stability, which is to be praised. However, it is essential to continuously engage countries to help implement recommendations of the FSAP. The infrequency of FSAP operations (and the heavy burden on the host country) should require a separate approach to doing so. While FIRST is designed to support capacity building, countries need to be engaged in a continuous policy dialog leading to the implementation.

Asian Development Bank (ADB) carries out financial sector program operations in its developing member countries, which provide a platform to support such a continuous policy dialog and capacity building. ADB, therefore, believe that it can contribute to this effort. To do so, however, it is essential for ADB to participate in FSAP itself for two reasons. One is that much of FSAP results, except for FSSA (and other occasional reports), is kept inaccessible for ADB. This creates a danger that ADB supports reforms in contradiction to FSAP recommendations. The other is that ADB doing a sector assessment comparable to FSAP is not an option as it would cause an excessive burden on the host country while requiring a duplication of effort and resources which ADB can neither justify nor afford.

ADB has been occasionally invited or suggested to participate in FSAP when it was to be done in ADB's member countries. ADB believes that the systematization of its participation would contribute to the effectiveness of FSAP. ADB sees neither a need nor a possibility to be a formal partner to IMF and WB in this global program. ADB instead can systematically contribute to the FSAP by sending an appropriate expert (s) to join the IMF-WB team whenever it is done in any of ADB member countries. ADB understands that this would not fully resolve the issue of ADB's inaccessibility to FSAP results because of the confidentiality required of the participants in the FSAP team. Nevertheless, ADB thinks it will significantly help improve the coordination between ADB operations and the FASP and will be beneficial for our member countries. ADB, therefore, suggests that IMF (and WB) consider putting such an arrangement into practice. ADB also wishes to request our member countries as well as IMF and WB to allow ADB to access full results of FSAP based on appropriate confidentiality arrangements.

Keynote Address

Financial Stability and FSAP : Practice and Experience of China

Zhou Xiaochuan, PBC

☐ Zhou Xiaochuan

Governor, PBC

Financial Stability and FSAP : Practice and Experience of China

Ladies and Gentlemen, good afternoon,

Financial stability has been a top priority issue among policy makers and international financial standard setters since 2008, and the uncertainty surrounding the Euro area since last year has added more dimensions to it. In China, policy makers and the financial community had taken to heart the importance of promoting financial stability through deepening financial reform and strengthening regulation in managing and preventing financial risks since the Asian financial crisis. And this recognition has only heightened since the latest global financial crisis.

This symposium offers an opportunity for representatives from the region and beyond to share experiences undertaking the FSAP and in related efforts for financial sector stability, and discuss how to make improvement based on past experiences. And I would like to take this opportunity to share with you a few thoughts on the FSAP, financial reform, financial stability and what we did in these areas.

I . Importance of macro economic stability and financial risk assessment is widely recognized after the global financial crisis

The crisis exposed weaknesses of major economies in areas such as monitoring and assessing systemic risks, political willingness to act on them, and crisis management framework. Strengthening financial stability assessment and early warning capacity has become the consensus of the international community.

As a program of comprehensive assessment of financial stability in member jurisdictions by the IMF and the World Bank in the aftermath of the Asian financial crisis, FSAP has gradually become a well-accepted assessment mechanism producing independent results and can be used by national authorities as a significant complement to their self-assessments. Since the crisis, both the G20 Summit and the FSB have given FSAP a timely boost in enhancing its legitimacy and strengthened the mandate of the IMF in conducting it. The G20 leaders committed to undertake FSAPs in their own jurisdictions at both the Washington and London Summit. FSB members made a unanimous commitment to lead by example by conducting FSAP every five years.

The crisis also called for improvement of the program. Along with the modernization drives of the IMF's surveillance framework, the FSAP has gone through reviews and its assessment scope and focus have also been modernized, particularly in crisis management, cross-border contagion, among other things. For example, the geographical focus has shifted from emerging markets before the crisis to systemically important economies and financial centers, and conducting FSAP now becomes mandatory for 25 jurisdictions with systemically important financial sectors.

Though FSAP participation rate is relatively low by the number of jurisdictions in Asia, major economies have undertaken FSAP, including China, India, Indonesia, Japan, Korea, and Hong Kong SAR, with Japan and India going through update assessments currently. With broader participation from Asia, we believe that FSAP will play an increasingly important role in helping monitor and maintain financial stability in Asia and the world.

II. Strengthen and implement international standards for financial sector soundness

Modifying and raising financial standards to higher levels has been the consensus minimum step to address lessons from the recent financial crisis. Implementing the new financial standards means each member country need to further reform domestically and also cooperate internationally in the process.

A. FSAP as a driving force for observance of international standards

The FSAP pays special attentions to the compliance and observance of the core principles in banking, securities and insurance sectors, which is important in promoting regulatory effectiveness and soundness of financial sector. It is a consensus that higher standards and observance are critical in reducing financial risks at both the micro and macro levels. For example, the newly adopted Basel III requires higher quality of capital, higher ratios of both capital adequacy and liquidity, counter-cyclical buffers and surcharges for G-SIFIs. We support strict implementation of Basel III worldwide, and support conducting peer reviews and thematic reviews at appropriate time on implementation progress to promote adherence. With higher requirements for capital and liquidity, Basel III will reduce probabilities of failure of banks. However, it will not make the probability of bank failures decrease to zero. It means that we still need to consider the tail risk, which becomes hopefully smaller but still exists, and to design the crisis management mechanism accordingly.

At the same time, we believe that importance should be attached to consistency and fairness in the standard-setting process. When setting new standards or revising existing ones, it is necessary to avoid the urge to tailor-make rules for the advanced economies and then apply them to the whole world indiscriminately. That means we still need to consider the specific development stages and specific situations of different countries.

B. China's practice in adopting international standards

China has benefited from rigorously introducing and implementing international standards. Starting from the banking reform since the beginning of this century, we have attached great importance to the implementation of Basel capital accords, particularly with respect to strengthening capital adequacy and high quality common equity capital. During Asia financial crisis, China's commercial banking sector was in a very stressed situation. A lot of journalists commented that China's banking sector was technically insolvent. In this background, strong determination was needed to push forward the reform. The reform was not only an economic transition from center-planned economy to a market-oriented economy, but also a reform implementing relevant international standards in China's banking sector and financial market, aiming to raise our own standards to international level for having healthier development of financial sector and financial stability.

Before that reform, there were many problems in China's financial sector——domestic accounting standard was from center-planning period, loan classification was not accurate, no external audit was applied, leverage and liquidity management was not good enough, risk management standard was low. There was widespread skepticism about the truthfulness of the commercial banks' financial data. It was necessary to strengthen and implement these standards and enhance transparency so as to maintain the confidence of international community on the financial reform in China. Given this background, in the round of reform from 2003, China persistently enforced the implementation of international standards, which was taken as one of the major reform tasks. The reform enhanced capital requirement, information disclosure, accounting standards and external audit standards. High standards for listed company such as international accounting standards, the core principles of corporate governance and risk management were also employed since major financial institutions were eventually listed in HK stock exchange and other financial centers.

Before the financial crisis hit in 2008, the reform of large commercial banks, securities firm and insurance companies in China was largely concluded. These efforts laid a good micro foundation for the financial sector, which proved to be resilient and was able to provide adequate credit expansion and financial services for economic recovery during the crisis. However, in overall, we still have some gap from fully implementing the standards. This is one of the reasons we welcomed FSAP to employ the high international standards in assessing China's financial sector. It shows the direction for us to have a further effort to reach the high standards.

C. Tackling financial crisis and central bank's role

The crisis management mechanism and the resources available to rescue the economy from the crisis is also an important topic. We know that in this round of crisis, especially in 2009 and 2010, there were a lot of voices criticizing the bailout of some financial institutions using taxpayer's money, saying this was unfair. However, when a serious problem takes place, authorities have to consider how to rescue the economy and the financial market. Then, when a rescue is needed, we should discuss what kinds of resources are available and what kinds of resources we can come up with to use. In the end, the fiscal authority, central bank and international organizations have to use some kinds of resources to rescue somebody. This can not be so fair to all——somebody wins and somebody loses. Although critics are inevitable, it is necessary for us to stop crisis from getting out of control. And, considering the negative impact from inaction on economy as a whole and the welfare of the larger population later on after the crisis, it is a worthy course of action.

People may argue that someone should be clearly authorized to do something. That is, who is authorized to use these resources? The answer is different across countries. In China, the authorization comes from the State Council. Unfortunately, in some countries, there's no pre-set answer to this question, especially for the central bank. As the Lender of Last Resort, and in this regard, central bank may argue that the government, the fiscal authority, and even the international organizations should do something before the LoLR. However, if finally nobody takes right actions, the economy will go down the drain and financial market collapse. Because of this concern central banks should at least do something. We notice there is a contradiction between the rescue action and the low inflation targeting as central bank's mandate. So it is an art for the central bank to minimize the negative impact on inflation target and, meanwhile, try to maximize the positive effect of the rescue actions. This should be an important topic for studying financial stability issues.

III. Improve macro-prudential and crisis management

We know that the micro-level supervisory standards and the micro-level health of financial sector are not enough to prevent financial failure, let alone sufficient to prevent systemic crisis. Based on strengthened micro-level standards, macro-prudential management, risks monitoring and early warning as well as crisis resolution capability should be enhanced. As highlighted by the financial crisis, counter-cyclical adjustment is the key to strengthening macro-prudential management.

A. China's practice in macro-prudential and counter-cyclical management

In the spring of 2009, China's economy started to show some sign of recovery. So at that time China started to consider new counter-cyclical measures under macro-prudential policy framework. Starting in late 2010, the PBC conducted very clear counter-cyclical macro-prudential policies which could tame rapid credit growth and help lower inflation. So far the result has been encouraging, with inflation tending to descend in the recent months.

The macro-prudential policy framework of China set up a formula for banks to calculate their needs for buffers based on their capital adequacy requirements, among others. For example, the financial institutions' SIFI status, credit expansion speed in the previous year, risk management situation, prudent management and provision level against the risk-weighted asset are also considered in the calculation. Besides the formula, some discretionary judgments about business cycle and incentives and restrictions imposed by the central bank are also included in the framework. The purposes of the framework are to maintain financial stability and to make counter-cyclical adjustment of financial market.

Many countries have already set up macro-prudential policy frameworks, with different type for different country. For China, we've already adopted such a framework and benefited in this regard, and the objective of "establishing counter-cyclical macro-prudential policy framework" was included in the Government's document. The process is dynamic and some of coefficients in the formula can be quarterly adjusted. This macro-prudential measure is exploratory in nature so far and we look forward to improving on it going forward.

B. SWAP as regional currency arrangement in crisis

In the crisis period, US had currency SWAP arrangement with several countries that experienced difficulties in US dollar liquidity. Recently, US has also signed SWAP arrangements with six other European countries. For many Asian economies, if US dollar liquidity problem takes place, they may also hope to solve the problem by using currency SWAP. This can be made through two ways: one is to make SWAP arrangement with the US Fed; and the other is to make regional SWAP arrangement inside Asia. For the latter one, also there are two forms available: one is SWAP between local currencies bilaterally. Although some of our local currencies are not widely used internationally, we have a lot of trade and investment activities. For instance, ASEAN plus East Asia is now the first trade bloc partner of China. So there is a potential that local currency SWAP is also useful to alleviate foreign currency liquidity stress and maintain financial stability. And the other is a multilateral arrangement like the Chiang Mai Initiative Multilateralization (CMIM), which was originally a set of bilateral arrangements initiated during Asia financial crisis but later was multi-lateralized. To some extent, these approaches helped to complement the resources of the IMF.

Ⅳ. Conclusion

Chinese government has always attached great importance to the monitoring and management of financial stability. The People's Bank of China has started to publish *Financial Stability Report* annually since 2005 in order to monitor and analyze the overall health of the financial system. At the same time, the PBC and other financial authorities have strengthened timely monitoring and reporting of the risk conditions in the financial system as they arise. Also, we have made a great deal of efforts in financial sector reforms which take account of both international experience and realities of China, and have achieved positive results so far. China views FSAP assessment as an important complement to our own financial stability monitoring and a thorough examination of the soundness of China's financial system. Going forward, we will remain devoted to the adoption of international financial standards and codes, deepen financial sector reform, improve regulation and supervision and the financial stability and crisis management frameworks. Meanwhile, we are also ready to cooperate with the IMF to promote participation in the FSAP in Asia Pacific area and jointly promote financial stability, economic prosperity and sustainable growth in the region.

Thank you!

Session II

New International Regulatory and Supervisory Standards
—Their Role in Addressing Systemic Risks

- How prepared is the region in implementing Basel III and Solvency II and the new guidance from IOSCO on securities markets, and in addressing the market infrastructure weaknesses highlighted in the ongoing crisis?

- How do we ensure that regulatory reforms and higher prudential standards are applied consistently across countries and without undue disruption to the ability of the financial system to support growth?

- What more needs to be done to improve the quality and effectiveness of financial supervision in the region?

□ Xuan Changneng

Director General, Financial Stability Bureau of the PBC

Gentlemen, let us get started on the second session, which is the New International Regulatory and Supervisory Standards—Their Role in Addressing Systemic Risks. On the agenda for this afternoon's session Ⅱ, we have, four distinguished speakers and they would talk about several aspects of regulatory standards, for example, what are the key aspects of Basel III. Governor Zhou just talked about it, the higher standards for liquidity, higher quality of capital, and particularly the macro-prudential elements in it, the counter-cyclical capital buffer and surcharges for SIFIs and so forth, and the assessment methodology for SIFIs and the strengthened or heightened crisis management framework.

We also talked about the Fund's take on the Basel III framework. We've heard from the experts and from IMF, what might be the impact of adopting the Basel III in the emerging market. We know that extensive studies have been conducted on the impact of adopting Basel III for the global economic growth, how that implementation impacts the banks' ability to extend financial services to the economy. But in emerging markets, generally, the quality of capital, the ratio of quality capital is higher, as Governor Zhou mentioned and Deputy Governor Liu also mentioned in the morning about China. When China initiated the banking reform, we attached great importance to high quality capital, which is common equity capital. Particularly, since starting the capital injections from the government as well as the strategic investor's investment and also eventually public listings, common equity capital accounts for more than 80% of the capital adequacy. It's not a problem for China to adopt Basel III going forward, but of course, it is still a challenge to maintain high capital adequacies. However, in that respect, I think everybody was on the same page across globe.

About what are the standards being adopted for the securities and insurance sectors, last week the Steering Committee of FSB invited experts from IAIS and IOSCO,

Session II

New International Regulatory and Supervisory Standards-Their Role in Addressing Systemic Risks?

talking about how to implement or design a methodology or a frame for G-SIFIs or SIFIs in the securities business and how to extend that frame to insurance groups as well. So I think that is a very important topic today. And also actually in that connection, we noticed it's quite widely followed that the joint-forum, established by BCBS, IOSCO and IAIS, had done a series of work on financial conglomerate supervision. And in that respect, maybe somebody wants to touch upon that point as well, because increasingly, financial groups control directly or indirectly or make investment into securities and insurance sector. So I think that would come to play as we move forward.

Finally, we also talk about whether the new regulatory standards alone will be sufficient? As Governor Zhou mentioned, higher standards, higher capital adequacy will certainly reduce the probability of failures, but will not absolutely reduce the probability to zero. Therefore, other framework or complementary, macro-prudential, crisis management readiness and monitoring and early-warning systems would need to take place as well.

As we talk about all these issues this afternoon, on this topic and beyond, I look forward to insightful comments and suggestions and analyses from all the experts and also from the people on the floor. With that, I would like to first invite our first speaker to talk about his take, please. Thank you.

□ Wayne Byres[1]

Secretary General, Basel committee on Banking Surervision

Good afternoon everyone. Let me start by thanking both the People's Bank of China and the IMF for the invitation to be here, not just to attend this conference but also to offer some remarks on an important topic.

There were three areas that I was asked to address in my presentation today. Those areas are (i) the preparedness of the Asian region for the new regulatory standards, (ii) issues associated with the consistency of implementation of those new standards, and how we make sure they are implemented in an orderly fashion which doesn't create more disruption, and (iii) what else we could do to improve the quality of supervision.

In framing my remarks, I am going to focus my comments on banks and bank supervision, although I suspect many of the comments are equally applicable to other sorts of financial institutions and other sorts of regulation. Also, for the record, I'm still speaking as an Australian rather than a representative of the Basel Committee, although I don't think there is anything that I plan to say that I wouldn't be happy to say in my new role as well.

Preparedness of the Asian region for the new regulatory standards

The goal of the regulatory reforms is simple and non-controversial: we are looking for a more stable financial system, built upon more resilient financial institutions. My observation, and it has already been touched upon by a couple of other speakers today, is that Asian banking systems are generally quite well-placed, given their strong starting points, to implement the reforms. Indeed, in many cases they are probably already compliant.

---

[1] At the time of the Symposium, Mr. wayne Byres was Executive General Manager of Australian Prudential Regulation Authority.

Session II

New International Regulatory and Supervisory Standards-Their Role in Addressing Systemic Risks?

To the extent there is a silver lining from any crisis, banks and regulators in this region have already learnt many of the lessons that are now being learnt elsewhere. There is no doubt that the benefits of strong regulation and strong supervision were recognised after the Asian financial crisis, and hence the importance of strong prudential standards has been well known in the Asian region for some time. So as a general rule, banks in this region that have higher capital buffers and better funding profiles than in many other parts of the world. As a result, the new reforms will probably have less impact, and lower transition costs, in this part of the world than elsewhere. Added to that, the Basel Committee has provided fairly generous transition arrangements for its reforms. Although there is a lot of focus on the 2013 introduction of the Basel III framework, in 2013 itself the new requirements that need to be met are actually fairly limited.

Given the transitional impact from the new minimum standards should be small, and that many banks in this region would already meet those requirements by a considerable margin, it is not surprising that we have seen a number of countries aiming for higher standards and faster implementation. This reflects confidence in the underlying strength of their banking systems.

Consistency in implementation

The issue of consistency in the implementation of the new standards is an interesting one, as I think the word "consistency" means different things to different people. If you talk to bankers, they will aspire to a common set of rules in all countries. When you talk to regulators, however, consistency means something quite different. The consistency of implementation that regulators are striving for is that minimum standards are applied robustly in all jurisdictions.

I think it is very important that we do not get drawn into a debate about consistency in a way that leads us to discourage jurisdictions from doing more than the minimum if they believe it is warranted for their local circumstances. Indeed many countries, including a number in the Asian region, have already signalled that they can and will do more than the global minimum reforms. They are doing that for a range of reasons: some are responding to specific local market features, some to the problems created by systemically important financial institutions, and some to broader macroprudential issues. But regardless of the reason, it is critical that, in promoting consistency, we do not take away the capacity of regulators and supervisors to respond to these issues if they judge it necessary to do so.

I also think it is inevitable that there will be inconsistency in transition speeds and in implementation timetables. Each country needs to look at its own circumstances, and obviously needs to balance benefits with transition costs. As I have already said, in the Asian region there is probably capacity to implement the reforms faster and with less cost than in many other parts of the world. The Basel III transition plan is quite generous. That said, the Governors and Heads of Supervision have made it clear that supervisors should encourage banks to meet the new standards as soon as practicable. And I suspect that we are also going to see varying degrees of market pressure that is going to drive different bank behaviour in different markets.

So to sum up, the question we were asked is what we could do to promote consistency in implementation. My response is that too much consistency is not necessary a good thing, and that some inconsistency is both inevitable and positive.

Improving the quality and effectiveness of supervision

Nothing as complex and as dynamic as a financial system can be regulated simply by setting some rules. So in my view, the most important of the three issues that I was asked to speak about was how to improve the quality and effectiveness of supervision. A lot of the post-crisis reform work has been devoted to re-writing the rulebook and establishing new rules by which banks and other institutions will need to play in future. But clearly there is also a need to improve the quality of supervision if we really want to achieve our objective.

Our goal is to have supervisors with the willingness and ability to act when needed. "Willingness and ability to act" was a phrase certainly that was used in the FSAP for the United States. I was part of that assessment team that looked at banking supervision, and we used that phrase in our assessment report in highlighting some weaknesses in the US supervisory system. The phrase has also been picked up by the IMF in its excellent

Session II

New International Regulatory and Supervisory Standards-Their Role in Addressing Systemic Risks?

report on what is needed for high quality supervision.

In saying we want supervisors to have a willingness and an ability to act when needed, I should add that "when needed" is often. Active supervision is not something that is occasionally used: it is regularly used. Supervisors have to be able to influence banks behaviour. To do that, they must be persistent in their intervention. I want to be clear, however, that I am not suggesting that supervisors should run banks. But they need to be able to regularly question and prod and poke and intervene to get banks to justify that they know what they are doing, they have accounted for risk, and they are appropriately managing their business in a prudent way with a long-term objective in mind.

There is an important link between rule-making and supervision. In looking to improve the quality of supervision, we need to make sure that when we write regulations, we draft them in such a way that empowers, and not limits, active supervision. An example to try to illustrate this point is the capital conservation buffer that has been introduced by the Basel III regime. Many of you will know that it is a buffer of capital that banks will have to hold over and above minimum requirements. If their capital ratio declines such that they eat into that buffer, various restrictions are put on their capacity to distribute profits to shareholders and alike.

There are two ways that the capital conservation framework could be interpreted. One way is a framework that says supervisors are encouraged to intervene early, but that the triggers within the capital conservation range are the very last point at which a supervisor should intervene. Or the rules could be drafted in such a way that banks are free to do what they like unless they have reached one of those limits, and it becomes the first point at which the supervisor is able to intervene. Clearly, in looking at the way those rules are drafted, one way empowers supervisors, and one way severely limits them. We need to pay particular attention to careful crafting of rules to make sure we set up our regulatory frameworks to promote active supervision.

Another example in the Basel framework is the countercyclical buffer, which introduces a macroprudential aspect into the capital regime. Here again, there is a need to think about what is the best way to respond to, in this case, excessive credit growth in the system. Is it better to use a macroprudential tool which will necessarily apply to all banks in a fairly blunt manner, or should we be encouraging supervisors to deal specifically with those banks who are the most aggressive and who are growing most quickly and are therefore more likely to be the ones that are generating the vulnerabilities. In all likelihood, the ideal response is for supervisors to do both: to use the macroprudential tool, but to also deal individually with institutions. The important thing is to make sure that we do not create a situation where supervisors are discouraged from acting on problem institutions and simply hide behind the blunt macroprudential tool.

The final point I will make on improving the quality of supervision is a personal hobby horse of mine. A lot of emphasis has been put in the post-crisis reform agenda on improved information sharing by supervisors and strengthening supervisory college arrangements. I know that a lot of supervisors, with a great deal of goodwill, have done a lot of work to improve the amount of information they share with their supervisory colleagues. Supervisory colleges are much more rigorous and frequent than they used to be. But most supervisors are still bound by statutory powers with respect to information sharing which were written in a pre-crisis world. The expectation of, and pressure for, a much freer flow of information amongst supervisors has grown enormously, but quite frankly the supporting infrastructure has not kept up: indeed, significant impediments remain within the legislative framework that many supervisors continue to operate under. It is a important issue that needs to be addressed.

□ Suhaedi

Advisor at Banking Research and Regulation
Directorate, Bank Indonesia

Role of the New International Regulatory and Supervisory Standards in Addressing Systemic Risks: Indonesian Perspectives

It is really a great pleasure and honor to be here. Please allow me to thank the International Monetary Fund and the People's Bank of China for giving the opportunity to share our views on the role of the international regulatory and supervisory standards in addressing systemic risks as well as safeguarding financial stability.

Trilogy: prudential standards, risk mitigation, and crisis prevention

Discussions on this issue are both relevant and timely. However, we may note that these discussions are always connected to financial crises at national or global levels. It is widely recognized that implementation of standards, risk mitigation, and crisis prevention are interlinked. This "trilogy" has the tenet of the greater compliance to standards and risk mitigation; the lesser occurrence of financial crises.

The new international regulatory and supervisory standards we are discussing today-are directed to strengthen financial sectors——as a response to the recent global crisis. At the national level, Indonesia's experience in dealing with the financial crisis in 1997—1998 emphasized the importance of the consistent implementation of regulatory and supervisory standards. One of the driving factors which propagate the banking crisis during 1997—1998 was the lack of appreciation with regard to importance of banking sector policy and supervision in accordance to best practices. Such negligence with respect to the role of regulatory and supervisory standard has cost the Indonesian economy dearly.

171

Based on such painful experience, the Government embarked on comprehensive economic and financial reforms focused on the bank restructuring program, banking system resilience and recovery of intermediation. Bank Indonesia has continually engaged in improving the regulatory and supervisory frameworks and promoting the implementation of good corporate governance and risk management principles with the primary aim of maintaining a sound and resilient banking system that effectively plays its role of financial intermediation.

Indonesian FSAP findings

Thanks to comprehensive economic and financial reforms undertaken since the Asian crisis, the Indonesian economy proved resilient during the global financial crisis, and has since continued to grow at a robust rate. Growth has also become more balanced, with investment adding to consumption and exports as the main engines of growth. Financial system stability has been maintained. The banking system had a large capital buffer, ample liquidity, and remained profitable. Stress tests found that a limited number of banks were vulnerable to extreme liquidity shocks and a few large banks susceptible to concentration risks. Exchange rate and contagion risks were also at a manageable level.

This favorable condition is also exhibited by the FSAP findings concluded in 2010. Indonesia was lucky enough to have an FSAP in the middle of the global crisis. The crisis emphasized many of the assessments' strengths. In other words, FSAP assessments were generally useful in pinpointing the key sources of risks that we had to mitigate. Therefore, Indonesia was prepared to mitigate the crisis by taking necessary measures to establish a crisis management protocol, including a financial sector safety net law. As the crisis outspread, FSAP teams were adaptive to focus on critical issues, such as crisis management, liquidity support arrangements, and cross-border cooperation. The recommendations generally helped mitigate some of the adverse impacts of the crisis.

A general observation on the FSAP in Indonesia reveals positive findings. By this, we mean that the assessment was effective in helping authorities identify vulnerabilities

Session II

New International Regulatory and Supervisory Standards-Their Role in Addressing Systemic Risks?

of our financial system and develop key recommendations to mitigate systemic risks including those related to macro-prudential policies. In financial stability assessment, FSAP assessors examined the soundness of the banking and other financial sectors; conducted stress tests; rated the quality of bank, insurance, and financial market supervision against accepted international standards; and evaluated the ability of supervisors, policymakers, and financial safety nets to respond effectively in case of systemic stress. It was successful in identifying the main vulnerabilities.

Implementation of new regulatory and supervisory standard

With respect to the global financial sector reforms, as member of the G20, Indonesia has committed to adopt the new regulatory standards. With the economic and financial circumstance in mind, we strike the optimal balance between preserving financial stability and promoting economic growth. Indonesia will implement Basel II in 2012 and is working on adopting several aspects of Basel II. 5 into its regulatory framework. Quantitative Impact Study (QIS) for Basel III is also currently being run and the adoption of select aspects of Basel III into the regulatory framework will commence in 2013. Regarding SIFIs, we are conducting studies related to methodology and modalities to determine domestic systemically important banks (D-SIBs) . Indonesia is also studying the possibility of adopting key elements of resolution regime on our financial sector safety net (FSN) scheme. Regarding the OTC derivative markets, we are preparing a policy paper related to OTC derivative products transacted by banks.

With regard to macro-prudential supervision, over the last several years the central bank has developed its capacity by identifying internal and external sources of vulnerability, assessing resilience of the financial system, and forecasting financial stability. This macro-prudential supervision framework helped BI handle the liquidity crisis of November 2008 rather well. Bank Indonesia will complement its current macro-surveillance tools with the tools it needs to carry out the macro-prudential supervision mandate it will carry. These tools will also facilitate early identification of systemic risk build up in the financial system with serious negative consequence for the economy at large.

173

National priorities and challenges ahead

We believe that the new regulatory and supervisory standards will provide a strong foundation for a better global economy in the future. In this regard, we are committed to implement all of agenda consistently and in a timely fashion to safeguard financial stability to pave a sound foundation in achieving strong, sustainable and balanced growth. It is necessary to note that the new regulatory standards have limited impact on the Indonesian financial sector. Capital levels in Indonesian banks are well in excess of Basel III levels and, while, liquidity rules may challenge some smaller banks. Our large institutions will meet this challenge without any change in their behavior. Regarding securities markets, we do not see that new rules will have significant impact on the current activity of our markets.

As an emerging economy, we have immediate priorities and challenges in reforming our regulatory and supervisory regime which may be different than those reflected in the global regulatory reforms. Let me offer a few examples of the issues which are of greater priority to us. First, development challenges. About one half of our population has no access to the formal financial system. This group encompasses the poorest of our population. Our challenge as a bank regulator is how to balance our regulatory regime with the need to reach this population with financial services that can play a part in alleviating poverty. In this regard, we will focus on enhancing intermediary function of domestic financial system and promoting financial inclusion & education to generate broader deposit and lending base for strong and inclusive economic growth.

Second, implementation of macro-prudential for managing credit expansion. Our credit to GDP ratio is about 30%. Such is much lower compared to those of neighboring countries. However, there are some sectors which have rapid credit growth (such as motor vehicles and property) which must be monitored carefully. Constructive guidance on designing and implementing macro-prudential policy to address specific sectors would be helpful.

Third, competency and consistency in conducting supervision oversight. In many cases, the collapse of banks are not only caused by lags in availability of appropriate regulations but also are related to supervision capacity and consistency. Therefore, improvement of regulatory standards should be complemented by the efforts to strengthen supervisory oversight.

Finally, institutional cooperation. Related to the previous point, the growing relevance of a financial stability function means that we need to design effective institutional structures. In this area, guidance drawing on international best practices would be helpful. In the case of Indonesia, the Law on the establishment of integrated financial supervisory agency (OJK) was passed last month. In this regard, one of the most critical issues was how to harmonize macro and micro supervision carried out by the OJK and the central bank to address systemic risks, as well as, maintain financial stability especially during the transition period. At the regional level, we must strengthen our cooperation under home-host supervision, supervisory colleges, and regional surveillance, crisis prevention and resolution mechanisms.

Thank you for your kind attention.

☐ K. C. Chan

Secretary for Financial Services and the Treasury, HKSAR

Thank you for inviting me to speak at this session. In the next hour, we will be discussing the readiness of our region to implement Basel III, Solvency II and the new guidance from the International Organization of Securities Commissions (IOSCO) on securities markets. We will also share some of the lessons each of our markets has learned from the never-ending financial crisis which began in 2008.

Basel III for banks

Let me start by giving you an overview of Hong Kong's plans for the future. First of all, we intend to implement the Basel III framework in full and meet the Basel Committee's time frame. We do not expect our local banks to have any major problem with complying with the new Basel III requirements given their existing capital levels and composition of capital base.

Solvency II

On the solvency regime, we are aware that the international trend is moving towards a risk-based capital framework for the insurance sector. The EU, for example, has developed Solvency II, which sets out quantitative, qualitative and disclosure requirements, as well as the risk levels and risk management in assessing solvency adequacy. Hong Kong is formulating policies in that direction whilst taking into account our local needs.

New guidance from the IOSCO on securities markets

In the aftermath of the financial crisis, regulators are expected to contribute to monitoring, mitigating and managing systemic risk. I am glad to say this is not foreign to Hong Kong——in fact reducing systemic risk has always been a statutory objective of our securities regulator.

The Securities and Futures Commission (SFC), our regulator, looks at a wide

Session II

New International Regulatory and Supervisory Standards-Their Role in Addressing Systemic Risks?

range of indicators when assessing the potential risk posed by institutions, markets or instruments to the orderly and effective functioning of the securities markets. In many ways, the monitoring of systemic risk is already embedded in the daily work of the SFC.

Needless to say, no matter how capable a regulator is, it cannot predict all the threats that a financial system may be faced with. Any sudden and unexpected financial turmoil or the demise of any major overseas financial institution will send the financial system into tremors, particularly in times of high market volatility and low levels of investor and consumer confidence.

What we can do is mitigate that threat.

(a) For exchange traded products, our regulator is looking at concentration of trades, distribution of outstanding positions and volatility. We study the interplay among different market segments and assess their associated risks. For exchange traded funds in particular, we have imposed a counterparty exposure limit and collateral requirements.

(b) Corporate credit rating agencies and their individual rating analysts are now subject to greater oversight via a licensing requirement and are regulated by the SFC.

Clearing houses are subject to our close oversight. Reform of the over-the-counter (OTC) derivatives is under way and will be consistent with the G20 objectives. A local trade repository (TR) is also being set up by the Hong Kong Monetary Authority, and the Hong Kong Exchanges and Clearing Limited is building a local central counterparty (CCP) for OTC derivatives in Hong Kong. The TR and the CCP are scheduled for launch in 2012.

How do we ensure that regulatory reforms and higher prudential standards are applied consistently across countries and without undue disruption to the ability of the financial system to support growth?

It is all very well that each country is putting in place its own regulatory regime. However, potential differences in the scope and application of rules could encourage regulatory arbitrage and increase systemic risk and market fragmentation. Co-ordination among international regulators is a must if we want to ensure an internationally consistent approach in implementation of the G20 commitments.

The IMF-World Bank Financial Sector Assessment Program （FSAP） offers by far the most comprehensive and in-depth analysis of the financial sector. It assesses an economy's actual implementation of financial sector standards and codes, including the IOSCO Objectives and Principles of Securities Regulation and the Basel Core Principles for Effective Banking Supervision.

The Financial Stability Board （FSB） has also put in place a peer review mechanism for more focused and detailed monitoring of implementation progress. Various standard setters such as the Basel Committee have established their own monitoring programmes.

The chances of successfully and smoothly implementing new policies depend to a large extent on whether there was effective engagement of relevant jurisdictions in making policies in the first place. In this regard, we note that the Basel Committee expanded its membership in 2009. In addition, the FSB has recently established regional consultative groups to further engage non-FSB members in six different regions. Meanwhile, regional economies are also encouraged to make more use of regional platforms, such as the Executives' Meeting of East Asia-Pacific Central Banks, to discuss issues of their common interests and relay their views to the international setting's bodies when appropriate.

A more resilient financial system with well-capitalised and liquid financial institutions goes a long way in reducing the risk of future crises and promoting sustainable growth in the long run. However, it is important to ensure that the regulatory reforms themselves will not introduce new risks and additional procyclicality to the financial system. The macroeconomic impact and effects on market dynamics and liquidity of the new capital and liquidity rules under Basel III must be carefully assessed. Consultation with the industry must be done to ensure normal economic activities are not disrupted inadvertently. Phased implementation would allow the kinks to be ironed out in an orderly fashion. A good example is the transitional arrangements for Basel III implementation: the two newly introduced minimum liquidity ratio requirements （i. e. the Liquidity Coverage Ratio and the Net Stable Funding Ratio）, which will only

Session II

New International Regulatory and Supervisory Standards-Their Role in Addressing Systemic Risks?

be implemented on January 1, 2015, and January 1, 2018, respectively after an observation period that started on January 1, 2011.

What more needs to be done to improve the quality and effectiveness of financial supervision in the region?

The global financial crisis has exposed a number of weaknesses in financial supervision. We welcome the work of the FSB on enhancing supervisory intensity and effectiveness by coming up with important findings and recommendations for financial supervision.

In one obvious area, minimising the data gap would lead to improvement in financial supervision. For example, data from banks on their credit exposure may not show their largest exposure by economic sector. Regulators may not have sufficient information on the sources of bank deposits to determine the stability of banks' funding sources. Closing data gaps and improving the information systems of banks and supervisors would allow risks to be identified at an early stage and facilitate better understanding of interconnectedness between financial institutions.

Supervisors need tools such as unambiguous mandates, appropriate powers and sufficient resources for their functions. They also need to constantly upgrade their technical expertise and understanding of the latest market developments, so that they are able and willing to challenge banks' business models and act early if necessary.

Supervisors should also adopt a more forward-looking approach to supervision and stand ready to employ prudential tools to "lean against the wind". There has been a growing recognition of the use of macro-prudential policies to reduce the procyclicality of the system. A good example is the introduction of the countercyclical capital buffer under Basel III. In Hong Kong, we have been cautious about the build-up of an asset bubble and the rapid credit expansion, so we have proactively deployed various prudential tools such as raising the levels of banks' regulatory reserves, lowering mortgage loan-to-value ratios and tightening credit underwriting standards.

Given the interconnectedness of our financial system and the global nature of systemically important financial institutions, financial supervision can only be effective if it is supported by strong cross-border co-operation. Supervisory colleges and crisis management groups have been set up for banks and other financial institutions with significant international operations to enhance information sharing, supervisory co-operation and crisis resolution. Hong Kong's regulators, as the major host supervisors of the banks and financial institutions concerned, have been participating constructively in the relevant supervisory colleges and crisis management groups.

☐ Noritaka Akamatsu

Deputy Head, Office of Regional Economic Integration, ADB

Since the 1997 crisis, banks in Asia have continuously strengthened their capital, provisioning, liquidity and risk management while reducing non-performing assets. As a result, they appear sound even based on new Basel III standards. Asia ex-Japan also do not have Global SIFIs at least at this stage. Going forward, a key challenge for developing Asia in implementing the more stringent prudential standards will be to balance the stability with the growth and development. Of particular interest to the region in this regard may be the treatment of trade finance and repos under Basel III. The Basel Committee has recently relaxed the capital charges (via leverage ratio) on trade finance supporting the trade with developing countries. Yet, it otherwise insists on the need of those against trade finance. Repos are also included in the calculation of leverage ratio, thus making the transaction more expensive. Asia has been working on developing the bond market for which repos are critical. Asia would face a dilemma in implementing these rules. On the other hand, guidance on repos with government securities of an economy with distressed fiscal finance or public debt situation is still awaited. ①

When looked at the global or international level, it is not convincing that Basel III or Solvency II as microprudential measures is a final answer to the challenge to achieve financial stability. The tighter prudential requirements introduced in Europe share the spirit with Basel III. The ongoing implementation of those requirements together with fair value accounting is causing a deleveraging effect on the balance sheet of its banks. It is partly taking the form of liquidation of assets and repatriation of funds from the rest of the world including Asia, thus causing capital outflows from Asia. ② Asia earlier

---

① ASEAN + 3 is considering to promote the use of cross-border collateral as part of its Asian Bond Market Initiative (ABMI). In this regard, appropriate treatment of government securities of an economy with distressed fiscal/public debt situation will be critical.

② In this regard, even the Vienna Initiative does not seem helpful for Asia.

suffered from massive capital inflows due to the QEs in the US and Europe. [1] If an effort to strengthen the financial stability based on what is supposed to be the international best practice in one part of the world has to cause capital flows in the rest of the world, countries need to be well equipped to deal with them. Without such a preparation, the microprudential measures alone would be incomplete in achieving true financial stability.

ASEAN is now working on the integration of the banking and financial sector as part of the agenda of ASEAN Economic Community 2015. ASEAN aims to introduce a common banking framework in which appropriately qualified banks are to be allowed to operate on an ASEAN-wide basis. While the effort will likely bring substantial benefit to ASEAN, it can also create risks. In particular, it can be seen as a process of creating SIFIs. So far, the Basel Committee defined domestic SIFIs and identified global ones. ADB wonders if it makes sense to define regional SIFIs and provide some regulatory and supervisory guidance for them. If not provided at the global level, ASEAN may need to look into this at the regional level. It would call for closer supervisory (as well as regulatory) cooperation among the authorities in the region.

Several Asian countries participate in the APEC process where the importance of central clearing of OTC derivatives and leveling the playing field in achieving it is emphasized. [2] However, developing Asia is generally behind in establishing derivatives markets themselves. With an exception of higher income countries, the region lacks a domestic capacity to handle central clearing of OTC derivatives. When it has, it is often part of a silo led by a stock exchange. A requirement to clear OTC derivatives trades at such clearing houses could lead to breaking up of the silos and allow more competition among the exchanges. That may facilitate ASEAN's effort to integrate their capital markets. However, some member countries do not seem ready to allow concentration of OTC derivatives clearing only in few clearing houses in the region. It remains to be seen

---

[1] Since yet earlier, it has been suffering from the depressed export due to the contraction of external demand caused by the subprime loan problem, Lehman Brothers' failure, etc. .

[2] Based on Dodd-Frank Act.

how these motives may be played out in accelerating or slowing the region-wide implementation of central clearing of OTC derivatives and / or imposing higher capital charges on not centrally cleared OTC derivatives trades consistently with Basel III.

Session III

Prevention and Response

—How Prepared Are We for the Next Crisis?

- Are effective mechanisms in place to identify systemic vulnerabilities, including those related to sovereign risk, contingent liabilities, and volatile capital flows?

- What are the practical issues in extending the perimeter of risk monitoring beyond the banking sector to the broader financial system?

- How could contingency planning and interagency coordination be made more effective at both national and international levels?

- How adequate are existing global financial safety nets, and what regional and supra−regional initiatives could help support these efforts?

☐ Je Yoon Shin

Vice Minister, Ministry of Strategy and Finance, Korea

Korea has experienced three crises, 1997, 2008 and nowadays. Fortunately I was on the front line, so let me share the experiences on how to prepare for the next crisis.

I think there're four important components to detect a crisis. The first one is early detection of a crisis. The second one is financial regulations without loopholes. The third one is competent regulators. Lastly and most importantly, is full-fledged financial safety nets. I want to focus more on the global safety net of the last component.

A. Systemic Risk Identification

As you may know, the US sub-prime mortgage triggered the global financial crisis, which nobody exactly predicted. The sub-prime mortgage had a serious impact on global financial markets, even on the real economy. So it's very important to detect these kinds of risks earlier. I think there're two tiers of risk identification. One is at the international level, and the other one is at the national level. In the earlier session this morning, many people talked about the early warning exercise which G20 initiated, and the spillover effects of the collapse of Lehman Brothers, while I would like to focus on efforts at the national level.

As G20, FSB and IMF recommended, we need some institutional set up to detect risks in advance. They also recommended stress tests on banks. However, as you see, the euro area debt crisis occurred. Even though the G20 leaders declared that they did not expect any kind of crisis in the future like the 2008 crisis, but in April 2010, the sovereign risk in Greece occurred. We can not perfectly forecast or detect systemic risks, but we should try our best to detect them in advance. We have had a lot of discussions on the Early Warning Exercise, but I should ask the IMF to do more to design some macro-economic models to detect risks precisely in advance. Now they are focusing on assessing key risks, but it's not sufficient yet. We also should strengthen bilateral surveillance at the international level, and build the early warning framework at the national level, that's the importance.

Nowadays the sovereign risk is a hot issue in the global economy. The point is how to mediate the market sentiment, especially regarding public debt sustainability. I want to introduce Korea's case. We revised the regulatory standards after the 1997 crisis, which can be one of the factors why we overcame the 2008 crisis. We have the Early Warning System in place, and it is monitoring five areas; external stability, financial stability, raw material, real estate and labor market. Within the Early Warning System, along with sector-specific quantitative model, we have introduced some qualitative approaches to assess the possibility of a crisis. And recently we have established the Fiscal Risk Management Committee in order to better address and manage fiscal risks. Fortunately, the debt to GDP ratio of Korean government is very stable, only 34 percent. But since there remain many potential risk factors, such as an aging population, we are going to closely monitor how the new welfare system impacts our fiscal status.

B. Shadow Banking

The second component is financial regulations without loopholes. Since many people have discussed shadow banking so far, I don't want to mention it in detail. But I would like to emphasize that it's very important, in some sense, to monitor and regulate shadow banking, and to harmonize shadow banking with traditional banking.

As for Korea, there was a small crisis of credit card distress in 2003. At that time, many people argued that regulations on the credit card industry were not necessary because there was no deposit and it was based on market principles. But suddenly some distress happened in the capital market, and then it greatly impacted the whole financial market and the real economy as well as the credit card industry. Therefore at that time, the consumption went down rapidly. I don't want to confine this issue just to shadow banking. But even a small area is very important. Nowadays in Korea, MSBs, mutual saving banks, are typical in the financial sector. But some problems even in a small part may shake the whole. That's the lesson from our recent experiences. The share of MSBs is only 1.7% in Korea. But it shakes the whole in terms of some social issues.

How are the risks of the financial sector transmitted to the real economy? One possibility might be through the confidence channel. When there's a problem in a small area, like MSBs, then it might be channeled to the whole market as it would shatter the confidence of the participants. We put a lot of efforts to mediate the sentiment of the market. As you may know, the volume of shadow banking is 20 trillion US dollars, while that of traditional banking is only 10 trillion US dollars according to the FSB report. The FSB and other standard setting bodies should step up efforts to address these issues.

C. Competent Regulators

The third one is competent regulators. At the international level, since the G20 Washington Summit in 2008, there have been some architecture achievements from G20 and from standard setting bodies. I think it has well progressed. At the national level, in the morning session our colleagues from China mentioned that they have three "C" components, including communication, cooperation and coordination, which have progressed well too.

I think we should intensify our efforts concerning some institutional building issues. Communication is very important. The banking regulators, securities regulators and insurance regulators do not want to tell their real stories to others. We should recommend them to be more open-minded, and then the communication and coordination among them will be improved much better. What I want to highlight is that we need to pay attention to some small areas. Many staffs in the regulatory agency like to be involved in some typical sectors, like the banking sector. But they don't want to get involved actively in certain small areas, like MSBs and credit unions, because it's very hard work, but not highlighted as a regulator. They are required to work in the banking division, instead of in the credit union department. That's the regulation gap in one agency. In case of Korea, we set up one agency, that's the Financial Supervisory Agency, to regulate all the banking, securities and insurance sectors. When I was Vice Chairman of the FSA, I rotated staffs periodically among different sectors. I recommend that the FSB should try to address these issues, filling the regulation gap and human resources gap in the market.

Session Ⅲ

Prevention and Response – How Prepared Are We for the Next Crisis?

As in many other countries, Korea sets up some oversight committees. I'm the chairman of these regulatory bodies, including the central bank, the FSA, FSS and FDIC. We frequently communicate with each other and make policies together if necessary. We announce policy measures together so that it's a good implication to the market by showing that there is no conflict among the regulatory bodies. I think it's a good example that soothes the market sentiment.

D. Financial Safety Net

Lastly, financial safety net; actually there're three tiers of financial safety nets, which are national, regional and global. There're some arguments about the national safety net and the foreign exchange reserves accumulation. Many emerging countries learned the lesson that the more foreign exchange reserves they have, the better it is for them especially in a time of crisis. But it deteriorated the global imbalances, which induced a big argument in G20 process and other international forums. What is the optimal level for foreign exchange reserves? It's a dilemma. From the emerging markets' point of view, our domestic interest rate is almost 4%, but the investment yield of our foreign reserves on the US treasury is below 2%. Then why the emerging markets still try to accumulate foreign reserves? If every country accumulates foreign exchange reserves to prevent a future crisis, it will be a prisoner's dilemma. So the only solution to address this issue is to set up a regional financial safety net.

Recently Korea has made agreements with Japan and China to increase the currency swap, which are 70 billion US dollars with Japan, and 56 billion US dollars with China respectively. This is for precautionary purpose. We don't need to aggressively accumulate foreign exchange reserves just to prevent a future crisis. For the Chiang Mai Initiative Multilateralization (CMIM), nowadays there's only 120 billion US dollars for the safety net, but it will increase soon, maybe to 200 billion US dollars. So the first step is the national safety net, the second step, which is complementary, is the regional safety net, and the third and final step is the global safety net.

Whenever we talk about the global safety net, there're some issues about moral hazard. Korea initiated some safety net issues at the G20 level in 2010. At that time there

189

was a hot debate on how to prevent moral hazard. Recently the IMF has improved the conditionality on some new lending facilities, and we need to constantly strengthen the global safety net. There should be some methods to prevent moral hazard.

Nobody knows how we can predict the future. We should spare no effort in detecting risk factors in the future. It's still a long way to go.

☐ Nestor A. Espenilla, Jr.

Deputy Governor, Bangko Sentral ng Pilipinas

We do not have the advantage of foresight which will tell us where, when and in what form will the next financial crisis be. Furthermore, financial markets are themselves evolving, both with newer (more complex) instruments as well as with scaling back on previous products/practices that have been shown to have unintended consequences. Taken together, by definition, we will never know if we are prepared for the next crisis until such a crisis does occur.

The lack of perfect foresight should not prevent us from being pro-active in reforming the system. However, we should not change for the sake of change. Instead, we need to have a more categorical appreciation of the market landscape features which we believe are not aligned with the best interest of our publics or will simply be too untenable to effectively manage moving forward. This is where the challenge lies: we need to set the prudential parameters before difficulties arise, recognizing that we cannot foresee the future while accepting the financial markets are both inherently risky and intrinsically laden with conflicts of interest.

1. *Are effective mechanisms in place to identify systemic vulnerabilities, including those related to sovereign risk, contingent liabilities, and volatile capital flows?*

Not likely. We do not yet know how to properly scope the transmission of risks from transactions/products/processes/institutions into system-wide risks. This is an issue of not knowing how micro-specific risks become macro-prudential concerns and the channels through which such risks operate within our respective systems. To the extent that local financial markets are structured to address domestic issues, there will be a lot of differentiation between one financial market and another and therefore, between one transmission system (combining both the evolution of specific into systemic risks and the channels they are transmitted) and another.

191

The reality is that the impact of the same (external) sovereign risk on 2 jurisdictions need not be identical. We can identify prototype effects of some stimuli but it is not likely that we can anticipate the exact magnitudes, the extent of spillovers and the sequencing of effects through different channels. The same argument holds for other stimuli such as contingent liabilities and volatile capital flows.

2. *What are the practical issues in extending the perimeter of risk monitoring beyond the banking sector to the broader financial system?*

Banking risks are complicated on their own and to extend the risk perimeter beyond the banking sector will certainly expand complexity and coverage. However, this distinction is artificial even though the escalation in risks is certainly a tautology. It is doubtful that a banking regulator will be indifferent once the risks involved spillover into the securities or insurance markets. The fact that the risks can extend outwards of the banking sector can only suggest the sector is itself vulnerable to the same risks reversing its direction.

It is in this context that one can argue that risk mitigation is more about minimizing the expected impact than it is about etymology. Since the financial market is itself risky, generating risks is less the problem than it is the magnification, transmission and impact of such risks. For this reason, financial stability—whether it is simply the absence of instability or the maintenance of a set of conditions that spur the system forward—is really a collective responsibility of all types of financial regulators.

It then follows that while the objective is coordination, the practical problem is defining accountabilities at the cusps of where the tri-markets (banking, securities, insurance) are traditionally segmented, how product regulation is delineated (in the case for example of derivatives), or how the market conduct of institutions are supervised (investment banking versus broker/dealer).

The same coordination problems will exist within central banks where monetary policy, bank supervision and market infrastructure are all lodged.

3. How could contingency planning and interagency coordination be made more effective at both national and international levels?

At the national level, it is always useful to have a pre-defined framework that can be relied upon in the event of financial crises. This framework should define, at the minimum, the responsibilities of each regulator/agency-stakeholder as well as the working arrangements that are in play under the stressed situation. This avoids confusion and ensures that each agency-stakeholder is at the business of regulation/supervision/oversight/governance in the soonest possible time.

Unfortunately, we cannot always have a good sense of what can go wrong which prevents us from anticipating such working arrangements. It is in this context that crisis simulation exercises can be most helpful. Run properly, these exercises should flag weaknesses in working arrangements as well as the limitations of the existing intervention toolkit.

At the international level, crisis simulation exercises are no longer practical. This is where metrics and models take on a bigger role. The models in question need to be grounded on actual data since they are expected to provide suitable guidance on behavioural (not necessarily textbook) relationships, including magnitudes and contagion sequencing.

One can imagine a hierarchy of models. Domestic models need to be first established and only then can they be linked to a more global model. Network analysis will be appropriate for the latter task. The key however is to make the global network model accessible to all so that stakeholders have a common view of the international exposures and inter-connections while being provided sufficient technical assistance to replicate the same locally.

4. How adequate are existing global financial safety nets, and what regional and supra-regional initiatives could help support these efforts?

The current safety nets are structured either as outright prohibitions or as limits. The implicit principle is that the attendant risks to the former are incompatible with collective interests while the risks with the latter are acceptable up to some cap. If the former is left as it is（i. e. , what is not tenable to some is untenable to others）, the challenge then is whether the caps in the latter are sufficiently flexible to account for the differentiation across jurisdictions and across circumstances.

Risk-based limits provide a workable relative base that recognizes idiosyncrasies in domestic markets while defining a common cap in risk-terms. The viability of this approach depends to a large extent on stakeholders' adherence to international best practices so that outright outliers can be delimited. This necessarily raises the question of whether "international best practices" are in fact "best" for all occasions.

On balance, it is not very likely that absolute standards can ever stand scrutiny across jurisdictions and circumstances. Instead of relying on global safety nets, the international community is perhaps better served by stronger domestic prudential regulations. This need not mean tighter controls but:

a. a clear enunciation of the domestic policy framework and how this aligns with the agreed international order; and

b. a credible regulatory framework that can effectively address breaches in market misconduct and can realistically intervene for a certain level of systemic difficulties.

The main point of the above is that in choosing between extreme options local prudential guidelines are more effective than purely global safety nets. The former is expected to address the issues before they can magnify while the latter may be already reactive in nature. However, one can very well argue that some combination of the two extremes is the idealized situation. What is less obvious is whether the combination is itself an absolute mix or relative to jurisdictions. This is where the debate will truly be.

☐ Hiromi Yamaoka

Associate Director-General, Financial System and Bank
Examination Department, Bank of Japan

Financial Crisis Prevention and Response
——Japan's experiences

Preface

First of all, I would like to express my sincere gratitude to the PBC and the IMF for organizing this excellent event. I am especially grateful to the staff of the PBC who took the toil of translating my presentation documents into Chinese!

Chinese characters, which Japan imported a long time ago, have been a wonderful gift to us, but they sometimes cause nightmare to school children. They have to learn around 1,000 characters while in the elementary school! Owing to such tough works, however, we Japanese can understand the meaning of most Chinese characters. Although I do not know the pronunciation of Chinese language, I can still understand how wonderful the Chinese version of my slides is!

Financial Crisis – Endless Circle of "Transmigration"?

Apparently, global policymakers are placed in a challenging situation. The global economy is still facing an immediate crisis, that is, the European sovereign debt problem. Today, even If policymakers talk very eloquently on how to prevent future crisis, people might say, "Well, if you are a good doctor, give me a good medicine for my stomachache right now. If it works, then I will listen to your advice on how to avoid over-weight and high blood pressure in the future. " So, in my presentation, I will try to withdraw as much implications as possible that could be applied to the

195

immediate crisis.

Figure-1 shows the famous *Taijitu*, symbol of Kung Fu Panda. (Undoubtedly, for Japanese school children, pandas are the best imports from China!) This symbol is widely shared in Asia with a variety of interpretations. The most widespread interpretation is that the dark side (*Yin*) always has its origin in the bright side (*Yang*) and vice versa, and that dark side and bright side continuously and eternally give place to each other.

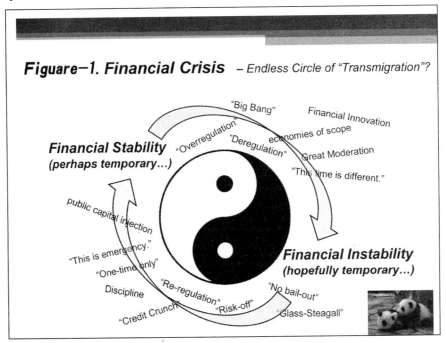

This symbol gives us an insight about financial crisis. First, some economists, in their models, tend to assume financial stability as stationary, and instability as exceptional. If we frankly look back on our history, however, it might be more appropriate to consider financial stability and instability as two phases of an eternal cycle. I dare say, financial stability itself could even be a source of another crisis.

The Best Prevention may not be the Best Response

Also, I would like to emphasize that the best crisis prevention may not be the best response to a crisis. It is good for health to do a jogging in the morning, but a reasonable doctor will not recommend it to a patient who is now in bed with flu. In a similar vein, more capital may contribute to more resiliency of a bank over the medium term, but tightening capital constraints in the midst of deleveraging may lead to a catastrophic credit crunch. It is easy to argue that public capital injection and blanket deposit guarantee give rise to moral hazard, but these measures are sometimes necessary for containing an immediate crisis. As such, all the policy tools have both a bright side and a dark side, and thus, the most difficult task for policymakers is to strike a right balance between them, based on accurate assessment of the state of a patient.

Japan's Experiences

After the financial crisis, public opinions may be against the use of taxpayers' money for bail-out. In Japan, although the idea of public capital injection was proposed by then-Prime Minister Miyazawa as early as in 1992, it took more than three years to implement large-scale capital injection. In hindsight, the losses stemming from deleveraging and economic slump was much bigger than taxpayers' direct losses, in view of the fact that most of the injected public money has already been repaid to date.

(Push on a String? ——Macro-prudential Easing)

Another challenge for policymakers after the financial crisis is how to "push on a string. " In the discussion on macro-prudential policies, economists tend to consider "tightening", such as by raising counter-cyclical capital buffer, rather than macro-prudential "easing". Indeed, emerging Asian economies, which weathered the recent crisis relatively well, have been in a position to think about macro-prudential tightening so far. For the economies that have recently experienced a crisis, however, bank loans to GDP ratio is likely to decline due to deleveraging, and their economy is likely to suffer strong downward pressure owing to financial malfunctioning. Moreover, in crisis countries it is very likely that policymakers have already exhausted available "macro" tools, with deteriorated fiscal situation and monetary policy under "zero bound". Thus, an actual challenge for policymakers in these countries is to find out the way to ease financial conditions and to stop deleveraging in a severe constraint of policy tools, instead of raising countercyclical buffers or reducing LTVs.

Indeed, after Japan's financial crisis, the BoJ's macro-prudential efforts, such as its stock-purchasing program introduced in 2002, were intended to stop deleveraging and to ease financial conditions, and it seems to me that European policymakers are now facing a similar challenge. Undoubtedly, it is important that we have prudential tools, but more important is WHEN we use each of them.

Interactions and Feedback Loops——Risk Games

Figure-2 illustrates another challenge for policymakers. Since any economic activity accompanies risk-taking, the needed quantity of risk-taking is determined largely by the size of the aggregate economy (as the slide illustrates that the volume of air inside the air bed is constant). If micro-focused prudential policies try to "squeeze" the volume of risks in the banking sector, such policies may simply transfer risks to other sectors, such as shadow banks, households, or public sectors including SWFs and central banks. In this respect, it is imperative for us to have comprehensive strategy on how we should achieve appropriate risk-sharing so as to facilitate sustainable economic growth.

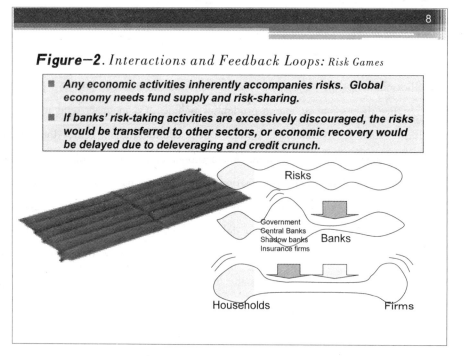

In this regard, Figure-3 illustrates another famous symbol shared in Asia. This symbol illustrates how closely the elements of the nature such as water, soil, plants and fire are interlinked with each other, and cause complicated feedbacks among them. Such complicated feedbacks among financial systems, markets and the economy are what macro-prudential policies are expected to focus on.

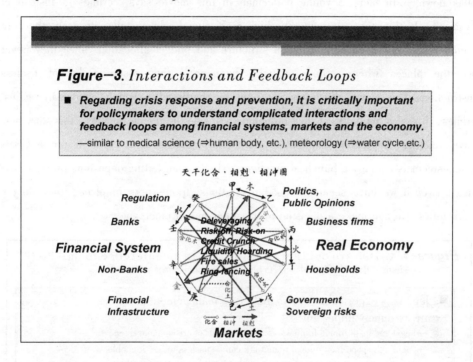

Figure-3. *Interactions and Feedback Loops*

■ *Regarding crisis response and prevention, it is critically important for policymakers to understand complicated interactions and feedback loops among financial systems, markets and the economy.*
—similar to medical science (⇒human body, etc.), meteorology (⇒water cycle.etc.)

Prevention and Response: What is needed?

Lastly, in view of Japan's experiences, I would like to raise a couple of issues that is important for both crisis prevention and response.

First, it is imperative to avoid "overconfidence".

In past crises, risks were always accumulated under various forms of "overconfidence", such as that in productivity growth, policy frameworks and risk management skills, just as the dark side originates from the bright side in *Taijitu*. Indeed, Japan's asset price bubbles developed in a co-existence of high growth and low inflation.

Second, I would like to emphasize the importance of good "practices" in crisis

199

prevention and response.

The title of Figure-4 (*"Crises are out there on-site, not in a conference room!"*) is a famous catch phrase of a Japanese mega-hit police movie series, "Bayside Shakedown". In fact, a young policeman in this movie says "crimes", instead of "crises". In this story, bureaucratic high-rank officials always talk with each other, in a conference room, on organizational structure and budget allocation. Since they never see the places where crimes actually happened, they issue a lot of useless instructions. This movie illustrates not only the battle of a young policeman against crimes, but also his battle against bureaucracy inside the police. Indeed, this story may have another important implication for crisis management and response. Crisis management is actually a bunch of practices, such as not letting depositors queue in the street. Even if we have seemingly-good institutional frameworks in place, they do not work unless we can make a decision over a weekend in emergency.

Figure-4. "Crises are out there on-site, not in a conference room!"
–from "Bayside Shakedown" (a blockbuster police movie in Japan)

- ■ Japan's experiences shows that crisis management practices are extremely important.
  —Legal and institutional frameworks are just a part of crisis management.
  —Seemingly-good institutional framework can be useless unless it enables swift decision-making and execution (e.g., within a weekend), since markets developments are quick and investors attack any delay in response.

(Several Practices for Crisis Prevention)

✓ NEVER let depositors make a queue on a street.

　　—If people see a queue on a street or on a TV, they will JOIN.

　　—If depositors come very early in the morning, open the branch and let them in!

✓ NEVER cause the "out of stock" of cash.

　　—CB will be required also to "physically" provide sufficient liquidity (=banknotes) swiftly!

✓ Effective communication strategy by the authorities is critical.

✓ CB's daily monitoring of bank's liquidity position is useful.

The Great East Japan Earthquake

Figure-5 shows our experiences of the tragic Great East Japan Earthquake. Indeed, people there had taken various measures against *Tsunami*, and at *Kamaishi Port* there was the world-largest breakwater of 1960 meters long and 63 meters deep. Nonetheless, the size of the actual *Tsunami* far exceeded their expectations, and the breakwater was completely broken down. I would also like to emphasize that milliard of sound practices and dedicated efforts of widely-ranging entities have played an extremely important role in the recovery from the disaster.

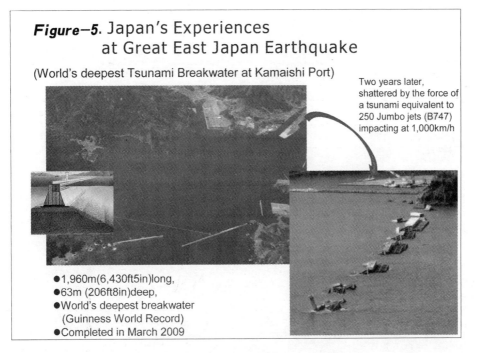

Figure-5. Japan's Experiences at Great East Japan Earthquake

(World's deepest Tsunami Breakwater at Kamaishi Port)

Two years later, shattered by the force of a tsunami equivalent to 250 Jumbo jets (B747) impacting at 1,000km/h

● 1,960m(6,430ft5in)long,
● 63m (206ft8in)deep,
● World's deepest breakwater (Guinness World Record)
● Completed in March 2009

In the context of financial stability, a breakwater can be macro-prudential policies, G-SIFI frameworks, or high-rank committees. In any case, over reliance on a specific methodology, such as the belief that macro-prudential policy will always be very effective, can be another source of a future crisis.

In terms of FSAP, I believe that FSAP can and should play an important role in maintaining financial stability. At the same time, from an Asian perspective, IMF's Article IV and FSAP are often very keen to recommend brand-new policies and frameworks adopted in some advanced economies, such as " Financial Big-Bang" and inflation targeting that does not "lean against the wind" . Although I pay respect to western cultures, I would also like to reiterate that Japan has imported many ideas and frameworks from Asian countries during these two thousand years (as my presentation slides illustrate), benefiting a lot from them. I believe that it is imperative for FSAP to pay maximum attention to its even-handedness and flexibility, so as to be beneficial to all the members including Asian economies.

I wish all the best for IMF FSAP, and thank you very much.

□ Noritaka Akamatsu

Deputy Head, Office of Regional Economic Integration, ADB

ADB is impressed by the frameworks for financial supervision including domestic inter-agency coordination developed by Asian countries. In particular the countries directly hit by the 1997 crisis seem to have consciously built sound and comprehensive frameworks to supervise the domestic financial sector. ADB fully appreciates the emphasis on watching the real estate market and asset bubbles and, in particular, the usefulness of debt to income (DTI) and loan to value (LTV) ratios in doing so. The countries seem to be well prepared to cope with possible instability or shocks in the future as far as financial sector regulation and supervision are concerned. This is based on an assumption that in a foreseeable future, Asia is unlikely to be faced with a sovereign debt crisis that interacts with and complicates the financial sector stability, as it is happening in some European countries today.

Yet, there may also be room to strengthen the supervision of inter-market links. Links between the banking sector and the insurance sector are now well known from the case of mono line insurance and AIG in the context of the subprime loan problem and securitization. Beyond those, real estate market bubbles could drive stock prices of companies holding substantial assets in real estate, as market prices in the unrealized capital gains. This category of companies could include banks with extensive branch networks. At the same time, banks in some countries in the region[1] were providing margin financing for stock investors, thus getting exposed to stock market bubbles. For the sake of stability, it is easy to say that banks should not be allowed. But developing Asia is often faced with a dilemma of not having other alternatives when it does not have a well functioning repo market where securities companies can participate and obtain liquidity. On the other hand, a functioning market for REIT could contribute to rationalizing, if not stabilizing, the pricing in the real estate market by connecting

---

[1] E. g., PRC and Vietnam.

the price to the underlying rent cash flows.

ADB also sees Asian countries' struggle in dealing with the capital flows impacting on the domestic money supply and inflation and causing the exchange rate volatility. Chronic excess liquidity could invite unhealthy behaviors of financial institutions and professionals aggressively extending credits and/or promoting investments particularly when they are driven by salaries / bonuses based on short-term performance. Those could undermine the integrity of corporate governance at the financial institutions, creating a major challenge for financial supervisors. ADB thus believes that sound monetary management including the management of capital flows is necessary to make the financial regulation and supervision effective. Some countries have used macroprudential measures such as credit growth targets to control banks' excessive lending, which seemed effective. [1]

To formulate effective measures to manage capital flows, the first step would be effectively monitor the flows to timely understand the nature of the flows. Korea seems to offer one of the best models for it in the region if not in the world (although it was not expressly discussed in the presentation by Vice Minister Shin).

---

[1] E. g. , PRC and Vietnam.

Keynote Address

The Future of the Global Financial
Architecture: An Asian Perspective

Choongsoo Kim , Bank of Korea

□ Choongsoo Kim

Governor, Bank of Korea

The Future of the Global Financial Architecture:
An Asian Perspective

Good evening, Ladies and Gentlemen.

It is a pleasure and a privilege to have this opportunity of delivering the keynote address at this high-level regional symposium in the noble city of Shanghai, a symbol of the openness and prosperity of today's China. I am most grateful to Governor Zhou of the People's Bank of China, to Deputy Managing Director Min Zhu of the IMF and to Financial Counsellor and Director José Viñals of the IMF.

The global financial crisis has cast a long shadow over the world economy. Financial disruptions in advanced economies, triggered by the bursting of housing bubbles, spilled over into the real economy and then crossed borders to adversely affect emerging economies, many of which were innocent bystanders. Asian countries including Korea have dealt relatively well with the global financial crisis on the basis of the conspicuously healthy economic fundamentals.

In retrospect, Asia's sound economic fundamentals were hard earned by painstakingly undertaking structural reforms after the 1997 Asian crisis. Many countries in the region liberalized financial markets, strengthened prudential regulations, improved fiscal soundness and increased foreign reserve buffers. In short, Asia did not waste its own crisis but learned valuable lessons from it. I am hopeful that our European partners will do the same.

If the importance of sound economic fundamentals was a key lesson from the 1997 crisis, what is the most important precept for Asia to draw from this global financial crisis? I think it is to face the reality that Asia, despite its acclaimed status as the engine of growth for the world economy, cannot escape from the risk posed by critical shortcomings of the global financial system, and go beyond to play a more active role in shaping the future global financial architecture.

As we all know, reform of the global financial architecture has been extensively debated over the past three years or so. In relation to regulatory policy, some progress has been achieved through the framework of Basel III. Even so, there are still many remaining gaps including volatile global liquidity cycles and the lack of effective global financial safety nets.

I should like to set out my views in this connection as to the challenges we are facing in formulating a new global financial architecture, and in what aspects Asia can contribute to it.

Regulatory reforms: striking the right balance

I will begin with policy challenges in financial regulatory reform.

It is widely agreed that regulatory failure was one of the main causes of the global financial crisis (IMF 2009, Truman 2009). Therefore there is no question about the need for the strengthening of prudential regulation with a greater focus on systemic risk and a multilateral perspective. However it is also critically important not to swing the pendulum too far the other way because over-regulation would risk undermining long-term growth potential by discouraging even productive leveraged risk-taking.

The literature on economic development suggests that the quality and volume of financial intermediation matters a great deal for long-term growth. Existing studies also suggest that financial deregulation can easily be a double-edged sword—enhancing growth by promoting financial innovations on the one hand but also killing growth by increasing the likelihood of financial crises on the other (Ranciere et al. 2008). Taken together, this evidence implies that we should have a good regulatory framework that strikes the right balance between financial stability and economic growth or efficiency. It is certainly true that financial crises more often than not result in a discernable decline in long-term growth. It is also true that declining and stagnant growth provides a fertile breeding ground for financial crises.

There is yet another balance that requires a due consideration in pursuing regulatory reform, namely the balance between prudential policy and monetary policy. The global crisis has clearly demonstrated that price stability is not sufficient for financial stability and also that financial stability matters for price stability. Of course monetary policy is distinct from macro-prudential policy in terms of objectives, transmission mechanism and effects. However, the intrinsic link between price and financial stability suggests that these policies should be appropriately coordinated. In this regard, I think this is the right time to depart from the Tinbergen Principle and seek an optimal mix of monetary and prudential policies (Committee on International Economic Policy Reform 2011).

It is easier said than done, however, to strike the right balance between macro-prudential and monetary policy. In theory, the former is better suited to deal with asset price bubbles in an isolated financial market while monetary policy is more effective in controlling overall credit supply and stabilizing the broader economy. In practice, however, it may be difficult to distinguish between a credit *boom* supported by productivity gains and a credit *bubble* created by irrational exuberance. So far there is little practical guidance on this matter. I believe the best approach is to establish best practices by exchanging ideas and pooling national experiences. I look to the IMF to play a leadership role in this respect.

Global jurisdiction for global solution on spillovers

Let me turn to policy challenges posed by global spillovers.

In an increasingly integrated world, cross-border spillovers, both financial and real, are key aspect of any financial crisis and particularly so if the crisis has global dimensions. Indeed, they are what made the 2008 financial crisis and the more recent and on-going eurozone debt crisis truly global in their reach and impact.

In this respect, global liquidity has received particular attention not only as the underlying trigger of crises but also as the conduit of cross-border spillovers. Global liquidity is created and destroyed through complex interactions among many players, both private and official and also advanced and emerging. And a myriad of factors matter for global liquidity, ranging from the monetary and regulatory policies of reserve currency countries to risk appetite and innovation in financial markets, and further to the pro-cyclical behavior of global banks.

Evidence suggests that excess global liquidity is often associated witha significantly higher frequency of financial crises. Such association is even stronger and the resulting crises prove more costly when that global liquidity is funded largely by unstable short-term financing. More importantly, recent studies show that the 2008 global crisis was more of a consequence of the "global banking glut" or the "global liquidity imbalances" as manifested in gross financial flows than of global savings glut or global imbalances in net flows (Shin 2011, Gourinchas 2011).

It is thus vital for global financial stability to keep global liquidity at a stable and sustainable level. Under the current international financial architecture, however, there is no effective mechanism that can offer a global solution to this problem. Simply speaking, the sum of uncoordinated policy efforts by individual countries falls significantly short of achieving global financial stability. This is why a global jurisdiction is needed that can monitor and control global liquidity effectively.

In a similar vein, a global solution is needed to leave behind us the eurozone debt crisis once and for all. Incremental and delayed policy responses have proven ineffective in forestalling contagion from the periphery to the core, making it only worse. I believe our European partners' approach is flawed in that it has sought a local solution with domestic focus. Missing from their equation are the negative spillovers of the debt crisis into emerging and other advanced economies. A global solution that internalizes such externality would prove far more effective in addressing the unstable debt dynamics. For instance, strong growth and stable funding conditions in emerging economies will contribute positively to an orderly deleveraging in the eurozone and else.

In this regard, I look forward to a greater role and stronger leadership of the G20, along with enhanced surveillance by the IMF and other international financial institutions. The G20 is particularly well suited for global policy coordination as proven by its prominent role in formulating concerted macroeconomic policy response to the

2008 global crisis. Such a role in crisis management can and should be extended to crisis prevention policies including global liquidity management. Moreover, the G20 offers a high profile platform for Asia to advocate its strategic interest in addressing the global liquidity issue and, more importantly, shaping the future financial architecture.

Need to strengthen Global Financial Safety Nets (*GFSNs*)

The third policy challenges that I will address is related to the global financial safety nets.

While most emerging market crises prior to the recent global crisis are considered home-grown crises, with few exceptions, the underlying vulnerabilities were related to surges in global liquidity originating in advanced countries and reaching the shores of emerging economies. The basic policy advice offered thus far has always concerned what emerging economies should do with little discussion of what advanced economies can or should do to stabilize the global liquidity cycle. And while international policy discussions since the global financial crisis have addressed a variety of policy issues related to global liquidity, their focus still lies on North-to-North capital flows, rather than North-to-South flows.

At present, and in the future as well, one of the most pressing issues for emerging economies will be how to guard themselves against the contingent risk of foreign exchange liquidity shortage and negative spillovers from advanced economies. Improved oversight of capital inflows and macro-prudential regulations will help address the danger of global liquidity surges and the attendant risk of asset price bubbles. But emerging economies will still be vulnerable to sudden reversals or disruptions of global liquidity.

Global liquidity disruption has always been a unidirectional process in that it starts from advanced economies and spills over into emerging market economies. But its real consequences are not. Retrenched growth and depreciated exchange rates of emerging economies ultimately feed back into lower economic growth for advanced economies. There are thus good reasons to argue that major central banks and the IMF should bear greater responsibility for strengthening global financial safety nets (GFSNs). Indeed, the currency swap arrangements that the US Fed offered to several emerging economies during the global financial crisis proved highly effective in calming the markets and stabilizing exchange rates. The recent renewal of China-Korea and Japan-Korea currency swaps, I believe, represents an important step toward finding a global solution for financial safety nets. I also commend the IMF's decision to offer a new Precautionary Credit Line in this regard.

The existence of well-functioning GFSNs would also help reduce emerging economies' temptation to hoard large foreign reserves, and thereby mitigate the problem of global imbalances. Some may argue that to prevent moral hazard, constructive ambiguity is warranted as to access to central bank swap lines. I agree with the merits of constructive ambiguity but have good reasons to believe that the risk of moral hazard is exaggerated. We should be keenly aware that GFSNs aims at addressing liquidity disruptions of a global nature, and not idiosyncratic or home-grown liquidity crises. Moreover, financial crises have proved very costly to countries, not only economically but also politically. The high cost of a financial crisis is by itself an effective deterrent to debtor moral hazard.

Asia's strategy for financial development

The last point that I should stress relates to Asia's strategy for financial development.

Asia accounts for a considerable and growing proportion of the world economy in terms of GDP and trade. In terms of finance, however, Asia does not measure up at all to its position in world trade and income. Asia's trade is invoiced and settled in a handful of reserve currencies with the dominant role of the US dollar. The same goes for Asia's cross-border capital transactions.

Heavy dependence on foreign currencies in trade and finance has been considered a key source of Asia's financial vulnerability. And such heavy dependence is a reflection of Asia's limited or underdeveloped capacity to create safe assets. By developing a financial industry commensurate with its real economic clout, therefore, Asia should be able to supply its own safe assets in sufficient scale. This will contribute to not only Asia's financial stability but also that of the world by mitigating Triffin's Dilemma.

Financial development is a complex and multifaceted process. It requires good financial regulation, sophisticated human capital and technology, and even supportive culture. At the current juncture, most important for Asia is an effective and sustained learning on how to do finance. And the key to learning is financial liberalization and market opening. Asian countries should not give up their efforts to liberalize their capital account even when the world is discussing how to improve financial regulation following the global crisis. In fact, regulatory reforms in advanced countries may well offer the best window of opportunity for Asia to further liberalize its capital accounts at lower risk of sudden stops or volatile capital flows.

I firmly believe that the first step toward capital account liberalization should be to allow greater flexibility in the exchange rate. A well-sequenced transition toward a floating exchange rate regime with an open capital account will contribute to the development of a resilient financial industry while minimizing the likelihood of a costly crisis. Historical experience has shown that intermediate exchange rate regimes have tended to be crisis prone (Ghosh 2010, Bubula and Otker-Robe 2003). And during the recent eurozone fiscal crisis it has become apparent that even a currency union, the hardest peg, is also vulnerable to external shocks.

Concluding remarks

Now let me conclude.

The global crisis has changed the financial landscape of the world in many important respects. New regulations will be implemented for crisis prevention, while debt-ridden countries will strive to achieve orderly deleveraging to return to financial stability and solid growth. The road ahead is full of challenges, however. Global spillovers will continue to be a fact of life while the risk of trade and financial protectionism will not go away easily. In this interconnected world, we need a global solution. And we need a global jurisdiction to make a global solution a real possibility.

In the last half a century of Asian history, prosperity and growth have largely resulted from openness and a forward-looking attitude. Where the markets for trade and finance are closed or self-contained, there can be no process of learning. By consistently pressing ahead with financial liberalization, Asia should upgrade its financial sector and correct the imbalances between the financial and the real sectors. By doing so Asia should be able to emerge as the self-sustaining engine of growth for the world. I am sure that now is the time to act upon this premise.

Thank you.

References

Bubula, Andrea and Inci Otker-Robe. 2003, "Are Pegged and Intermediate Exchange Rate Regimes More Crisis Prone? IMF.

Committee on the Global Financial System. 2011, "Global Liquidity-Concept, Measurement and Policy Implications," BIS.

Committee on International Economic Policy Reform. 2011, "Rethinking Central Banking".

Ghosh, Atish, Jonathan Ostry, and Charalambos Tsangarides. 2010, "Exchange Rate Regimes and the Stability of the International Monetary System," IMF.

Gourinchas, Pierre-Oliver. 2011, "Global Imbalances and Global Liquidity".

IMF. 2009, "Lessons of the Financial Crisis for Future Regulation of Financial Institutions and Markets and for Liquidity Management".

Ranciere, Romain, Aaron Tornell, and Frank Westermann. 2008, "Systemic Crises and Growth," *Quarterly Journal of Economics*.

Shin, Hyun Song. 2011, "Global Banking Glut and Loan Risk Premium".

Truman, Edwin. 2009, "The Global Financial Crisis: Lessons Learned and Challenges for Developing Countries".

Special address

Challenges for Macroprudential
Supervision

Barry Eichengreen,
Professor of Economics and Political Science,
University of California, Berkeley

□ Barry Eichengreen

Professor of Economics and Political Science,
University of California, Berkeley

Challenges for Macroprudential Supervision

I have been asked to address the role of central banks in macroprudential supervision. I am happy to do so because this gives me an opportunity to promote the first report of the Committee on International Policy and Reform, entitled "Rethinking Central Banking," and recently published by the Brookings Institution. [1] I draw on the conclusions of that report in what follows. The views that follow are therefore my own, but they are inspired by those of my fellow committee members: Mohamed El-Erian, Arminio Fraga, Takatoshi Ito, Jean Pisani-Ferry, Eswar Prasad, Raghu Rajan, Maria Ramos, Carmen Reinhart, Helene Rey, Dani Rodrik, Ken Rogoff, Hyun Shin, Andres Velasco, Beatrice Weder di Mauro, and Yongding Yu.

The global financial crisis shook confidence in microprudential tools of regulation as the primary tool for ensuring financial stability. Yet I think it is fair to say that many central bankers still subscribe to the traditional dichotomy between monetary policy and financial stability, except that *microprudential* tools have given way to an embrace of *macroprudential* tools of financial regulation (countercyclical capital adequacy requirements, for example) . These tools or policies are to be developed and implemented by specialists in financial stability, not by central bankers responsible for the conduct of monetary policy.

---

① Committee on Internatinoal Economic Policy and Reform, *Rethinking Central Banking*, Washington, D. C. : Brookings Institution (2011) .

The case for this separation rests on the belief that interest rates are too blunt an instrument for the effective pursuit of financial stability. The question is commonly framed as whether the central bank should raise interest rates in response to asset bubbles. In the 1990s and early 2000s, central bankers discussed at length whether and how to respond to asset market developments. The conclusion of that debate was that central banks had a mandate to react to bursting bubbles but not to target asset prices.

The case against attempting to prick bubbles rests on two arguments.

- First, identifying bubbles is hard.

- And, second, even if there is a bubble, monetary policy is not the best tool with which to address it. An asset price bubble will not respond to small changes in interest rates; only a sharp increase will suffice to prick a bubble. However, a drastic increase in interest rates can cause more harm than good by depressing output growth and increasing output volatility.

The first argument is unquestionably correct. But the second one is more dubious. The claim that an asset price bubble will not respond to a small change in interest rates has been made in the context of stock market bubbles, where the proposition is most plausible. When the stock market is rising by 20 percent a year, a small increase in interest rates will not outweigh the effects of rapid asset price increases. However, the stock market may not be the best context in which to discuss the financial stability role of monetary policy. The housing market, with its more prominent role for leverage and credit, and markets in the derivative securities associated with housing investment may be more pertinent. Monetary policy is central the leverage decisions of banks and other financial intermediaries involved in lending for housing-related investments. In this setting, even small changes in funding costs may have an impact on risk-taking and funding conditions. Financial intermediaries, after all, borrow in order to lend. The spread between borrowing and lending rates is therefore a key determinant of the use of leverage and has important implications for the interaction between banking sector loan growth, risk premia, and any ongoing housing boom.

Focusing on risk taking by banks and other financial intermediaries will lead the policy maker to ask additional questions about risks to the stability of economic activity. Rather than waiting for "proof" (whatever that may be) of a bubble in housing markets, for example, a policy maker could instead ask whether benign funding conditions could reverse abruptly with adverse consequences for the economy. Even if policy makers are convinced that higher housing prices are broadly justified by secular trends in population, household size, and living standards, policy intervention would still be justified if the policy maker also believed that, if left unchecked, current loose monetary conditions significantly raise the risk of an abrupt reversal in housing prices and of financing conditions, with adverse consequences for the financial system and the economy.

Not responding in this way has led to a dangerously asymmetric response. Central banks have allowed credit growth to run free, fueling booms, and then flooded markets with liquidity after the crash, bailing out financial institutions and bondholders. This asymmetry has contributed to stretched balance sheets, with faster lending growth and leverage in times of low risk premia, more violent deleveraging when risk premia rise, and frequent booms and busts.

For all these reasons, there is a case for central banks to guard against credit market excesses. An inflation-targeting central bank may argue that it does so automatically insofar as higher asset prices boost aggregate demand through wealth effects and create inflationary pressures. However, some additional leaning against credit market developments would be advisable even in the absence of aggregate demand effects once it is determined that funding conditions and reduced risk premia indicate a nascent credit boom. Put differently, inflation-targeting central banks may want to stray below target when conditions are "boom-like" ——when rapid asset price growth is accompanied by substantial credit expansion——since policy would otherwise become asymmetric and execerbate macroeconomic volatility.

A consequence of this doctrine of leaning against the wind is that the neat Tinbergen assignment of different tools to different objectives becomes more difficult to implement in practice. Interest rates affect financial stability and, hence, real activity. Equally, macroprudential tools impact credit growth and external imbalances with consequences for macroeconomic and price stability. When consumer credit is growing rapidly and the household debt ratio is high, for example, restraining credit growth by changing guidance on loan-to-value or debt service-to-income ratios over the business cycle will have important macro-stabilization effects.

Rather than viewing the allocation problem as having a corner solution where one instrument is devoted entirely to one objective, I believe that the macro-stabilization exercise must be viewed as a joint optimization problem where monetary and regulatory policies are used in concert in pursuit of both objectives.

True believers in Tinbergen separation will of course object that blurring the assignment of instruments to targets will jeopardize the central bank's operational autonomy, the central bank's mandate will become fuzzier, and its actions will become more difficult to justify.

I would acknowledge that these are valid concerns. Central bankers will experience more political pressure than if monetary policy were primarily targeted at price stability. Here, however, it is important to remember that central bank independence is a means to an end rather than an end in itself. Limiting the scope of monetary policy purely for the sake of defending central bank independence risks undermining the institution's legitimacy by giving the impression that the central bank is out of touch and that it is pursuing a narrow and esoteric activity that does not square with its democratic responsibilities.

Ultimately, political reality will thrust responsibility for financial stability on the central bank. As happened in the UK following the failure of Northern Rock, the central bank will be blamed for financial problems whether or not it was formally responsible for supervision and regulation. As lender of last resort, it will be charged with cleaning up the mess. It follows that it would be better off devoting more of its resources and attention to attempting to prevent the crisis, the elegance of the Tinbergen principle notwithstanding.

Macroprudential Policy Tools

So what should central banks as macroprudential supervisors do specifically? Here I think it is useful to distinguish the time-and cross-sectional dimensions of risk.

In terms of the time dimension, the macroprudential supervisor should develop a range of tools address financial procyclicality. Countercyclical capital buffers are an example, although they are not enough, since they are confined to the banking system. A supplement would be to impose a systemic levy for all levered financial institutions—that is, an additional charge levied on the unstable (non-core) portion of a financial institution's funding, as suggested by the IMF. This levy could be varied over the cycle.

Restraints on bank lending such as loan-to-value or debt service-to-income guidelines could usefully complement traditional tools of bank regulation, such as capital requirements. Capital requirements can themselves consist of a core of long-dated equity or equity-like instruments supplemented with an additional buffer of contingent capital instruments.

Some measures (like capital requirements) are likely to have implications for cross-border competition and therefore may need to be harmonized across countries. Others like loan-to-value guidelines do not have to be harmonized across countries and could vary substantially with the cycle.

In terms of the cross-sectional dimension, policy should focus on systemically important financial institutions (SIFIs). Better resolution regimes to deal with failing financial institutions could reduce the need for reliance on ex ante buffers such as capital. The obvious complication is that many systemically relevant institutions are active across geographical and product borders. These new laws have not been coordinated, and they are unlikely to be adequate for dealing with a large cross-border or cross-market failure. The new resolution regimes consequently do not solve the moral hazard problem implicit in "too big to fail" (TBTF). It follows that the implicit public subsidy for too-big-to-fail institutions remains intact; hence the need for ex ante measures.

It follows that macroprudential tools should be used to reduce this incentive to become too big to fail. These could include a systemic risk tax. Doing so of course presupposes more progress in quantifying systemic risk exposure, and agreement on who would impose this tax, on whom, and under what circumstances.

Alternatively, surcharges on capital requirements that vary with the systemic risk they create could be applied to SIFIs. The Swiss government commission on too-big-to-fail institutions has shown how this could be done. In addition to increasing capital buffers to nearly double the level of Basel III, the Swiss proposal as I understand it makes the surcharge sensitive to systemic risk, calculated as a function of the balance sheet size and the market share of the institution.

Proposals have also been mooted to eliminate certain activities of SIFIs (e. g. , proprietary trading), ringfence certain activities (such as retail banking, as discussed in the context of the Vickers Commission in the UK), or even break up SIFIs. Personally, I am not a fan of these proposals. They are likely to shift the risk in question outside the ringfence but not to remove the problem of too big to fail.

Institutional Responsibility

So let me return to the question of who should be responsible for financial stability at the national level? There are two answers to this question. One gives multiple institutions (central bank, systemic risk boards, micro-and macroprudential supervisors) interlocking mandates, their own instruments, and a directive to cooperate. The other vests one institution, possibly the central bank, with multiple mandates and instruments.

The first approach dominated prior to the financial crisis and, despite its failures, has largely survived the reform process. In countries like India and the United States, administrative bodies have been set up to coordinate the efforts of multiple supervisory and regulatory bodies, although these bodies tend to lack enforcement power. In Europe, the push for greater regional coordination has been further complicated by the superimposition of an additional layer of supervisory institutions with few powers of their own. Supervisory colleges, which collect relevant home and host-country supervisors of a large cross-border institution, are one of the tools for coordination among countries. But overall, the problem of incomplete coordination remains. In particular, it remains in Europe.

While there is little consensus as to the best model, the argument that financial stability should be a core objective of the central bank increases the weight of arguments for giving central banks primary responsibility for regulatory matters. If central banks have a mandate to ensure financial stability and also the powers needed to wield macroprudential corrective instruments, they can optimally choose trade-offs between the use of the interest rate instrument and macroprudential measures. Moreover, the central bank should have its finger on the pulse of financial markets through its monetary policy operations. It possesses a staff with macroeconomic expertise. It is the one institution with the balance sheet capacity to act as lender of last resort.

There are also compelling arguments against a unified model. One disadvantage is that it makes the central bank more susceptible to political interference. The central bank will have to work hard to establish the legitimacy of its actions in circumstances where the nature of threats to financial stability may be poorly understood and its actions are unpopular. The public and its elected representatives may not be happy, for example, if the central bank curbs credit growth and causes asset prices to fall, and they will pressure the authorities to reverse course.

The unified model may also pose a conflict of interest for the central bank, which may, for example, be tempted to keep interest rates aritificially low in an effort to aid distressed financial institutions, or to treat a bank facing a solvency problem (a matter properly addressed by the fiscal authority or its agents) as if it were facing a liquidity problem.

If, on balance, the decision is to make the central bank the macroprudential supervisor, it should go hand in hand with measures to strengthen its independence from political pressure. To this end, it is important for the central bank to participate in the public discussion of how its performance will be evaluated. More regular communication of the rationale for its policies will also become increasingly important.

In sum then, there are advantages to both models, and individual countries' institutional characteristics and political settings will determine what works best. Whatever the mechanism, it is clear that effective coordination between monetary and financial regulatory policies will be the lynchpin of financial stability.

Session IV

Macroprudential Policy
—What Are the Implementation Issues?

- Systemic risk identification and monitoring—What models and indicators are most useful?

- Macroprudential instruments—What seems to work and why?

- Institutional setup—Who does what, and what are the best mechanisms to ensure accountability and coordination?

- International coordination—Do we agree that international coordination for macroprudential policy is useful? What would be a possible and promising form of coordination in Asia?

□ Keith Hall

Assistant Governor, Reserve Bank of Australia

First of all, let me thank the People's Bank of China and the International Monetary Fund for the opportunity to return to Shanghai and to participate in this Symposium.

Unlike some of my colleagues from other central banks here today, I've no direct experience with macro-prudential instruments to lay out before you. Australia doesn't have a macro-prudential toolkit as such. But we are a country that the recent FSB Peer View Report described as "having an implicit macro-prudential orientation to financial system oversight——one in which the monitoring of systemic risks is matched by day-to-day supervision of individual institutions". So in the few minutes available, let me highlight the main features of our arrangements and some of the key implementation issues. Many of these came up yesterday: they relate to issues of governance, in particular the adequacy of institutional arrangements and the appropriateness of agency mandates. They also involve more practical issues such as the quantity and quality of resources devoted to financial surveillance and financial stability analysis.

The foundations for the current regulatory arrangements in Australia were laid in the late 1990s when the Government of the day accepted one of the key recommendations of a Financial System Inquiry, which was the establishment of an integrated financial regulator to (amongst other things) facilitate the better oversight of financial conglomerates—a decision that ultimately involved the transfer of bank supervision responsibilities from the central bank to a new agency, the Australian Prudential Regulatory Authority (APRA). We recognised at the time——at least we in the central bank did——that this initiative had the potential to jeopardise the Reserve Bank's ability to fulfil its long-standing responsibility for promoting and maintaining financial stability——a role that the Government had been very careful to underscore when announcing the new institutional arrangements. These concerns on our part were an acknowledgement that bank supervisors are a source of vital information about financial risks and that those central banks that conduct a supervisory function are able to extract some important synergies from this work in support of their stability mandate.

Nevertheless, both the Reserve Bank and APRA were determined from the outset to make the new arrangements work. Our joint objective was to ensure that APRA was able to deliver enhanced oversight of individual financial institutions—and so provide better protection for depositors and policy holders—but without diluting the RBA's capacity to contain systemic risk.

To my mind, two initiatives, in particular, seemed to hold the key to achieving this objective.

The first was the establishment of **strong and effective inter-agency co-ordination arrangements**. We saw it as vital that the Reserve Bank had access to APRA's skill set and vice-versa, particularly in times of stress. And it was similarly critical that both agencies, together with our securities regulator, ASIC, and the Government's financial policy arm, the Australian Treasury, could work together to craft the types of policy initiatives that would keep pace with financial innovation and help contain any of the associated systemic risks.

In Australia we believed that the best way of achieving the desired level of co-operation was by way of a Council of Financial Regulators that had a mandate for:

• identifying important trends in the financial system, including those impinging upon overall financial stability; and

• Ensuring the existence of appropriate co-ordination arrangements for responding to actual or potential instances of financial instability and helping resolve any issues where members' responsibilities overlap.

It's worth emphasising, however, that from the outset there was unanimous agreement that this Council should operate as an informal body with no separate legal personality or powers separate to those of its four member agencies. But its importance within the new regulatory architecture was signified by its membership, which was to include the financial agency heads, with the Governor of the Reserve Bank in the chair. It was also agreed that the Reserve Bank should provide the secretariat—an acknowledgement of the central bank's "firepower" in terms of financial stability analysis. The commitment of each agency was further underpinned by a Joint Memorandum of Understanding setting out respective roles and responsibilities within the new arrangements. And in addition, each agency set about establishing bilateral MOUs to underpin an adequate flow of information from one agency to another in pursuit of their individual policy objectives.

I certainly don't want to leave you with the impression that a Council became the "be all and end all" of effective inter-agency co-operation in Australia; nor, that we think a similar arrangement is the answer for everyone else. It is equally, if not more important, that regular informal working level meetings are put in place. But we certainly did see the Council as the key to promoting a shared view of risks and thereby reducing the potential for our respective macro and micro-prudential policy settings to become misaligned. Of course, the case for formalised inter-agency co-ordination arrangements may be far less compelling in other countries, most obviously those with regulatory central banks which continue to conduct supervisory functions "in-house". But as we heard yesterday, many regulatory central banks have also been working hard to strengthen their institutional arrangements in support of financial stability.

The second initiative that seemed to hold the key to containing systemic risk was to provide APRA with an **explicit financial stability mandate**—so that in framing its policies it was charged with promoting overall stability of the system, as well the safety and soundness of individual financial institutions. In one sense this does no more than acknowledge that a systemic crisis is the event that is most likely to jeopardise the interests of depositors and policy-holders.

APRA made this stability mandate operational by building a number of specific systemic elements into its supervisory practices——so that its efforts would be directed towards those institutions that posed most threat to the financial system——those institutions that we now commonly describe as SIFIs. This is achieved by combining a probability and ratings impact methodology with an oversight and response system so that the intensity of supervision rises with the assessed systemic impact of the regulated institution; and may, in some circumstances, trigger additional prudential measures such as higher capital requirements.

From the outset, APRA also subscribed to the view that its greatest contribution to financial stability would come about through taking a pro-active approach to supervisory oversight——one in which the wrong institutions are prevented from lending too much to the wrong people at the wrong time—the type of pro-activity that might have done much to contain the US sub-prime lending debacle. And the same holds true for just about any other property-related credit crisis that I can think of. In other words, good supervision is a micro tool which strengthens individual financial institutions. But at the same time good supervision has an important macro dimension by helping to limit the build-up of excessive leverage by households, companies and, even in some circumstances sovereigns. After all, there is only very short-term joy to be gained from presiding over strong financial sector balance sheets when the rest of the economy is very obviously distressed.

What I have described so far is a macro-prudential approach to supervision rather than a macro-prudential approach to regulation——one in which regulations are explicitly targeted at financial imbalances——those imbalances within the economy that, if left unchecked, are so threatening to financial stability. In this context, it's noteworthy that APRA has announced its intention to introduce a pro-cyclical capital buffer in 2016 as part of the Basel III reforms. The implementation details have yet to be worked out and—we at the Bank at least—don't underestimate the practical challenges of finding the right degree of mechanical linkage to a particular variable such as credit, with an appropriate degree of short term flexibility. Those of you familiar with the old debates about rules versus discretion in monetary policy might find an echo here. If so, you won't rule out the possibility of combining rule-like behaviour with a sensible degree of discretion, but you won't be expecting it any time soon. After all, in the case of monetary policy this balance took a couple of decades or more to achieve.

Which takes us on to the role of monetary policy within the macro-prudential framework more generally, and the all too familiar policy conundrum—touched on by

Governor Kim last night and again this morning by Professor Eichengreen. Which is how to use one policy instrument in support of two important policy objectives, namely low inflation and financial stability? Like most central banks, we believe that a stable price environment is ultimately our single most important contribution to financial stability. But at the same time, one of the most important policy lessons of the past decade is that unless you take the greatest of care, the very success of delivering low, stable and predictable inflation rates can sometimes underpin a hazardous build-up in risk-taking——a build-up that manifests itself as a run-up in asset prices followed by a destabilising collapse. To our mind this isn't an argument for using monetary policy to aggressively reverse asset price developments—but nor is it one for passively accepting them. In our view this latter position is no longer credible. Monetary policy will need to move, at least somewhat, in a more "responsive" direction in the future.

Finally, let me emphasise a practical challenge to effective macroprudential policy—whatever the chosen institutional arrangements—which is that of developing **a systematic approach to surveillance**, including early warning methodologies, so that we can do a better job of identifying the risks and vulnerabilities within our financial systems. I would be very surprised, indeed, if there was any central bank in this room today that hasn't substantially increased the resources devoted to financial stability analysis in recent years and isn't anticipating some further increase.

Unfortunately, lifting our game around surveillance doesn't guarantee that we will find it any easier to contain systemic risks than we have in the past—for some of the reasons Mr. Yamaoka outlined yesterday. But in finance as in life, early diagnosis should make for a better prognosis. And in this context, it is fitting to end with a compliment to the work of the IMF and MCM in particular. There is no doubt in my mind that some of the best work on systemic risk measurement and on financial stability analysis is now being done within the Fund. So even though we all have far too much to read, time reading the Fund's Global Financial Stability Report— exhausting though it can sometimes be—is time well spent!

And with that bit of free advertising for one of our hosts let me stop!

Thank you.

☐ Andrew Khoo

Assistant Managing Director, Monetary Authority of Singapore

Today, I wish to share with you Singapore's approach to macroprudential policy. Some of the measures I will highlight were implemented for prudential reasons before the term macroprudential became a common regulatory word.

My presentation will focus on our property market measures, but our macroprudential work extends beyond the property market. Vulnerabilities and risks from both outside and within Singapore are monitored closely. Effort is devoted to understanding how risks may transmit to our financial system and institutions, as well as to assessing our financial system's resilience to these risks.

There are several elements in our macroprudential policy framework. Indicators suggestive of risks building-up, e. g. credit growth, asset price inflation, capital flows, funding tightness, currency mismatches, are monitored to determine whether and how we should address emerging trends. Banks are stress-tested for resilience, and surcharges have been applied on locally-incorporated banks on account of their domestic SIFI-ness. Surveillance of the shadow banking sector helps to surface risks and their linkages to the banking system.

Presently, we have been tracking system-wide exposures to the EU, and also identifying FIs with the largest exposures. Establishing the role of EU banks in domestic credit provision, specifically to see whether such banks have large market shares in particular lending segments, allows us to assess the implications of deleveraging. Some EU banks are large in trade financing. We have hence been watching closely developments in this area, especially in terms of withdrawal by EU banks and capacity of other banks to pick up the business.

In terms of set-up, MAS has a Macroprudential Surveillance Department that sits within our Financial Supervision Group. Two divisions support the department's functions. The Financial Surveillance Division leads the effort to identify risks and

231

transmission channels, and is closely complemented by the research efforts of the Financial Studies Division.

The latter has been tasked with investigating macro-financial linkages, so as to design an appropriate counter-cyclical capital buffer scheme to meet Basel III. We are supportive of a counter-cyclical capital buffer because it addresses procyclicality in financial systems. But more work needs to be done to design such schemes, to ensure it will complement the property market measures that have already been taken.

The property market is a key source of risk for Singapore. The possible impact of the property market on the balance sheets of households and banks is not small. Home buyers and the construction sector together account for more than a quarter of total non-bank loans. From a macroprudential perspective, there is a need to ensure that households are not overly leveraged, and banks maintain both good underwriting standards as well as a sufficient cushion against a property correction.

Property price corrections can have a severe impact on households and banks. As the asset quality of banks worsen with falling property values, the availability of credit to households and developers may also decline. This feeds back negatively on property values, creating a downward spiral that could have negative consequences for the real economy.

Let me turn your attention to the measures taken. These have targeted both the demand and supply sides of the market.

The loan-to-value (LTV) ratio cap has been adjusted downwards in a series of steps. Across the board, the LTV cap was reduced from 90% to 80%. For those with second mortgages, the LTV cap was further lowered from 80% to 70% and then to 60%, so as to target buyers who are investors. The LTV applied on borrowers who are not individuals, such as funds, is more severe at 50% because we assume these are investors.

Simple mathematics underlies how LTV caps work. An LTV cap of 90% means the borrower can borrow a maximum of $ 9 for every $ 1 he has, if the bank is willing. An LTV of 80% means that the borrower can borrow a maximum of only $ 4 for every $ 1 that he has. Therefore, LTV caps limit household leverage. A seemingly small change in LTV can have a potentially large effect on borrowing. Furthermore, lower LTV caps also mean a larger cushion for banks when property prices fall.

Other measures taken include minimum cash payments, which we increased from 5% to 10%. Property buyers in Singapore are allowed to use savings in the state-run pension scheme (Central Provident Fund) to pay for property purchases. By stipulating and increasing the minimum cash outlay, purchasers have to be less reliant on pension savings and bank loans to purchase a property.

"Innovative loan" schemes have been disallowed to address speculation. Deferred payment schemes that allow buyers to flip property purchases before the completion of construction, with minimum cash outlay, have been disallowed. Transaction costs have been increased. The Government introduced a Seller Stamp Duty[1] for buyers who sell their properties within a specified period after purchase. Together with the already-present 3% Buyers' Stamp Duty, short term speculators face an increased hurdle rate.

The Government also recently introduced an Additional Buyer Stamp Duty (ABSD). Foreigners have to pay 10% ABSD, Permanent Residents 3% for the second property and citizens 3% for the 3rd property onwards. This was targeted at a small segment of the buyer market, to shift the incentives away from investment in property.

The current low interest rate environment has raised concern that borrowers are taking larger loans than they can repay. As a part of increasing consumer awareness, banks will be required to provide a Housing Loan Fact Sheet to borrowers from early 2012. A two-pages in plain English will highlight to potential borrowers the impact of rising interest rates on their loan repayment obligations.

Finally, in conjunction with demand measures, the Government has expanded its land sales program to increase the supply of private properties in Singapore.

---

[1] Currently, it is 16% if the buyer sells within the first year; 12% if sold within second year, and then 8% and 4% if sold within the 3rd and 4th year.

So have our measures worked?

Overall transaction activity has declined. Sub-sales[①], a proxy for speculative activity, have also gone down. Growth in the property price index has moderated, although the rate of growth is different in different segments of the market. But growth is still positive. Property prices are still increasing and are presently at record levels.

However, outstanding housing loans growth has moderated. The share of loans with LTV above 80% is now low, at about 5%. This means that banks would face stresses to asset quality only if property prices collapsed by more than 30%. In fact, when the market dropped substantially during 2007—2009, banks were not materially affected. The IMF Article IV team at that time said Singapore went through a real stress test.

Our approach to macroprudential policy has been to respond to emerging risks with a range of relevant tools, which are each applied in a targeted manner.

The property market was identified to be a source of risk, and multiple tools have been used to mitigate the risk. Our approach is fairly simple and non-rules based. We believe targeting measures at the source of risk has a direct and faster impact. Unintended consequences that may arise from broad measures that affect lending to all sectors are also avoided, especially if there is no evidence of excessive credit growth in other sectors.

Measures are calibrated to target different segments of buyers. The LTV rules for first-time home-buyers are the least stringent, although prudence is still encouraged. For those buying subsequent properties, the LTV cap is stricter. For the short-term speculators, the high transaction costs are intended to deter them from participating in the property market.

There are challenges. The threshold or step-size we set for each of the measures as well as the timing of implementation is a matter of judgment. And this is an implementation challenge.

---

① Sub-sales refer to sales that take place before completion of construction.

A better understanding and modelling of financial and real sector linkages is required for policymaking of a more rigorous fashion. Chapter 3 of the recent GFSR titled "Toward Operationalising Macroprudential Policies: When to Act" has attempted to do so. It recognises that this is still work in progress. We welcome more research by the Fund in this area.

Another challenge of macroprudential policy is the absence of a clear target. How do we measure financial stability? Policymakers cannot be proven right. Once we choose to act, we will never know the counter-factual. We would never know if our actions had preempted a price hike and subsequent destabilising correction.

Enforcement is also a challenge. Let me give an example. We intended to impose a lower LTV cap for investors. But this is difficult to enforce because banks have no way of ascertaining the true intent of the borrower. Banks will probably want to offer a higher LTV loan if the borrower's credit standing is good. We eventually settled on imposing a lower LTV cap for those with an existing mortgage. Banks are required to do a prior check with the credit bureau to confirm if a borrower has an existing housing loan. But this affected those who have a single property and wanted to upgrade, as it meant that they have to first sell the existing property, or face the lower LTV cap.

Finally, coordination is needed to implement macroprudential policy successfully.

The MAS is both the central bank as well as the integrated financial supervisor, so we do not have some of the agency coordination issues faced by other jurisdictions. MAS has a statutory responsibility for financial stability. Within the MAS, the Financial Stability Meeting brings together both the supervision and central banking functions of MAS. We also have periodic meetings with the Ministry of Finance. While MAS is the lender of last resort, if bank recapitalisation is required, the money must come from the Ministry of Finance.

In the case of property market measures, we take a "whole of Government" approach. There is an inter-agency workgroup comprising the Ministry of Finance (who can raise/impose transaction costs) and the Ministry of National Development (who is responsible for land supply policy).

This brings me to the end of the presentation. Property market measures are important but are not the only aspect of our macroprudential policy framework. Our policy responses reflect what we consider is needed in our context, and may not be appropriate in another jurisdiction. Thank you.

☐ Tongurai Limpiti

Assistant Governor, Bank of Thailand

Good morning,

First of all, let me thank the IMF and the People's Bank of China for inviting me to speak at this session on "Macroprudential——What Are the Implementation Issues?" —the issue that captures the attention of academia and policy makers alike, especially in the post-crisis world. To stimulate the discussion later on, I organize my presentation today into three parts:

1) Lessons drawn from the recent global financial crisis

2) Thailand's experiences on macroprudential policy implementation and

3) Macroprudential policy formulation process at the Bank of Thailand

Before summing up the lessons learned from the global financial crisis, I would like to briefly touch on its causes and what comes after the crisis.

Main causes of the Subprime crisis

Monetary Easing: Sustained monetary easing resulted in asset price bubbles in many developed countries.

Inadequate Financial Regulations: Financial institutions lowered the bar in terms of credit origination due to fierce competition, coupled with weak financial discipline of households; To make the matter worse, it was propagated by financial innovation (e. g. CDOs, ABS) that distorted accountability and governance of credit approval process. Moreover, financial institutions investing in CDOs and ABS lacked sufficient risk management; Shadow banking (e. g. investment banks, pension funds, insurance companies, and hedge funds) sector was inadequately supervised, and thus, expanded rapidly as a result of regulatory arbitrage.

237

Global Financial Crisis

Sharp decrease of housing prices and rise of NPLs ensued after the asset price bubble burst; Then, liquidity shortage was followed by huge losses and insolvency of US financial institutions. The collapse of Lehman Brothers, and other high street banks thereafter, eventually caused contagion that triggered the global financial crisis; In response, we saw willingness and capacity of the authorities to take series of decisive measures.

Lessons learned

The recent global financial crisis highlights the need for sound microprudential policy, among other public policies. It is critical for the maintenance of financial stability to have in place sufficient prudential regulations to address the build-up of systemic risk, and thus, prevent the future crisis. At the same time, macroprudential regulations should have greater role in enhancing the soundness and risk absorption of the whole financial system.

In the post-crisis world, macroprudential policy is more of a norm than an exception toolkit to maintain financial stability with increasing international recognition.

The case in point is Basel III's macroprudential elements of countercyclical capital buffer to deal with procyclicality and more stringent capital rules and supervision for SIFIs.

In addition, the FSB, IMF and BIS highlighted three main aspects of macroprudential policy framework, namely, identification and monitoring of systemic financial risk, designation and calibration of macroprudential instruments, and building institutional and governance arrangements in the domestic and regional context.

Now, let me turn to Thailand's experiences by first outlining some key principles of macroprudential policy implementation.

First, macroprudential policy is meant to be preventive of systemic risk by addressing directly to the root cause, rather than dealing with the symptoms afterward. For us, it requires taking measures earlier on to ward off macroeconomic imbalances or financial vulnerabilities such as excess leverage, over indebtedness in certain economic sectors, or price bubble in various asset classes.

Second, it is applied as a leaning-against-the-wind policy to preempt the build-up of systemic risk and strengthen resilience of the financial system.

Third, we need to exercise judgment in implementing macroprudential policy with flexibility in response to change in macroeconomic and financial circumstance. For example, we recently postpone the LTV ratio policy on low-rise residential property due to impacts of the flood on the real estate sector.

Last, implementation of macroprudential policy in harmony with monetary policy and microprudential regulation is also critical for policy consistency and hence, effectiveness in achieving overall financial and macroeconomic stability.

In a nutshell, when implementing macroprudential policy we should ask ourselves three questions: 1) does the policy itself make sense? 2) is it practical to all the stakeholders? and 3) is it implemented at the right time? As you listen on to illustrations of the policy experience of Thailand, these principles will come up time and again.

The Bank of Thailand has long used macroprudential policy as a financial stability policy toolkit in complimentary with rigorous microprudential regulation and supervision. This along with flexible inflation-targeting framework contributed to the resiliency of our financial system that stand against the recent global financial crisis and domestic turmoil in the last few years.

Examples of macroprudential policies implemented are:

1) Net Foreign Exchange Position implemented in 2002;

2) Loan-to-Value ratio on mortgage loans in 2003, 2009, and 2010;

3) Tightened regulation on credit card loan and personal loan in 2002, 2004, and 2005; and

4) Loan-loss provisioning in 2006 and 2007.

239

Net Foreign Exchange Position implemented in 2002:

Regulation on net foreign exchange position helps contain FX risk in the Thai banking system. Complementing the regulation on limits of overbought and oversold FX position, the Bank of Thailand also has in place net FX regulation, for both individual currency and aggregated basis, in line with the BIS shorthand method.

As evidenced, both individual and aggregate currency limits of financial institutions have remained well below the regulatory requirement. In particular, the net FX positions significantly declined during the crisis in 2008, reflecting financial institutions' ability to manage FX risk and adjust their exposures appropriate to the changing global environment.

Loan-to-Value ratio on mortgage loans in 2003, 2009, and 2010:

I would like to spend some moment on the implementation of Loan-to-Value ratio in Thailand since it is based on some key principles of macroprudential policy implementation I mentioned earlier. The use, and adjustment thereafter, of the LTV ratio by the Bank of Thailand demonstrates its preventive nature and, more importantly, the flexibility to fine tune the policy in response to changing economic circumstance.

The 70% LTV limit for mortgage with value of at least 10 million baht was first introduced back in 2003 to preempt speculation in luxury real estate segment. Then, amid global downturn in 2009, we removed the 70% LTV limit, and replaced it with a more risk-sensitive rule by imposing higher risk weight capital charge for mortgage with LTV greater than 80%.

Having seen its effectiveness, in late 2010 the Bank of Thailand extended the LTV rule to mortgage with value less than 10 million baht. There are two policy considerations in designing such rule. First, it serves as a preventive action of excessive risk taking by banks from intense competition in the mortgage market, although there was no obvious sign of property price bubble. Second, the rule was purposely made more stringent with one year earlier effective date for high-rise mortgage than low-rise mortgage, taking into consideration of more intense competition in the high-rise segment.

The LTV rule for high-rise mortgage is already in force beginning of this year; however, we decided to postpone the implementation date for low-rise mortgage by another year from the original date of 1 January 2012, in light of the recent flood situation in Thailand.

Tightened regulation on credit card loan and personal loan in 2002, 2004, and 2005:

The next example demonstrates the use of macroprudential policy to address sectoral imbalance and in alignment of monetary policy and microprudential regulation.

The excessive growth of consumer credit in early 2000s and imbalance in the household sector observed in some emerging economies prompted us to introduce tightened regulation on credit card and personal loans. This was implemented successively from including non-bank credit card companies in the scope of supervision, followed by minimum requirements for credit cardholders, maximum credit line and minimum repayment, and eventually, similar rules also applied to personal loans.

These measures bear fruits as we have seen the growth of credit in these markets coming down remarkably. This experience shows that macroprudential policy, when implemented properly, can tackle the sectoral imbalance directly, rather than resorting to the use of conventional monetary tightening that might have broad-based effects, with unintentional, undesirable results on other economic sectors.

Loan-loss provisioning in 2006 and 2007:

This leads us to the last example of Thailand's experience on macroprudential policy implementation in the context of "leaning against the wind".

During extended periods of profitability in mid 2000s, the Bank of Thailand implemented tightened loan loss provisioning rules of IAS 39, in steps, so that banks have buffer against impaired assets, as evidenced by rising NPL coverage ratio.

Before moving to the last part of my presentation on macroprudential policy formulation process at the Bank of Thailand, I would like to mention the financial stability work process, commonly faced by us all. That is: (1) identification of vulnerability in key sectors；（2）surveillance of systemic risk and impact assessment；（3）appropriate policy response；and （4）fall short of all three, crisis resolution and management.

As macroprudential policy resides across many departments, comprehensive surveillance and risk assessment are made by the Subcommittee on Financial Stability, chaired by the Governor, with members including all deputy governors, and assistant governors overseeing prudential regulation, supervision, monetary policy and money market operation. Such governance structure promotes comprehensive systemic risk assessment and balanced decisive preemptive action. Once policy recommendation reached, the Subcommittee delivers it to relevant committee for decision making.

The financial stability review is reported to the Subcommittee in a regular meeting where any vulnerabilities and risks to the financial system can be raised. The Subcommittee discusses the concerns not only on a specific sector but also on the linkages between different parts of the financial market, capital market, financial institutions, and the macroeconomic conditions. Our recent exercise is the assessment of the impact from EU debt crisis on Thailand's financial system. The analysis covered both impacts through the financial and trade linkages. The networking model has been used to achieve deeper understanding of the interlinkage among financial institutions. We found that the direct impact through the Thai financial system is limited because of our low exposure to European countries. However, our main concern is on the indirect impact from trade channel due to our reliance on exports. The Subcommittee also monitors the situation closely through our daily macro surveillance focusing on the development of crisis and the impact on financial market and financial institutions. Additionally, the Subcommittee has ready a set of policy tools in order to stabilize the financial system.

In addition, we have two levels of policy coordination：

Domestic policy coordination：As a lead regulator, the Bank of Thailand supervise mainly the banking sector, and at the same time sits in the committee that supervise insurance and security business, while heads of SEC and Office of Insurance Commission also sit in FIPC. Such cross-directorship ensures absence of regulatory arbitrage and thorough supervision of financial conglomerates.

Cross-border coordination: As a member of EMEAP WGBS, we meet regularly to exchange experiences on macroprudential policy implementation, as well as form common stance on global regulatory rules.

In order to complete our financial stability work process as mentioned, I would like to share with you our crisis resolution process. Bank of Thailand, as the lender of last resort, can provide liquidity to banks according to Bank of Thailand Act. For solvency problem, NPLs and NPAs are bought at fair value by the national AMC, namely Bangkok Commercial Asset Management (BAM), which will be privatized later on. Additional capital could be injected to financial institutions in need through the process proposed by Bank of Thailand to FIPC and then to the Financial Institutions Development Fund (FIDF), who will then propose to the Cabinet for resolution on fiscalisation. Upon approval from the Cabinet, the FIDF will carry out the capital injection. However, if any financial institution has to be closed, the Deposit Protection Agency will come into play and disburse each depositor one million baht as enshrined in the law.

Thank you for your attention.

□ Alex Gibbs

Executive Director （UK）, IMF

General Comments

Plan to focus on the third set of questions on institutional setup and illustrate them by saying something about how the UK is handling them——not to say we have all the answers because we certainly don't, and we recognise that we will need to learn lessons both from our experience and from others and adapt as necessary over time. In this context will also touch on the fourth on international coordination.

First thing to say is that we are——at least in UK——in very early days for macroprudential policy. The UK FSAP struck a note of caution when it said that which said that to be credible we had to be realistic about what macroprudential regulation can achieve, particularly in the early days of implementation.

The challenges are significant. If you compare monetary policy to macroprudential policy, in the UK the Bank of England has a single symmetric, numerically defined target, one policy instrument at least in normal times, a wealth of expertise and detailed modelling of the relevant underlying relationships, an established voting procedure to make decisions and a track record of communicating its actions.

We are now asking the FPC to consider and take decisions （hopefully by consensus） to meet an objective defined in terms of a concept that you can't define in numbers, with potential overlap or conflict with other policies, a variety of potential policy levers, with much less research underpinning the various relationships.

So plenty of reasons to be cautious as the IMF comments imply. In the aftermath of a crisis there is a natural dynamic among policymakers to look and what new things can be done, and the UK is full part of that debate. But at the same time, mustn't lose focus on getting more traditional macro and supervisory policies right, because arguably the crisis has shown that we got those wrong as well.

Institutional set up

Turning to the institutional setup issues, in there UK we are in the process of moving to the "triple peak" model, which includes a Financial Policy Committee (FPC) within the Bank of England that has a clear macroprudential remit to identify and address systemic risks. Since June we have had an interim version of this up and running. The legislation to put it on a firm statutory basis and give it legal powers should be in place by the end of next year.

General institutional set up

We decided it was important to have a separate, stand-alone macroprudential body. A lesson we take from the crisis is that without this, you risk not having a clear focus on systemic stability issues. Micro prudential supervisors have a natural incentive to always focus on firm-specific issues. Ultimately that is what they are responsible for. So we think the separation is important, although of course the prudential authorites need to be fully involved and are the source of much of the information that underpins thinking about system wide issue.

A lot of work has gone into how to set up the objectives, the functions, the membership and the accountability of this new body.

On the objective——we think of it in terms of the resilience of the financial system, and the goal is therefore to monitor and take action to remove or reduce systemic financial risks. But straight away this goes to one of the challenges which is how to ensure the right balance between financial stability and economic growth, because there are trade offs, which——unlike with monetary policy——you can imagine might exist even in the long term. An economy with a repressed financial system may not experience financial instability but it will have plenty of other problems. At some level we have to accept that financial systems are prone to bouts of instability reflecting the balances sheet fragility of some of the participants and the complex networks through which they are connected.

245

One way to think of the challenge is that we should aim for enough resilience in the system that is suited to potential tail events, without impairing the wider functioning of the economy. And the FPC will be asked to apply a test to its interventions that they avoid damage to medium to long term growth.

But arguably we need to go beyond that and be able to adjust the resilience standard upwards when it looks as though the world has become a more threatening place. This is not about fine tuning the business cycle, it's about recognising that different states of the cycle potentially call for recalibrating the policies we use to achieve resilience.

So there are two potential sets of policies in play, those that address structural issues in the financial system and those that react to cyclical developments. And it is important to remember in all this that the cycle itself is affected by developments in the structure of the financial sector, as we have seen in the crisis.

This is broadly the thinking behind the way we are setting up the new macroprudential body in the UK.

The FPC will be able to offer advice to the microprudential and market regulators , and in a more limited field subject to further discussion, to give them directions. The scope of its powers to direct the supervisors powers is going to be big part of the legislation that is still to be discussed. But however that debate goes it is clear that the FPC will have a range of tools and courses of action, depending on the nature and scale of the risk.

Accountability

Accountability is particularly important as the policy levers potentially go well beyond the levers that people are used to being the responsibility of an independent agency, for example in restricting individuals and corporates access to credit.

The key mechanism here is transparency.

The governments proposals involve requiring the FPC to set out clearly how and why it intends to use instruments and as it does so to provide assessments of how they are working. It will have to demonstrate that is acting proportionately and transparently, taking into account international law.

The FPC will present published biannual Financial Stability Report to the Treasury and Parliament. Records of quarterly FPC meetings will be published. All FPC directions issued to the microprudential authorities will be laid in Parliament.

The role of Parliament in this is likely to be a big focus of discussion when the legislation is debated.

Expertise / composition

Another set of issues is around where to locate the authority and who do you actually get to do the work.

The expertise required is mainly at central banks and microprudential regulators. The FPC will be made up of 11 members, including six Bank of England representatives and the heads of the microprudential regulators.

But you do still need a challenge function, and a link back to the government. In the UK the other members of the FPC will include four highly experienced, independent external members; and a non-voting Treasury member.

Finally on the institutional side, word about coordination.

Given the scope for overlap of policies, important question is how to deliver effective coordination with other institutions in the broader architecture.

The key link is with the microprudential regulator. In the UK it should help that the two institutions will be part of the same institution——the Bank of England. But the FPC must also stay plugged in to policy developments at the Treasury.

But there is also the potentially complex issue of interaction with monetary policy, where it isn't hard to imagine circumstances where what might look on paper like a clear division of responsibilities becomes much less clear in practice.

We are tackling this in several ways. Firstly, it makes sense to have some overlap in the membership of the macroprudential and monetary policy committees. Secondly, the sequencing of meetings will be different, FPC meetings are less frequent, with a presumption that it will not be fine tuning instruments as frequently, and so that the MPC will be the "last mover" taking its decisions in the light of the less frequently changed macroprudential measures. But it remains to be seen how this will work in practice.

International coordination

Finally A few words on international cooperation and coordination which will be critical in ensuring macroprudential policy is successful. Obvious, given the level of global financial integration.

Given nature of financial services in UK we are very aware of this. We host many subsidiaries and branches of major global firms——our supervisors play an important role in the collective consolidated supervision of SIFIs. At same time nature of City is that there are significant institutions operating through a branch structure and outside scope of UK authorities.

Cooperation is particularly important for the implementation of cyclical instruments. If one country tightens capital requirements it will be ineffective if lenders not subject to its regulation step in to fill the gap. One potential solution would be reciprocal arrangements between national supervisors, under which authorities commit to ensure that the institutions they regulate do not undermine one another's policies. This is a complex but potentially important area which needs more analysis. Given the experience in the room, I would be interested in comments on whether this is likely to be a practical approach.

As with the Basel framework discussed yesterday, with macroprudential policies national regulators and supervisors need discretion to go beyond the minima when national circumstances require, to safeguard financial stability. One size will not necessarily fit all. This is a major issue in the UK, where we feel, given scale and nature of the industry, it is in the interests of both national and global financial stability that we have the power to go beyond what is agreed in Europe.

Finally, another key strand of coordination is——information sharing. IMF bilateral and multilateral surveillance will play a key role in developing the evidence base. Shouldn't underestimate how important this will be given how new the discipline is.

Session V

Connecting the Dots and Key Takeaways

☐ Liu Shiyu

Deputy Governor, PBC

At the outset, I would like to thank the International Monetary Fund for holding this important Asia-Pacific High-Level Symposium in Shanghai. I also thank colleagues from Asia-Pacific regions and regulators and specialists from the International Monetary Fund, the Financial Stability Board (FSB) and the International Association of Insurance Supervisors (IAIS) for participating in this conference. You arrive at a time when Shanghai's weather has turned from overcast to sunny. I hope this change in weather bodes well for the global economy, especially that of the European sovereign debt crisis.

The People's Bank of China, as the host of this symposium, has benefited a lot from the experiences and lessons shared by the participants. During the discussions, the pre-scheduled itinerary has been expanded from financial stability assessment to include financial risk monitoring, risk warning, risk resolution, international cooperation, roles of central banks and macro-prudential techniques and methods, etc. There is room for further discussion, but the discussions have come across neither disagreement nor intense argument. This reveals the very pragmatic nature of the symposium and the converging views about maintaining financial stability. From this we can also see that FSAP is in itself a complex, systematic and necessary process. In fact, FSAP assessment is a system engineering that requires professional staff of various fields and an integration of institutions. China's practices have illustrated that FSAP is very important in identifying, preventing and managing risks. We acknowledge the efforts made and the significant progress achieved in recent years by the International Monetary Fund in pushing FSAP forward. The assessment methods have also been greatly improved. Although countries have different views and suggestions of FSAP assessment due to their respective domestic conditions, there is no major disagreement as to this institutional arrangement.

China has just finished its FSAP assessment, which not only helps other countries and international organizations deepen their understanding of the stability and risk conditions of China's financial system, but also helps us identify existing problems in our financial system and enables us to put forward related reform proposal in *China's Outline of the Twelfth Five-Year Plan for National Economic and Social Development*. Leaders of the State Council value the work of the assessment team in terms of the problems in China's financial system and policy recommendations to the Chinese government. We will further discuss these problems, make schedules of improvement and propose reform goals during the next National Financial Work Conference to be held by the central government at the beginning of the next year.

In the following, I would like to share some of my thoughts with you:

Firstly, we should value the assessment conclusions of FSAP and let FSAP mechanism play a continuous role. The financial systems and financial markets of different countries will unquestionably bear the characteristics of these nations' economy, society, history and literature. As a result, the key is to respect the history and structure of each country and look at whether such a system can really address the practical problems faced by this country, instead of applying some fixed models on everyone. If there are no definite signs that certain institutional arrangement will cause risks, one shall accept that it has reasonable basis.

China's experience has shown that any reform should be supported by careful preparation and with references to wisdom from around the world in the globalization process. With regard to the reform suggestions proposed by the FSAP mission, especially those to which the government and financial regulatory agencies are committed, the assessed country should fulfill its commitment and push forward the reforms. As an old Chinese saying goes, "Actions speak louder than words". FSAP is a five-year cyclical assessment, during which unexpected things could happen. Therefore, the recommendations of the assessment mission, in particular those agreed upon with the assessed country, can be included in the Article IV Consultation of the International Monetary Fund, which is helpful in further promoting the resilience of a country's financial system. That is to say, monetary policy, fiscal policy and financial stability

251

policy should all become the focus of Article IV Consultation of the International Monetary Fund. This is my suggestion to help FSAP to play a continuous role.

Secondly, each country should manage its own business well. During the process of economic and financial globalization, the external impact, i. e. the so-called spillover effect, of a country's financial risks is significant. Meanwhile, the risks of a country's financial sector, sometimes even those of non-financial sector, can trigger turbulence in the entire financial system. In fact, this is the inevitable result of cross-product innovations and cross-market operations. Whether from a historical perspective or taking into consideration the complicated reality, any country or economy has to manage its own business well, first things first. Meanwhile, regardless of the development of the domestic financial market and the institutional arrangement, the financial soundness and governance structure of financial institutions at the micro level still play the key role. Without financial soundness of micro-financial institutions, a well-designed institutional arrangement will become castle in the air. Therefore, countries should ensure the healthy financial status of financial institutions at the micro level and secure the stability of their own financial systems, consequently contributing to the international financial stability.

Thirdly, attentions should be paid to preventing home country's spillover risks. Economic and financial globalization is an irreversible trend. Financial institution's cross-border operations, including setting up overseas branches and running cross-border agent business, have become a common practice. This requires stronger cooperation between home and host countries. The challenge was in front of national supervisors ever since the bankruptcy of the Bank of Credit and Commerce International. In the past few decades, when failed institutions had cross-market operations, there were always shortcomings in information sharing and coordination between home and host countries. While financial regulators always heed the market participants to moral hazards, there is another equally important issue, which is to emphasize the responsibility of home and host countries, to prevent moral hazards rising from incompetent supervision and self-interest behaviors, to minimize the cost of global financial crisis and to support a sustained global recovery. This is particularly true in the current world of financial globalization. Therefore, it is suggested that the evaluation of information sharing practices among financial supervisors, especially on high-risk institutions and businesses, be included into the IMF/WB assessment framework. This should become a mandate of the assessed country in maintaining financial stability and preventing financial risks.

Fourthly, we should enhance the regulation and supervision over shadow banking. As an emerging economy and developing country, China has a financial system that needs to be constantly improved. We will deepen financial reform based on China's circumstances, including promoting asset securitization for balanced development of the money and capital market. It is not sustainable for commercial banks to rely on the capital market for financing. Moreover, this limits the financing available for the real economy. Asset securitization will help banks diversify their business and contribute to balanced development of bond and credit markets. In China, the risks of local government financing platforms are in essence fiscal. Such risks, emerging from economic development, can no longer be resolved through approaches of the traditional planned economy. The only feasible solution to address the risks is by developing municipal bonds market. To do this, we need to have the courage to carry out reforms and make innovations and learn from mature markets to promote the development of China's municipal market.

About the shadow banking system, in the Chinese system, we have a comparatively wide range of financial regulation and supervision, with few areas remaining outside of the authorities' domain. The central bank's mandate is to maintain financial stability. By way of managing access to payment and settlement system and to the repo market, account management, financial market monitoring, the central bank is able to limit the financing capability of the shadow banking system, and monitor the activities of various banking institutions in the market to prevent potential risks. Moreover, the central bank needs to follow the developments of financial products, and instead of relying on the market unconditionally, should have a clear judgment on the performance and potential risks of the products, restrict or deny market access of "polluting" financial derivatives.

Fifthly, we should promote early warning of financial risks and improve the resolution regime. In dealing with risk of financial institutions at the micro level, and the spillover risk to other countries and regions, there is a conclusion that the earlier and quicker the counter measures are taken, the lower the costs will be. China has gained valuable experience in this aspect. If we have had launched reforms of state-owned banks a couple of years earlier, the financial costs would have been even lower. Bad assets in the balance sheet have a contagious effect. These bad assets are like rotten peaches among the good ones. The later you pick them out of the basket, the fewer good ones will be left. Therefore, when managing crisis through measures including market exit, liquidation of failed institutions, bankruptcy and restructuring, the faster the authorities move, the better the result.

To fulfill our mandate as central bankers, we need to have passion and wisdom, and take concrete actions. As we wind up this symposium, on behalf of the PBC, I want to thank the IMF for jointly holding it with us, and thank the participants for their valuable comments and suggestions. My special thanks go to the staff of IMF and the PBC Shanghai Head Office for their excellent work and service.

Finally, I would like to wish you every success in your work. For those who have come a long way to Shanghai, please enjoy your stay and have a safe journey home. We are ready to enhance cooperation with Asian colleagues to safeguard financial stability and promote the FSAP to a larger coverage.

Thank you!

☐ José Viñals

Financial Counsellor and Director, IMF

Good afternoon! After one-and-a-half days of intense and fruitful discussions, allow me to propose some preliminary conclusions, key messages, and personal views.

First of all, I would like to thank you—our distinguished participants—for contributing so generously to our discussions. Your views and suggestions will help us enhance the quality and relevance of the FSAP, which has become an essential part of the IMF's work. I would also like to express my sincere gratitude to our generous hosts— Governor Zhou and his staff. This meeting would not have been possible without their hard work, dedication, and keen interest in our discussion topic.

Yesterday, Min Zhu opened our meeting by saying that the improved FSAP represents a "win-win" situation. And I could not agree more. Not only has the program significantly strengthened the capacity and effectiveness of the IMF's surveillance function. But it has also greatly enhanced the authorities' ability to monitor and manage financial stability.

Let me briefly summarize some of the key issues that have emerged in the four sessions:

1. First, participants generally agree that the **FSAP can play a useful role as an independent review**. As such, It can help national authorities identify potential financial sector vulnerabilities and can help them design longer-term policies and reforms to ensure financial stability.

2. How do new international regulatory and supervisory standards address systemic risk?

3. How prepared are we for the next crisis?

4. Macroprudential policy.

Based on what we have discussed, allow me to propose **key messages** in two

255

areas：

（1）International financial reform and the role of the Fund

（2）Ongoing financial sector reform in Asia：How can the Fund help?

1. International financial reform and the role of the Fund

（1）Progress has been made toward repairing and restructuring the global financial system. The work underway is moving in the right direction, but there is much left to be done. Looking ahead, policymakers need to press ahead with structural solutions to long standing financial problems, focusing on the following key goals：

Nationally：

• Strengthen microprudential supervision, including supervision of systemically important banks. This requires boosting the authority, resources and capacity of supervisory agencies and emphasizing the need to intervene early.

• Diagnose and repair weak financial institutions. Where the diagnoses identify capital shortfalls, banks need to have credible and timely recapitalizations or be taken over. This process is less advanced than it should be at this stage, adding to the risk of moral hazard.

• Integrate macroprudential supervision in policy frameworks. Macroprudential policy needs to identify and highlight the buildup of system-wide financial risk.

• Put in place credible strategies for medium term fiscal consolidation to safeguard sovereign risk and financial stability.

Multilaterally：

• Reach agreement on how to limit the risks from Global Systemically Important Financial Institutions（G-SIFIs）.

• Work to make cross-border crisis resolution feasible by developing coordinated crisis management frameworks and clear principles to guide cross-border bank resolutions.

• Shed more light on the shadow banking system and, as appropriate, expand the regulatory and supervisory perimeter.

• Create a comprehensive framework for macroprudential policy and a consistent set of policy tools, and increase international cooperation to ensure their consistent application.

(2) The financial stability framework—what is the role of the Fund?

• Providing advice on how to rethink global regulation and supervision of markets, and working with its partners, the BIS and FSB, and with member countries, to complete the reform agenda.

• Taking steps to improve risk analysis with an early-warning exercise, carried out jointly with the Financial Stability Board, analyzing financial interconnectedness across borders and the spillover effects of financial and economic policies across borders.

• Taking a leading role in shaping the macroprudential policy framework.

• Closely working with country authorities through bilateral and multilateral surveillance and other international institutions in an effort to prevent future crises.

2. Ongoing financial sector reform in Asia: How can the Fund help?

• Closely working with country authorities in taking steps to improve risk identification, assessment and monitoring by improving data collection and analysis, using both TA and surveillance operations.

• Strengthening microprudential supervision, including supervision of systemically important financial institutions, and improving risk management capability.

• Putting in place credible strategies for managing the macro-financial aspects of sovereign risk and its interconnections with financial stability.

• Identifying and managing systemic risks and their financial stability spillovers, through macroprudential measures.

• Diagnosing and repairing weak financial institutions. Where the diagnoses identify capital shortfalls, banks need to have credible and timely recapitalizations or be taken over. This process is less advanced than it should be at this stage, adding to the risk of moral hazard.